Female Scripture Biography

Including An Essay On What Christianity Has Done For Women
Vol. I

by

Francis Augustus Cox

Double 9
BOOKS

Female Scripture Biography
Including An Essay On What Christianity Has Done For Women
Vol. I
by Francis Augustus Cox

ISBN: 978-93-61426-66-7

Published by

DOUBLE 9 BOOKS

2/13-B, Ansari Road
Daryaganj, New Delhi – 110002
info@double9books.com
www.double9books.com
Tel. 011-40042856

ABOUT THE AUTHOR

Francis Augustus Cox, a notable English Nonconformist pastor and author, is best known for his seminal work, "Female Scripture Biography: Including an Essay on What Christianity Has Done for Women." This landmark book, written in the early nineteenth century, demonstrates Cox's commitment to improving women's rights and acknowledgment in the Christian faith. In "Female Scripture Biography," Cox methodically explores the lives of famous women from the Bible, providing incisive comments on their relevance and contributions to religious history. Through extensive biographical biographies, he highlights the different roles and accomplishments of women such as Eve, Sarah, Ruth, Esther, and Mary, among others. Cox's portrayal of these biblical people goes beyond simple storytelling; it is a stunning testament to women's critical role in constructing religious narratives and communities. Furthermore, Cox supports his biographical narratives with an insightful article on Christianity's transformative impact on women's lives. He convincingly contends that, rather than maintaining patriarchal standards, Christianity has played a crucial role in lifting women's position, equipping them with dignity, agency, and spiritual equality.

CONTENTS

Preface

Notwithstanding the variety of theological publications of a devotional class, which are perpetually issuing from the press, the author concurs in the opinion of those who think they can scarcely be too numerous. It may reasonably be hoped, that in proportion to the multiplication of works of this kind, the almost incalculable diversities of taste will be suited; and that those who may be disinclined to one style of writing, or to a particular series of subjects, may be allured by their predilections to the perusal of others.

Amidst the general plenty, however, there is one department which experiences a degree of scarcity--a department to which these volumes properly belong. Pious families require a supply of religious reading, adapted to occupy the intervals of business, the hours of devotion, and the time which is often and properly appropriated to domestic instruction in the evenings of the Christian Sabbath. To have the minds of the young directed at such seasons, not only to the truths of religion in general, but the more attractive parts of Scripture in particular, seems highly important. By a happy combination of amusement and instruction, piety is divested of her formality, and clothed with fascination: the ear is caught, and the heart gained; while the narrative interests, the best lessons become impressed even upon the gay and the trifling; and he who, when summoned to the social circle, sat down with reluctance, may rise up with regret.

Whoever has been blessed with the advantages of a religious education, and recurs to his own years of juvenile susceptibility, cannot forget the strong impressions he received by these means; and must have had frequent occasion to remark the tenaciousness with which they have lingered in his memory, and sprung up amidst his recollections at every subsequent period. In many cases they have proved the basis, of future eminence in piety, and blended delightfully with the gladdening retrospections of declining life. In those instances, where all the good effects which might be anticipated did not appear, these early lessons have checked the impetuousity of passion, neutralized the force of temptation, and cherished the convictions of an incipient piety.

The writer of the following pages is aware of the just celebrity acquired by some of his predecessors in the same line of composition, and he might have felt wholly deterred from pursuing his design, by an apprehension of having been superseded by the elegant and comprehensive lectures of HUNTER, and the simple, perspicuous, and devotional biography of ROBINSON, had he not remarked that their notices of the women in Scripture formed but a small proportion of their respective works, and that the present performance might be very properly considered as a continuation of their volumes, particularly of those of the latter author.

It will be seen, that some of the same characters which have been given in preceding writers, appear in the "Female Scripture Biography;" but the reader may perhaps be conciliated to this seeming repetition, by being reminded that they were necessarily retouched, in order to complete the series; while the writer satisfies himself with the reflection that, whatever subjects are deduced from Scripture, are not only unexhausted, but will forever remain inexhaustible. The "wells of salvation," from which preceding ages have drawn, still afford to us, and will supply to far-distant generations, the same spiritual, copious, and unfailing refreshment.

The Introductory Essay to the second volume, respecting the influence of Christianity on the condition of the female sex, has been somewhat divested of that literary cast which it might have been expected to assume, the better to accord with the general drift of the work. The reader will, it is confidently anticipated, deem, it no unacceptable addition.

Eve Chapter I

What a glorious pre-eminence in the creation, has Infinite Wisdom assigned to the human species! As the skilful architect finishes his performance by the most exquisite specimens of workmanship, so "the great Builder of this varied frame," after the formation of *matter*, proceeded to impart *life*, to communicate *instinct*, and to inspire reason. "And God said, Let us make man in our image, after our likeness; and let them have *dominion* over the fish of the sea, and over the fowl of the air, and over the cattle, and over all the earth, and over every creeping thing that creepeth upon the earth. So God created man in his *own image*; in the image of God created he him; male and female created he them."

The superiority of man to *matter*, however fair, to *life* however pleasing, to *instinct* however perfect, appears in this, that he only is capable of contemplating and admiring the works of God--he only has an eye that opens upon the heavens, and a mind adapted to receive impressions from their diversified glories.

But even *reason*, in its present state, is so degraded, that the wonders of creative wisdom are, in a considerable degree, overlooked or undervalued. The heavens, with all their stars, and suns, and systems, exhibit few beauties to the great mass of inattentive spectators; and the observance of them, by day and by night, excites no correspondent emotions. All is a blank! Plunged into an abyss of cares and anxieties, chained to the oar of constant, unvarying labour; and solicitous only "to buy and sell, and get gain," to *them* "the heavens declare the glory of God, and the firmament showeth his handywork" almost in vain!

Nor can it escape observation, that valuable as the discoveries of philosophy are, the *mere discoverer* who converts his knowledge to no pious purpose, is the most infatuated of human beings. While he contemplates distances, magnitudes, and number--while he investigates the laws of motion, and the phenomena of nature--while he points the telescope to gaze on fiery comets, to pursue wandering planets in their orbits, to detect hitherto undiscovered globes of matter in the fields of space, merely to gratify curiosity or to acquire fame--the Christian contemplates the scene with another eye, and with far different sentiments. He sees GOD in all. "This," says he, "is *his* creation--this the work of *his* fingers--these the productions of *his* skill"--"by *his* spirit he hath garnished the heavens"--*he* hath appointed "the sweet influences of the Pleiades, and looseth the bands of Orion"--*he* "bringeth forth Mazzaroth in his season, and guides Arcturus with his sons." Yonder sun was formed and fixed by *his* mighty power--that moon, which walks forth in brightness, and those stars, which glitter on the robe of night, were kindled by *his* energy, and shine by *his* command.-- "Lift up your eyes on high, and behold WHO hath created these things, that bringeth out their host by number; he calleth them all by names."

The God of *nature* is the God of *truth*, the God of *revelation*, and the God of *Israel*. If the Christian contemplate the firmament, or look into the Bible, he sees the same Being. His operations are diverse, but it is the same God. If he go, like Isaac, "into the fields to meditate at the eventide," he meets with God in every leaf, in every stream, and in every star; if he enter into his closet to read the Scriptures, still he finds God in every page and in every truth; or if he pray, it is to "his FATHER who seeth in secret." He may change his place, but he can never remove from this lovely presence. "Nevertheless, I am continually with thee." Hence nature shines with new glory in his eyes. God in the *sun*, conducts him by a delightful association of ideas, and a frequent train of reflection, to "God in *Christ*, reconciling the world unto himself, not imputing their trespasses unto them."

[Sidenote: Years before Christ, 4004.]

Creation was the work of six days, upon the third of which, the earth was formed, and clothed with vegetative fertility; on the last "the Lord God formed MAN of the dust of the ground, and breathed into his nostrils the breath of life; and man became a living soul." It is for this reason that Eternal Wisdom is represented as "rejoicing in the habitable part of his earth, and her delights were with the sons of men." The *uninhabited* part of the earth is surely worthy of divine complacency. It forms a portion of that universe which the Supreme Architect at first pronounced to be "very good." The most retired places of this terrestrial globe, those extensive deserts which were never printed by the human foot, those dens and caves, deep valleys and cloud-encircled mountains, where silence and solitude have reigned from the beginning of time, contain innumerable manifestations of wisdom, power, and goodness. Wisdom might rejoice in a thousand wonders that lie concealed within the bowels of the earth, or in the caverns of the ocean, a world of mineral productions which our utmost research fails to discover; but the *habitable* part of the earth has ever excited the highest interest, as the residence of his intelligent creature, and the anticipated scene where the mediatorial work of his beloved Son was to be accomplished.

Man has been called "an abridgment of the universe," [1] uniting in himself in the extremes of being; in his body connected with the material, in his soul with the spiritual world;--by his corporeal constitution a fit inhabitant of the earth; by his intellectual faculties, a suitable tenant of the skies.

The soul of man constitutes the perfection of his nature, being destined to survive the dissolution of his body, and capable of everlasting progression in knowledge and felicity. And here a vast, an illimitable field of observation presents itself to view; but we must pass by it with only one practical remark. The welfare of this immortal soul ought to become the object of our principal solicitude. Considering the extent of its capacities, the indissoluble nature of its constituent principles, the novel and interesting circumstances under which it will hereafter exist, its total incompetency to provide for itself under those amazing vicissitudes which it is destined to undergo in a change of worlds, and the unalterable perpetuity of its future condition, how inconsiderate and how presumptuous must that individual be who neglects its interests, and acts in constant hostility to the first great law of nature, SELF-PRESERVATION! The protomartyr of the Christian age evinced a wise anxiety when he exclaimed in his dying moments, "Lord Jesus, receive my *spirit*." He was aware that his body would soon be consigned by the fury of persecution to its native dust; but this excited comparatively little concern. To him it was of no importance whether his grave was with the rich or the poor, whether his burying-place were an obscure or an illustrious spot: he was anxious for the salvation of his *soul*. Unhappily, mankind in general lavish all their cares upon the body, to embellish or preserve it, to pamper its appetites, or to minister to its artificial necessities: but what an infatuation is it, to provide for that which perishes, and to be careless of that which is immortal--to decorate the walls, and to despise the furniture--to value the casket, and to throw away the jewel!

The situation of Adam in the garden of Eden, shows that his Creator had adopted every proper expedient to promote his felicity. The place selected for his residence was in the highest degree rich and fertile, furnished with every suitable accommodation, and "well watered" by a large river which ran through it, and afterward divided itself into four considerable branches. In being directed to "dress" and to "keep" the garden, the goodness of God appears in providing him with an employment adapted to a state of primitive innocence, and calculated by a proper occupation of his time to promote his happiness. A slothful inactivity is not only incompatible with true enjoyment in our fallen state, but would have been inconsistent with the bliss of original paradise; and even when our nature shall have attained its greatest perfection in a future world, an incessant exertion of our intellectual powers and moral capacities, is represent as essential to the joy of heaven. There "his servants shall *serve* him."

"When we think of Paradise," observes bishop Horne, "we think of it as the seat of delight. The name EDEN authorizes us so to do. It signifies PLEASURE, and the idea of pleasure is inseparable from that of a garden, where man still seeks after lost happiness, and where, perhaps, a good man finds the nearest resemblance of it which this world affords." "What is requisite," exclaims a great and original genius, "to make a wise and a happy man, but reflection and peace? And both are the natural growth of a garden. A garden to the virtuous is a paradise still extant, a paradise unlost." [2] The culture of a garden, as it was the first employment of man, so it is that to which the most eminent persons in different ages have retired, from the camp and the cabinet, to pass the interval between a life of action and a removal hence. When old Dioclesian was invited from his retreat, to resume the purple which he had laid down some years before, "Ah," said he, "could you but see those fruits and herbs of mine own raising at Salona, you would never talk to me of empire!" An accomplished statesman of our own country, who spent the latter part of his life in this manner, has so well described the advantages of it, that it would be injustice to communicate his ideas in any words but his own. "No other sort of abode," says he, "seems to contribute so much both to tranquillity of mind and indolence of body. The sweetness of the air, the pleasantness of the smell, the verdure of plants, the clearness and lightness of food, the exercise of working or walking; but above all, the exemption from care and solicitude, seem equally to favour and improve both contemplation and health, the enjoyment of sense and imagination, and thereby the quiet and ease both of body and mind. A garden has been the inclination of kings, and the choice of philosophers; the common favourite of public and private men; the pleasure of the greatest, and the care of the meanest; an employment and a possession for which no man is too high nor too low. If we believe the Scriptures, we must allow that God Almighty esteemed the life of man in a garden the happiest he could give him, or else he would not have placed Adam in that of Eden." [3] Traditions of this state of primeval felicity are current among all nations; they are discoverable in the Roman and Grecian fables of the gardens of Flora, of Alcinous, and of the Hesperides; and in the pleasing fictions of the poets respecting the golden age.

Thus the Lord God formed the nature of man pure, placed him in a garden of delights, and poured around him rivers of joy. The heavens and the earth, the visible and invisible worlds, animate and inanimate, material and spiritual beings, conspired to replenish his cup of bliss; and, as the perfection of his felicity, God himself condescended to visit his creature.

Human transgression has disturbed the peace of human life; but man, in his primeval state, was exposed to no changes; his cup had no bitterness, his day no cloud, his path no thorn; the *past* had no regrets, the *present* no guilt, the *future*, no terror; the stream of mercy flowed into Paradise with uninterrupted course, and the beam of prosperity shone with unfading brightness and unsetting splendour.

In this exalted condition there was neither corporeal nor mental debility; and the body and soul were not more closely connected in the constitution of their being, than in the harmony of their friendship. There was no opposition between the flesh and the spirit, no internal warfare, no unhappy disagreement; the dictates of a pure mind were unreluctantly obeyed by the faculties of an uncorrupted body; for it appears to have been the established order of Infinite Wisdom in the constitution of the universe, that matter should be in subjection to spirit, body to soul, animals to rational creatures, and man to God; his understanding was clear, his judgment correct, his affections holy, his will free, his reason upright; he desired only what was desirable, he loved only what was lovely; the whole moral machinery was in the most complete order, the fine-toned instrument constructed by omniscient skill, was in perfect tune!

But notwithstanding the diversified means of enjoyment with which Adam was furnished, his paradise was still incomplete; one ingredient was wanting to his cup of joy. Although the place of his residence was, us the greatest of poets describes it,

"A happy rural seat of various view,--"

although diversified with "groves," and "lawns," and "level downs," and "flocks," and "irriguous valleys," and "umbrageous grots and caves of cool recess," and "murmuring waters," and "airs, vernal airs--"

"while universal Pan,
Knit with the Graces and the Hours in dance,
Led on th' eternal spring--"

the favoured lord of this unrivalled dominion was ALONE. The inanimate creation spread before his view its unparalleled beauties, and nature furnished a table to supply all his wants; the animal world acknowledged his superiority, and went to him to receive their names: his Maker condescended to hold communion with this excellent and intellectual creature, admitting him to that sacred intercourse, and imparting some of that divine knowledge which will no doubt constitute the future felicity of emparadised believers: still he had no COMPANION, no one to share his pleasures, no one upon equal terms to whom he could communicate his sentiments. Endowed with a social nature, he had at present no social means; he seemed as if placed in that solitary point, that fair, but desolate region, where he saw thousands of creatures below him and above him, but none upon that pleasing *level* which conduces to a delightful and profitable familiarity.

This defect, however, scarcely existed before the goodness of his Maker supplied it. "And the Lord God said, It is not good that the man should be alone; I will make him a help meet for him." The process by which this merciful intention was accomplished appears truly wonderful: Adam was put into a profound sleep, and the Lord God took out one of his ribs, from which he made a woman, and closed up the flesh. What must have been the emotions of our great progenitor, when, upon awaking from his supernatural slumber, this help meet was presented to him! He had, it seems, an intuitive perception of the kind purpose for which this female companion of his future days was made; or some immediate revelation disclosing both the manner of her formation, and the reason of his being presented with this invaluable gift. In the first transports of gratitude he exclaimed, "This is now bone of my bone, and flesh of my flesh; she shall be called woman (or *Ishah,*) because she was taken out of man." This name was afterwards changed by him to *Havah,* or EVE; assigning, as a reason, that "she was the mother of all living." This name we have placed at the head of the list of female characters in the present work; and while her brief history is replete with instruction, it possesses an additional interest, from the consideration of her being the *first* woman. We are conducted back to the infancy of time, to the origin of human being, to the cause of the present degradation of our race, to an impressive exhibition of the evil of sin, and to the dawn of redeeming mercy upon this world of transgressors. In this history we shall perceive reasons both for humiliation and triumph; we shall see human nature in ruins, and provision made for its reparation; we shall witness the effects of infernal agency, the loss of primeval glory, the power of female influence; and, above all, the INFINITE GOODNESS of our Creator.

It very much enhances the dignity of the female character to reflect, that of all created things the woman was selected as the only suitable companion of the first and fairest of men; she was made expressly to contribute to his mental and social pleasures, and not to be the slave of his will; if the *mother,* she was intended also as the *instructor* of his children; his assistant, at least, in the "delightful task" of "rearing the tender thought," and "teaching the young idea how to shoot:" she was qualified to counsel and co-operate with him in his daily occupations, to aid in the investigation of those laws which regulated the new-made world, to unite with him in acts of worship, and to enliven, as well as to participate, his devotional hours.

Revelation is the only system that assigns to woman her natural and proper elevation in the scale of being, and inspires a consciousness of her real dignity. The moment that an intelligent being is by any injurious treatment, or by any prevailing error, induced to form a degrading estimate of itself, that moment it begins to approximate a state of meanness which was hitherto only imaginary. Let such an one be conscious of being held in no esteem, or prized solely as the tool of servitude or the food of appetite, and all majesty of character is lost; all aim or wish to rise above the brute, to aspire after a station or character, to the occupation of which a tyrannic impiety has opposed an insurmountable barrier, is gone; and those great principles which confer a superiority upon the human kind, and point to a noble pre-eminence, cease to operate, and expire for want of action. This state of things is unnatural, contrary to the original purpose of creation, and in fact, more dishonorable to the usurper than to the degraded sufferer. In Mahometan and Pagan countries the rights of women have been sacrificed to the caprices of men; and, having plucked this fair flower of creation from its original and highly elevated situation, its beauty has faded, its glory been lost in the sacrilegious hands of its barbarian possessor. Abject slavery or base flattery have existed where woman has been displaced from her proper and original character, and the most mischievous consequences have ensued. [4]

The first woman is said to have been formed *out of man*; hence, as a *part of himself*, it seems the law of creation, that man should cherish the most affectionate sentiments for the woman:--"Therefore," says the inspired history, "shall a man leave his father and his mother, and shall cleave unto his wife; and they shall be one flesh."

It is observable, that the woman was neither taken out of the *head*, nor from the *feet*, but from the *side*, and near the *heart*! If, therefore, on the one hand, she ought not to assume pre-eminence, on the other she is not to be trampled on and despised, but received as an equal and a friend.

As the original arrangements of Infinite Wisdom were the most perfect in their respective kinds, the appropriation of *one* woman only, as the companion and *wife* of the first created man, indicates both the will of the Creator respecting marriage, and the circumstances in which it is most likely to produce the greatest sum of domestic felicity. Man is neither to live *alone*, nor to indulge that depravity of taste, which, by seeking enjoyment in diversity, not only ensures disappointment, but generates discord.

The advocates for celibacy and for plurality, equally betray an ignorance of Scripture and of human nature, and can find few supporters, except amongst the infidel or the barbarian classes of mankind. "They that will not connect their interests, lest they should be unhappy by their partner's fault, dream away their time without friendship, without fondness, and are driven to rid themselves of the day, for which they have no use, by childish amusement or vicious delights. They act as beings under the constant sense of some known inferiority, that fills their minds with rancor and their tongues with censure; they are peevish at home, and malevolent abroad; and, as the outlaws of human nature, make it their business and their pleasure to disturb that society which debars them from its privileges. To live without feeling or exciting sympathy, to be fortunate without adding to the felicity of others, or afflicted without tasting the balm of pity, is a state more gloomy than solitude: it is not retreat, but exclusion from mankind. Marriage has many pains, but celibacy has no pleasures." [5]

The original law is enforced in the New Testament by an infallible commentator: "Have ye not read, that he which made them at the beginning made them male and female, and said, For this cause shall a man leave father and mother, and shall cleave to his wife; and they twain shall be one flesh? Wherefore they are no more twain, but one flesh. What, therefore, God hath joined together, let no man put asunder." Thus Jesus Christ sanctions marriage by his authority, virtually interdicts polygamy, and absolutely prohibits divorce.

As the bestowal of one woman upon one man, at the creation of the human species, was sufficiently indicative of the divine will, so the near equality of the two sexes is a strong presumptive argument in favour of this division of society: if a different proportion were better calculated to replenish the world with population, the circumstances of Adam seemed particularly to require such an arrangement; or if it were calculated to promote human happiness, the Divine Being, who created Eve for the very purpose of enhancing the bliss of our first parent, would have superadded this to his paradisaical possessions. The reverse, however, was obviously the case. Polygamy violates the constitution of nature, and produces contests, jealousies, distracted affections, a voluptuousness which dissolves the vigour of the intellectual and corporeal faculties, neglect of children, with other lamentable evils, for which it furnishes no compensation. "Whether," says Dr. Paley, "simultaneous polygamy was permitted by the law of Moses, seems doubtful; but whether permitted or not, it was certainly practised by the Jewish patriarchs, both before that law and under it. The permission, if there were any, might be like that of divorce, 'for the hardness of their heart,' in condescension to their established indulgencies, rather than from the general rectitude or propriety of the thing itself. The state of manners in Judea had probably undergone a reformation in this respect before the time of Christ, for in the New Testament we meet with no trace or mention of any such practice being tolerated." [6]

Though man was created in the state we have been representing, encircled with the divine favour, rich in all the requisites of happiness, and the tenant of a glorious palace, a melancholy alteration soon occurred. Seduced by infernal temptation, he forsook his God and forfeited his paradise; and from the narrative of his fall in the book of Genesis, which immediately succeeds the account of his felicity, we learn that the WOMAN was the first transgressor. Assuming the form of a serpent, Satan presented himself to Eve, and entered into familiar conversation with her. To his artful inquiry respecting the divine interdiction of one of the trees of the garden, she at first gave a very proper answer. Satan insinuated that the terms which God had prescribed, were severe, if not capricious: but she replied in a manner indicative of her perfect acquiescence in the commandment, her untainted purity of mind, and such a sense of the beneficence of God, as prevented even a momentary doubt of his wisdom or goodness, in the denial of "one tree in the midst of the garden."

The tempter, in making a second attack, became more positive. In contradiction to the divine assurance, he affirmed, with unhesitating effrontery, that they should *not* die, even though they tasted the fruit of the interdicted tree; but on the contrary, that they should be "as gods, knowing good and evil." By the very same representations do the ministers of satanic malice in every age seduce mankind, suggesting that the commands of Heaven are extremely rigid, and flattering them that sin may be committed with impunity.

The fatal moment was come--she *looked* at *the tree!*--Ah! thou mother of all living! hadst thou looked at the *command*, and turned away from the attractive plant and the beguiling serpent, all would have been well--thine innocence had been uncorrupted, thy posterity uncondemned! But unhallowed curiosity prompted the fatal experiment--she wished to be wise--

> "Her rash hand in evil hour,
> Forth reaching to the fruit, she plucked, she ate.
> Earth felt the wound; and Nature from her seat,
> Sighing through all her works, gave signs of wo,
> That all was lost!"

It does not appear that any ill consequences resulted *immediately* from the criminal rashness of this sinner, so that she was encouraged to go to her husband, who, seduced by a fairer tempter, and one endeared to him by the tenderest ties, complied with her request to share the violated tree. Motives of curiosity and pride excited *her* to sin, and so far as appears from the history, blind affection influenced *him*. Alas! she who was given him as a *"help meet,"* is changed into his *seducer,* and from his *comfort* is become his *snare!* That influence which she naturally possessed over her husband, ought to have been exerted to *prevent* his compliance with any sinful intimation, in case of an unexpected solicitation, instead of which it was used to *induce* him to plunge into guilt and ruin. "We have a right to presume," observes Saurin, "that as no crime was ever connected with more melancholy results, so none was ever more atrocious than hers. The more we examine its nature, the more base it appears, and the more easy is it to exculpate religion from those reproaches which this statement has so often occasioned. Whatever tends to extenuate the guilt of other sins, is an aggravation of this.

"Sometimes a confusion *of the passions* obscures all the powers of the soul; a man who sins in this manner, is frequently less deserving of abhorrence than of pity; he acts from a sort of compulsion, and protests against the crime, even at the moment he is committing it. Eve possessed a dominion over those passions to which we are become enslaved; she could easily calm their turbulence, and they had no other influence over her, than what was on her own part voluntary.

"Sometimes *necessity* inspires the design of acquiring by unlawful methods, a supply which nature has rendered requisite, and which cannot be legitimately obtained. But, what could be wanting to satisfy the insatiable cravings of this woman? What could she need as an addition to her happiness? She might be said to be 'crowned with glory and honour;' she had dominion over the works of the Creator; all things were put under her feet; all sheep and oxen; yea, and the beasts of the field, the fowl of the air, and the fish of the sea, and whatsoever passeth through the paths of the seas. Even her love of variety could not yet be satiated, and this garden offered a thousand exquisite fruits which she had never tasted.

"Sometimes *doubt* blends itself with disobedience. There are but few sins totally unaccompanied with unbelief; some clouds always obscure our faith; some veils of concealment overspread the existence of the Creator. Among the previous pangs which sin occasions, when we deliberate respecting the commission of it, there always exist certain vague ideas in the mind, such as these--perhaps no superior being concerns himself about it; or, perhaps no one has forbidden it;--but Eve could not possibly doubt of the existence or the will of the Creator. She had herself heard this language from his mouth, 'In the day that thou eatest thereof thou shall surely die.'

"Sometimes our abuse of a favour proceeds from *false ideas of its origin*. Though every sinner be ungrateful, yet every sinner is not a monster of ingratitude. The first cause of our felicity is sometimes mingled with the second, which is serviceable in procuring it. Our industry frequently seems to share with Providence the glory of our condition, and the nature of a blessing sometimes leads us to forget the acknowledgments due to our benefactor; but Eve enjoyed no good which did not in some respect proceed *immediately* from the bounty of God, and which ought not to have induced her to glorify him.

"Sometimes a *pure motive* produces an *impure action*, and the love of virtue itself sometimes occasions our removal from it; but in the present case the action is aggravated by the motive. Pride, vain-glory, perhaps the desire of robbing God of his pre-eminence, his omniscience, or his jurisdiction over the creature, his most sacred and incommunicable distinctions, were the dispositions that actuated this woman.

"Can any imaginable pretext serve to palliate so atrocious a crime, or excuse the woman who first committed it, and the man who joined in the rebellion? Would they indeed have been less criminal, if a seraph of glory had proposed to them the impious deed? Was not the faculty of *reason* which they had received from God, sufficient to make them understand what revelation has taught us, that if an angel from heaven were to proclaim any thing contrary to what God has commanded, it ought to inspire us with no other sentiments than those of *anathema* and execration?" [7]

The general consequences of human transgression were:

1. *The loss of Eden*, and the subjection of our first parents to a mode of life both humiliating and painful. Ease was exchanged for toil, honour for degradation, peace for distraction and wo.

It is always painful to quit a favourite spot. The heart lingers long behind, and employs the pencil of memory to paint the absent scene. Adam and Eve must have experienced inexpressible emotions when driven from their primeval residence, where all the elements, all the seasons, and all beings had contributed to their enjoyment. Never, never, could they forget those landscapes on which the eye paused with rapture; never, never, could they cease to remember its rich productions, its often-frequented vales, and hills, and rivers, and woods; never, never, could they obliterate from their memory the bright sunshine of heavenly love that beamed upon them there--for by transgression they suffered.

2. *The loss of their God.* The divine favour can alone constitute the real felicity of a creature; this, in its full manifestation, is *heaven*--in its total absence, is *hell.* No place, however loaded with blessings, can constitute a desirable abode, unless God be there. The fairest Eden without this manifestation must be a melancholy dungeon to an intelligent and immortal being. It is this which was forfeited by original sin, and which occasioned "a flaming sword which turned every way, to keep the way of the tree of life."

It would be inconsistent with the nature of God not to manifest displeasure against iniquity, however high and dignified the being who commits it. An angel must lose his crown, if he dare to disobey that Being who is "glorious in holiness."

3. Mankind incurred by sin *the loss of life.*--"And the Lord God commanded the man, saying, Of every tree in the garden thou mayest freely eat, but of the tree of the knowledge of good and evil thou shall not eat of it, for in the day that thou eatest thereof, thou shalt surely die." This denunciation included an exposure not only to temporal, but to eternal death, as might be shown from the nature and demerit of sin, the means which were afterwards employed to destroy its effects in the work of Christ, the repeated declarations of Scripture, and the peculiar energy of the original expression; it is literally, "Dying, thou shalt die." The weight of the condemnation rested on the sinner's head, and in order to maintain the glory of his character, "the blessed God" rendered his punishment as extraordinary as his former mercies, and proportionate to his enormous guilt.--"Thou wilt by no means clear the guilty."--"These shall go away into *everlasting* punishment."

4. The sin of Adam and Eve involved the *ruin of their posterity.* As the first man and woman, they stood in a peculiar relation to all who should hereafter be born, the representatives of unnumbered millions, whose future condition essentially depended on their character and circumstances. Had they continued innocent, it cannot be doubted their children would have been placed in a far happier condition. They would have inherited purity and a blessing for the Father's sake, instead of being "shapen in iniquity." As the streams become polluted when the fountain is poisoned, or as the branches die when the root is destroyed, so the race of men are become degraded, accursed, and condemned by their parent's sin. They inherit a nature depraved by original transgression, and disposed to every wicked indulgence. Instead of becoming more assimilated to God, as man had flattered himself he should be by partaking of the forbidden fruit, he became from that moment assimilated to the devil. Every dishonorable and hurtful passion took immediate possession of the breast, and to this hour reigns in the carnal man with unrivalled influence. Whatever misery

results from the gratification of these passions, is solely attributable to the principle; for man, who is criminal by nature, is still more so by inclination and practice. The world is thrown into a state of anarchy. The unbridled dominion of the passions disturbs the peace of the individual and the harmony of society. Sin makes a man at variance with himself, with his neighbour, and with the whole constitution of things. He is restless as the ocean, impelled by every contrary wind, and tossed about by every sportive billow. The desire of happiness exists; but he is ignorant of the true means of it, and is perpetually pursuing it by a method which only plunges him into greater misery. To this cause must be attributed all the mental distresses and all the bodily afflictions of the individual--all the disturbances which prevent domestic enjoyment, the bickerings and jealousies of families with their various alliances--all the animosities which agitate social life--all the intestine broils, ambitious emulations, endless contentions, and opposing interests that distract a state--all the melancholy wars that convulse nations and desolate empires, the record of which has stained the page of history in all ages--with every particular, form, and mode of evil, discoverable in the world.

But sin extends its ravages beyond the present state. It has not only strewed the whole path of life with tormenting thorns, but enkindled "everlasting burnings." It has not only introduced disorder into the world, disease into the body, and distress into the condition of men, but exposed them to the agonies of death and of hell. It is sin which banishes every hope and excludes every ray of comfort from the realms of infernal despair. Justly, then, is it characterized by the apostle, as "*exceeding sinful.*"

There were two respects in which the woman became more deeply affected by the curse than the man; she not only participated, as a fallen creature, in the diversified calamities which, from the moment of transgression, were entailed upon humanity, but suffered as a *female* in the *conjugal* and *maternal* relationships which she was destined hereafter to sustain. Her husband was to "rule over her," and in sorrow "she was to bring forth children." The yoke of subjection, indeed, in the one case, and the pangs of childbirth in the other, are alleviated by the benign influences of Christianity, whose supplies are intended to heal the wounds inflicted by the poisonous serpent; but they nevertheless attach, in greater or less degrees, to the human constitution.

The reason of this marked difference in the dispensation of an avenging Providence to the two principal parties concerned, was obviously this; the woman was *first* in the transgression, and after listening to the deceptive counsel of her adversary, tempted when she ought to have warned her husband. It appears consonant to every principle of equity, that the atrociousness of her guilt should be characterized by appropriate expressions of displeasure; and that, in the future condition of mankind, all beings should recognize, not only the general purity of the divine administration, but its reference to the peculiarities of individual delinquency. Whatever mystery may at present involve the proceedings of Infinite Wisdom, and however incapacitated we may be to discover in every given case, or even in the majority of instances, the distinct traces of a justice that holds the even balance, and adjusts with nicety the proportions of sin and punishment, of this we may feel perfectly assured, that "every one" will eventually "receive the things done in his body, *according to that he hath done*, whether it be good or bad."

It should be a matter of serious consideration to women to employ the influence which they possess, as the gift of nature, to wise, holy, and useful purposes. Let the young female especially see to it, that her attractions are not dedicated to the service of sin, but to that of virtue and of Christ. Let her neither be tempted, nor tempt others, but close her ear against the voice of enticement, and make a covenant with her tongue, that it neither utter folly, nor propagate slander. Let the daughters of Eve imitate their mother in her state of unfallen rectitude, when she shone in all the purity of innocence, and in all the summer of her charms; but let them avoid that course which tarnished her glory, debased her nature, and withered her paradise. It is indisputable that society is materially affected by the character of women; and in very important respects the moral state, as well as the social comfort of the world, is at their disposal. Let them beware of the delusions to which they are exposed, and make virtuous use of the influence which is undoubtedly given them. Let them aim to be guides to piety, not seducers to sin; and, instead of presenting to others the forbidden fruit, refuse to taste, or even to *look* at it: so shall they regain the dignity they have lost, be admitted to partake of the untainted spring of happiness, and enjoy at once a peaceful conscience and an approving God.

The narrative which has here been briefly introduced, stands in immediate connection with a subject which abounds in considerable difficulties, and has produced, unhappily, many acrimonious controversies. These it would be improper to detail; but as our design is chiefly practical, if some of those objections which occur to almost every mind, can, by a few words, be in any degree obviated, it will be worthy at least of a short digression.

1. It has been alleged that the first man might have been created immutable by a necessity of nature, the consequence of which would have been his own perfect and unchanging happiness, and that of all mankind. The imagination seizes the transporting thought, and in a moment converts

every spot of this barren wilderness into "the garden of Eden." Does it, however, become us to prescribe rules to Omniscience? Was the Deity obliged to impose a miraculous constraint upon the human will, and compel his creature to choose whatever is best with invariable determination and promptitude? If a parent were to caution his child against a danger, into which he afterward plunged himself by his inadvertence or perverseness, would the child be justified in censuring the parent, because, in addition to advice, he did not employ bonds and cords? Adam might have been created immutable by a necessity of nature. True--but Adam would then have been another being, and not a man. It might with similar propriety be asked, why men were not created equal to angels, or beasts to men? This sentiment implies, that it was not proper to create such a being as *man* at all, an intimation sufficiently presumptuous. Adam possessed all the perfections essential to his nature, and conducive to his felicity, and all the motives to obedience, which a reasonable creature could demand. If he fell, it was *violating* and not *concurring* with the principles of his nature. And who was culpable for this violation? It is true he was *tempted,*--but then he was *forewarned*. He was *tempted*--so was the *second Adam*, the Lord from heaven, who effectually *resisted* the temptation.

2. Some have supposed that the punishment was disproportioned to the offence. A more attentive consideration of the subject, however, will demonstrate the contrary. The compliance with the seductions of the tempter, of which our first parents were guilty, betrayed many lamentable symptoms of degeneracy. Pride, ambition, discontent, unbelief, presumption, ingratitude, and an undervaluation of the divine favour, are all plainly discernible through the thin veil of an extenuating apology, with which they vainly attempted to conceal their baseness.--"The woman, whom thou gavest to be with me, she gave me of the tree, and I did eat." And the woman said, "The serpent beguiled me, and I did eat." Endowed as they were with knowledge, it was a sin against the greatest *light*; surrounded as they were with motives, it was a sin against the greatest *means*; warned as they were of danger and promised eternal blessedness, it was a sin against the greatest *reason*; and placed as they were at the head of a numerous posterity, and in a sense the depositories and trustees of their happiness, it was a sin against the greatest *public good*.

Besides, it was the *first sin*, and consequently justice demanded such an expression of the divine displeasure as would tend to deter future transgressors, and evince the purity of God to all holy intelligences. When justice seized upon the delinquents, and brought them to the equitable tribunal of Heaven, the whole intelligent universe may be considered as attentive spectators of the scene. Every eye was fixed--every ear open--

every tongue silent--every harp suspended. The great Judge with whom "a thousand years are as one day, and one day as a thousand years," saw, as it were, the unborn generations of men all present, and tremblingly awaiting the verdict. This was the solemn hour when the perfections of Deity were to be most sublimely illustrated, and ten thousand worlds were to learn in one eventful moment the character of their Creator, "Therefore the Lord God sent him from the garden of Eden."

The nature of sin in itself should also be considered. It is no trifling affair. From the habit of observing only its outward effects, we overlook its rancorous principle. The propensity to extenuate sin arises from ignorance of its vileness. We judge of every thing by comparison, and self-flattery always renders the comparison favorable to ourselves. But *small* and *large* are terms which, though we have chosen to adopt them, do not properly belong to the subject. The divine mind contemplates sin in its principle; and the *least* transgression, being a resistance of his command, an insult to his authority, an opposition to his truth, a violation, of general order, a perversion and misuse of the noblest faculties, whatever may be the force of the attack or the nature of the temptation, is infinitely offensive to the blessed God. It is an admission of that principle which, could it possibly prevail, would produce eternal discord, universal rebellion, and boundless misery.

3. If, however, we be accounted sinners in Adam, may it not be inferred that our guilt is incalculably *inferior* to his, and that in all our actions resulting from this inherent depravity, we are more *pitiable* than *culpable*? By no means.--It is sufficient to remark, that though our original guilt be less than his, not having been personally the perpetrators of the first crime, our *actual* guilt is equal, if not greater. For it is obvious we sin with all the experience of the past to forewarn us; we sin, though we witness the deplorable effects of his fall, and hear the denunciations of vengeance in the Scriptures.

Though it be true that sin originates in a depravity of heart, which is the fatal inheritance of the whole human race, will any one pretend that such a sentiment justifies its excesses? The perpetration of iniquity in the course of our daily practice, must not be confounded with the original tendency. These excesses are in no sense chargeable upon the principle as its necessary and unavoidable result, because thousands escape "the pollutions that are in the world." Nor are we less obliged to love God in consequence of the fall, though unhappily we are become more incapable and indisposed to it. You ask, why passions were implanted in human nature? The reply is, to extend the means of our happiness, by rendering us more capable of glorifying and enjoying God. If they have acquired a sinful bias, the obligation to devote them to their original purpose is by no means diminished: But their great Author, to whom we are responsible for every faculty, requires that we should oppose their perverse propensities, earnestly repent of the irregularities produced by their seducing influence, and solicit the aid of his grace to conquer them.

When the apostle of the Gentiles was reasoning before an unjust judge of "righteousness, temperance, and judgment to come," it is said, "Felix trembled, and answered. Go thy way for this time, when I have a convenient season I will call for thee." Unhappy man! Hadst thou but obeyed Paul instead of dismissing him, hadst thou but yielded to thy kindling convictions, confessed thy sins, and sought salvation through the blood of that Jesus whom Paul preached, the church of Christ would have hailed thee as "a brand plucked out of the burning."

Every one is conscious that, however corrupt his nature, he is under no irresistible impulse, no constraining necessity. If he commit sin it is voluntarily. Sin is his choice and his pleasure. He does not sin because he is *necessitated* to do it, but because he *loves* it: and however willing the carnal mind may be to avail itself of sophistical reasonings to quiet conscience, every one must, in the hour of dispassionate reflection, feel himself implicated in the charge, "all have sinned."

Listen to the case of a wretched prodigal.--Crime had reduced him to rags. He had a *home*--but through perverseness he banished himself from all its comforts. He had a *father*--but he undervalued his affection, in a moment of folly demanded his patrimony, and adventured abroad friendless and alone. A few years brought him to the very gates of death. O thoughtless sinner, "*Thou* art the man!" *Thou* hast forsaken God, the Father of mercies! *Thou* art "perishing in ignorance and unbelief!" But this moral lunatic came to himself, and resolved to return to his father; "I will arise and go to my father, and will say unto him, Father, I have sinned against heaven and before thee, and am no more worthy to be called thy son; make me as one of thy hired servants. And he arose and came to his father. But when he was yet a great way off, his father saw him, and had compassion, and ran, and fell on his neck, and kissed him." What a son! what a father! what a meeting! what sighs of penitence! what tears of fondness! what looks of tenderness! what words of peace! How were resentment and grief drowned in a sea of love!

God of all comfort, who art thyself this kind, forgiving, bountiful Father, grant of thine infinite mercy that every reader may prove himself this humble, sincere, and grateful penitent!

Sarah Chapter II

[Sidenote: Years before Christ, about 1920-1921.]

At a very advanced period of life, and in obedience to a divine injunction, Abraham went out from his country and his father's house, "not knowing whither he went." By this cheerful, prompt, and pious submission to the mysterious will of Heaven, he has acquired a high distinction in the sacred records, and presents a noble example for the imitation of all future ages. Here was no debate between a sense of duty and an inclination to sin--no disposition to question the wisdom or the goodness of the command--no effort to devise expedients for the purpose of procuring delay--and no unholy apprehensions respecting the possible or probable consequences of such a proceeding.

In this removal from Chaldea, the illustrious exile took with him his wife, his nephew, "and all their substance that they had gathered, and the souls that they had gotten in Haran." Upon their arrival in Canaan, the divine declaration respecting his future possession of the country was renewed, and he erected an altar to the Lord in the plain of Moreh. The same act of devotion was performed at the next stage of his journey, on a mountain to the east of Bethel; for no change of place could obliterate his sense of religious obligation.

This land of promise was soon afflicted with a grievous famine, in consequence of which, he was necessitated to provide for the subsistence of his family by removing into Egypt. This was a new trial to his faith; for by what possible means could a land at present so impoverished, become a place of plentiful subsistence to his posterity, when multiplied as the sands upon the sea-shore? Driven even from this promised inheritance, he did not, however, manifest a spirit of discontent or unbelief, but hastened to seek a temporary asylum, convinced that he to whose guidance he had committed himself and his beloved family, could, by the outstretched arm of his power, not only overcome every obstacle which to human ignorance might seem insurmountable; but by his concurrent wisdom render difficulties themselves subservient to the accomplishment of his purposes.

Alas! on his entering Egypt he is seized with apprehension. The faith which had hitherto been so conspicuous is mingled with distrust, and he engages his beloved SARAH, who is now introduced to our notice, in an act of most unwarrantable duplicity. The whole of this transaction is detailed with that perfect impartiality which characterizes the histories of the Scriptures, and which furnishes one very decisive evidence of their inspiration.

Sarah is represented as very beautiful. Her husband was aware that this circumstance would attract the notice of the Egyptians, not only because of the contrast her person would exhibit to the swarthy complexions of their women, but on account of their licentious character. He dreaded their illicit attachment, and the probable consequence that they might assassinate him in order to obtain his wife. This idea of Egyptian morals was no doubt correct, but how deplorable! They would not commit adultery; but for the sake of gratifying a guilty passion, were ready to perpetrate the abominable sin of murder! And thus, under the strange pretence of reverence for the matrimonial law, they would have violated at once the dictates of humanity, the principles of reason, and the constitutions of heaven. So common is it for transgressors to "strain at a knat and swallow a camel;" and so uniform the course of guilt, which never walks alone, but draws with it a train of complicated iniquities!

The preliminaries being settled, Abraham and his family entered Egypt. She was to say, when any inquiries were made, that she was his *sister*, hoping by this artifice to escape danger. This, it must be observed, was not a *direct* falsehood: it was such only by *implication*. It was true that, according to the Jewish mode of reckoning, Sarah was the *sister* of Abraham; but their intention in circulating this statement was, to conceal the whole truth of her being his *wife*. Notwithstanding the ingenuity which some learned men have displayed in attempting to vindicate this conduct, we must without hesitation pronounce it base, mean, and prevaricating. The purpose was to deceive, and it was the more censurable for being so deliberately premeditated and so perseveringly practised. There are cases in which persons have been overtaken in a fault, impelled by some momentary passion, excited by some brilliant temptation, or betrayed by some unexpected coincidence of circumstances, and of which they have deeply and almost immediately repented--a situation which cannot but excite our pity, as well as our disapprobation; but this was a transaction which it is impossible either to extenuate or justify. Let it be improved as a motive for self-examination, and a beacon to warn us from similar misconduct. "O keep my soul, and deliver me: let me not be ashamed, for I put my trust in thee. Let INTEGRITY and UPRIGHTNESS preserve me, for I wait on thee."

Prevarication of every kind partakes of the very essence of lying, being not only subversive of social happiness, by preventing all confidential intercourse amongst mankind, but diametrically opposed to the commands of God. Every species of wilful deceit, as the use of ambiguities in language for the purpose of misleading; the adoption of expressions which we know to be understood by another in a different sense from what we really mean; mental reservations; a studied suppression of part of the truth, as in the present example, is unworthy the character of any person who professes to be an honest man, much more of one who sustains the dignified character of a Christian. "Wherefore, putting away lying, speak every man truth with his neighbour."

In theory, it seems an easy thing to adhere to truth; but it is too frequently found difficult in practice. When motives of interest are balanced against motives of duty, it is well if the former do not sometimes preponderate. Are we always careful to state facts *exactly* as they exist; to avoid all false colouring; to swear even to our own hurt? If so, we need not fear investigation, because nothing can be detected but an honourable, undissembled mind.

When Adam disobeyed the divine commandment, and in consequence forfeited the bliss of primeval paradise, he was seduced by his fair partner, who had already listened to the wily suggestions of the serpent; but Abraham, so far from being tempted by his wife, appears to have been the sole contriver of this disingenuous artifice, and employed all his influence to induce her to transgress. In following him from his original residence into Canaan, and subsequently to Egypt, she obeyed the dictates of affection and of religion; but when she suffered herself to be persuaded into a deceitful action, she sacrificed the purity of her conscience. It became her, however painful the conflict, to resist the temptation; and, when the claims of heaven were opposed to those of affection or human authority, to obey God rather than man. It appears that we are not only in danger of being misled by those who are our avowed enemies, or by the pernicious example of the multitude who do evil, but the nearest and dearest relatives may become snares to our feet; and even those, in whose piety and wisdom we should naturally confide, may, under the influence of temporary delusion, incite us to do wrong. Our affections must not be implicitly trusted. There is a point where submission to man becomes treason against heaven. It were better to incur the displeasure even of the dearest friend and tenderest relative, than of Him who possesses supreme authority over conscience.

At the same time, let a woman, who thus ventures to disobey her husband, do it with that caution which results solely from a conviction of paramount duty, and from a well founded assurance that she is not mistaken. It is no trifling occasion that will justify opposition to the will of him whom she is commanded to obey; and if it be done in a proper spirit, it will be done with a degree of reluctance, and under an overwhelming sense of necessity.

Let the spirit of meekness be prevalent. Nothing in the *manner*, in which unwelcome opposition is maintained, must indicate a proud resistance, or an air of triumph. It must not be litigious, petulant, unconciliating; but the importance of those principles which occasion the difference, must be apparent in the temper of mind they produce. Thus, it will be possible to maintain the rights of conscience, and not to violate the claims of duty: the integrity of the heart will be indicated, not by words only, but by actions.--It is natural to feel indignant against a conduct which we suspect to proceed from improper motives, and a hostile spirit; but we extenuate even the mistakes of those who differ most widely from ourselves, provided we have sufficient evidence that their scruples result from conscientious feelings. While, therefore, in our differences from others, we are careful not to be actuated by mere frivolous pretences, we must be equally solicitous not to be deterred from showing a firm consistence of conduct, lest we should incur the charge of an affected singularity.

The fact was such as Abraham had anticipated. Sarah was the object of universal admiration. She attracted the attention even of Pharaoh's courtiers, who, with the view of pleasing their master, recommended her to the king. Supposing she had been the stranger's sister, she was taken into his house. Alas! what availed all this timid policy! The very means which had been devised for the preservation of Sarah from Egyptian licentiousness, nearly exposed her to all its dreaded consequences; and Abraham was duped by his own craftiness. His wife was endangered, his artifice detected, and the household of Pharaoh visited with divine chastisements on her account. And, in addition to the pain which both he and his beloved partner must have felt, from the consciousness of having acted wrong, they were dismissed from the country. "And Pharaoh called Abraham, and said, What is this that thou hast done unto me? Why didst thou not tell me that she was thy wife? Why saidst thou, She is my sister? So I might have taken her to me to wife: now, therefore, behold thy wife, take her and go thy way. And Pharaoh commanded his men concerning him; and they sent him away, and his wife, and all that he had."

The *beauty* of Sarah was obviously the occasion of her committing, in concert with her husband, the sin of equivocation, and of the misfortunes which attended their Egyptian journey. If she had not been distinguished for a fair exterior, she would have escaped the admiration of these strangers, and the difficulties which she and Abraham afterwards encountered. Solomon pronounces beauty to be vain; and the history of the world will show, that, in innumerable instances, as well as that of Sarah, it has betrayed its fair possessor into many snares. Experience, however, in this respect, does not seem to teach wisdom; for the wish to acquire the attraction which beauty confers, seems to be no less prevalent in the present age, than it was at the earliest period of the world. How many hours of the day, and how many days of the wasted year, do some females devote to the improvement of their persons! Impossible as it has ever been, and ever will be found, to make one hair black or white, to add one cubit to the stature, to bend one untractable feature into the admired curve to which common consent attributes grace and loveliness; the impossible transformation is nevertheless attempted. The treasures of opulence are exhausted; the more valuable possession of health is often sacrificed at the shrine of vanity: and while the noble distinctions of cultivated intellect and solid piety are neglected, the ostentatious decoration of exterior polish is sought with useless and guilty avidity.

The most effectual means of correcting this error, is in early life to commence the important business of moral discipline by a solid education. If a greater degree of attention be paid to showy, than to substantial acquirements; if young ladies be systematically prepared to shine and attract, instead of being assiduously formed to be useful in the stations to which Providence has assigned them; it may be expected that they should become solicitous of courting admiration, rather than of winning esteem. They will necessarily be unfitted for domestic management, and disqualified for the sober realities of life. If the matrimonial connexion be founded upon no better pretensions, and no superior reasons for attachment, it is incapable of securing solid happiness. It is, in fact, at the mercy of every breeze. The wind of adversity may blow upon the fair flower, wither its exterior charms, and leave nothing but prickles and thorns. A consciousness of insignificance on the one hand, and a perception of it on the other, will produce disappointment, and generate dissatisfaction; and it will be found, too late perhaps, that the *mind*, instead of the *face*, ought to have been principally regarded.

There is a species of parental vanity against which we would loudly appeal. Some persons are extremely anxious that their daughters should possess all the attractions of beauty; and from their earliest infancy, a concern for appearances is instilled into them, as of the first importance. If young persons, so unhappily circumstanced, should receive a wrong bias, we cannot feel surprised; and it will require a long course of salutary discipline, combined with the inculcation of religious principles, effectually to teach them that to see, and to be seen, are not the great purposes of human existence; that they must live for nobler ends, and secure the approbation of the wise and good by other accomplishments than a taste for the arrangement of a ribbon, or the harmony of a tune. Unless they should be unfortunate enough to meet with none but flippant and vacant admirers, to whose flattering nothings they are induced to listen, they will find, that persons of real worth are not to be attracted by tinsel decorations, nor a butterfly exterior, but that

"Man has a relish more refined;"

and will rather breathe the following sentiments, as the appropriate language of a noble enthusiasm, connected with rationality and religion;

"Souls are for social bliss designed--
Give me a blessing fit to match my mind;
A kindred soul to double and to share my joys."

That which constitutes the source of attraction to well regulated minds, does not depend upon the disposition of the features, nor the colour of the skin. It is possible to every kind of exterior form. "This beauty," it has been well observed, "does not always consist in smiles, but varies as expressions of meekness and kindness vary with their objects: it is extremely forcible in the silent complaint of patient sufferance, the tender solicitude of friendship, and the glow of filial obedience; and in tears, whether of joy, of pity, or of grief, it is almost irresistible.

"This is the charm which captivates without the aid of nature, and without which her utmost bounty is ineffectual. But it cannot be assumed as a mask to conceal insensibility or malevolence: it must be the effect of corresponding sentiments, or it will impress upon the countenance a new and more disgusting deformity--AFFECTATION. Looks, which do not correspond with the heart, cannot be assumed without labour, nor continued without pain: the motive to relinquish them must, therefore, soon preponderate, and the aspect and apparel of the visit will be laid by together: the smiles and the languishments of art will vanish, and the fierceness of rage, or the gloom of discontent, will either obscure or destroy all the elegance of symmetry and complexion.

"The artificial aspect is, indeed, as wretched a substitute for the expression of sentiment, as the smear of paint for the blushes of health: it is not only equally transient, and equally liable to detection; but, as paint leaves the countenance yet more withered and ghastly, the passions burst out with more violence after restraint, the features become more distorted, and excite more determined aversion.

"Beauty, therefore, depends principally upon the mind, and consequently may be influenced by education. It has been remarked, that the predominent passion may generally be discovered in the countenance; because the muscles by which it is expressed, being almost perpetually contracted, lose their tone, and never totally relax; so that the expression remains when the passion is suspended: thus, an angry, a disdainful, a subtle, and a suspicious temper, is displayed in characters that are almost universally understood. It is equally true of the pleasing and the softer passions, that they leave their signatures upon the countenance when they cease to act. The prevalence of these passions, therefore, produces a mechanical effect upon the aspect, and gives a turn and cast to the features, which make a more favourable and forcible impression upon the mind of others, than any charm produced by mere external causes.

"Neither does the beauty which depends upon temper and sentiment, equally endanger the possessor: it is, to use an eastern metaphor, 'like the towers of a city--not only an ornament, but a defence:' if it excite desire, it at once controls and refines it; it represses with awe, it softens with delicacy, and it wins to imitation. The love of reason and of virtue is mingled with the love of beauty; because this beauty is little more than the emanation of intellectual excellence, which is not an object of corporeal appetite. As it excites a purer passion, it also more forcibly engages to fidelity: every man finds himself more powerfully restrained from giving pain to goodness than to beauty; and every look of a countenance in which they are blended, in which beauty is the expression of goodness, is a silent reproach to the first irregular wish; and the purpose immediately appears to be disingenuous and cruel, by which the tender hope of ineffable affection would be disappointed, the placid confidence of unsuspecting simplicity abused, and the peace even of virtue endangered, by the most sordid infidelity, and the breach of the strongest obligations.

"But the hope of the hypocrite must perish.--When the factitious beauty has laid by her smiles; when the lustre of her eyes, and the bloom of her cheeks, have lost their influence with their novelty; what remains, but a tyrant divested of power, who will never be seen without a mixture of indignation and disdain? The only desire which this object could gratify, will be transferred to another, not only without reluctance, but with triumph.

"Let it, therefore, be remembered, that none can be disciples of the GRACES, but in the school of VIRTUE; and that those who wish to be LOVELY, must learn early to be GOOD."

In the next transaction, Sarah appears in a still more unfavourable light than in the former part of her history. In whatever degree the circumstances in which she was placed may seem to extenuate the guilt of her conduct in Egypt, they can no longer be pleaded on her behalf. She is not now overawed by the authority of her husband, or seduced by an affection, which would, at all hazards, endeavour to save his valuable life; but becomes the voluntary tempter to a violation of divine institutions, by which she not only manifested her unbelief, but sacrifices to unworthy motives her domestic peace.

Notwithstanding the divine assurance, that the posterity of Abraham should become a great nation, and possess the land of Canaan, Sarah begins to think that there is no probability of her becoming a mother. Ten years had elapsed, and no child was born. Reflecting on her advanced period of life, and incapable of an implicit reliance upon the power of God, she requested Abraham to take Hagar, her Egyptian handmaid, in order that she might obtain children by her. It is scarcely possible to imagine a proposal more calculated to subvert the comfort of her family, or more illustrative of an unbelieving spirit. She could not rely upon the slow but certain operations of a superintending Providence to fulfil those promises which had been given; although a humble faith would have cherished confidence in his word. He who has filled the volume of inspiration with "exceeding great and precious promises," will assuredly accomplish them, notwithstanding every apparent impediment. Omnipotence marches forward with a steady, undeviating step, to its predestined purpose; and that infinite wisdom which originally planned the future, can never be frustrated or confused by any contingencies or vicissitudes; for no possible event can occur which was not fully anticipated at the moment when the promise was given.

Sarah was not only under the influence of distrust, but of inordinate desire. She was impatient for one of those prime domestic comforts which it was seen fit at present to deny her; and because the time which had elapsed, exceeded her calculations of probability, she took upon herself to devise a plan to hasten the accomplishment of her wishes. Let us beware of an undue eagerness after the possession of any temporal enjoyment. It will not only produce distrust, but, probably, precipitate us into irregular means of gratifying our wishes. "Inordinate desires commonly produce irregular endeavours. If our wishes be not kept in submission to God's providence, our pursuits will scarcely be kept under the restraints of his precepts."

It is truly surprising, that the father of the faithful should listen to this insinuating request. Possibly he thought that, as Sarah was not distinctly mentioned in the promise, Hagar might become the parent of the promised seed; and by this specious pretence, being anxious for a son, he was induced to comply. We are easily persuaded, when our own inclinations already concur with a proposal; and even good men are very liable to misinterpret the intimations of Providence, whenever they consult their own feelings rather than the word of God.

It is remarked, that "Abraham hearkened to the voice of SARAH." This was his error. There was another voice he should have heard. If he had any doubts upon his mind, or any suspicion that his present wife was not the predestined mother of the numerous posterity that were to people Canaan, he should at least have betook himself to prayer. In a day of such remarkable revelations, and in an affair of so much consequence, he might reasonably have expected an express direction from heaven; and he who had been already so privileged, ought to have unbosomed his thoughts and explained his desires to the Lord. Let such as sustain the closest connexion, beware of becoming snares instead of helps to each other! Previous to a compliance with any important request that may lead to considerable consequences, Let us, from whatever quarter it proceed, or however justifiable it may appear, promptly avail ourselves of that gracious throne, which is always accessible to the humble petitioner. We are liable to so many misconceptions, exposed to the influence of so many prejudices, and subject to the attacks of such a variety of temptations, that our only security is in the exercise of a devotional spirit, our only help is in the Lord our God. If any man lack wisdom, let him repair to the fountain of intelligence, and solicit those supplies from heaven which are not only freely dispensed, but fully adequate to our diversified necessities.

The consequence of this unsanctioned proceeding, was precisely what might have been expected. Elated with the honour of her situation, Sarah is despised by her Egyptian handmaid. She treats her with contempt and impertinence, as if she were the peculiar favourite of Heaven, and hoping no doubt, that the ample promises of God were to be fulfilled by her means. Knowing what human nature is, we cannot wonder at this disposition, culpable as it was. Nothing is more common than for persons, when raised above the meanness of their birth, and the inferiority of their former circumstances, to be guilty of assuming airs of importance, and to forget their most obvious duties: and we would caution servants especially against such unwarrantable conduct. If divine favours should be conferred upon them; if by the grace of God they should be made partakers of that spiritual dignity which genuine religion confers, and be thus placed upon a level with their masters or mistresses in the Christian church, let them remember that they are not exempted from a civil subserviency. They are by no means elevated above their natural situation as *servants*, because they become *Christians*; but all the peculiar claims of domestic duty remain. An aspiring, or a haughty spirit, is unbecoming their newly acquired character, and shows that they have very imperfectly learned of him who was "meek and lowly of heart." Every person is respectable in his station, exactly in proportion as it is properly occupied; and real religion, instead of disqualifying for subordinate situations, is adapted to produce contentment, and to dictate an exemplary and uniform correctness of conduct in *whatever* condition we may be placed by Providence. "Servants, be obedient to them that are your masters, according to the flesh, with fear and trembling, in singleness of your heart, as unto Christ: not with eye-service, as men-pleasers; but as the servants of Christ, doing the will of God from the heart; with good will doing service, as to the Lord, and not to men: knowing that whatsoever good thing any man doeth, the same shall he receive of the Lord, whether he be bond or free." "Let as many servants as are under the yoke, count their own masters worthy of all honour, that the name of God and his doctrine be not blasphemed. And they that have believing masters, let them not despise them, because they are brethren; but rather do them service, because they are faithful and beloved, partakers of the benefit."

If Hagar behaved with impertinence and vanity, Sarah manifested a very censurable degree of resentment. Irritated by her handmaid's arrogance, she appealed to Abraham, protesting that she could not endure such insolence, and charging him with a secret connivance, if not an encouragement of her provoking behaviour. Thus we perceive a specimen of what will generally prove the case in family dissensions--both were in the wrong. Hagar was aspiring and rude; Sarah passionate and severe. If the former should have recollected her obligations, the latter ought not to have forgotten her own foolishness in raising her above her natural level, and placing her in circumstances of powerful temptation. The one should have known her place; the other have kept her temper. Let the modern mistress and servant take a lesson from this unhappy difference. How many intestine commotions might be prevented, if inferiors would not overstep the proper limits of their sphere; and if superiors in station would be conciliating in spirit; "The beginning of strife is as when one letteth out water; therefore leave off contention before it be meddled with."

Abraham wisely avoided all interference in this affair; and though his beloved Sarah had appealed to him in very intemperate terms, he gave a soft answer. "Behold thy maid is in thy hand; do to her as it pleaseth thee." He refrained from all self-vindication, to which he seemed called by the violent appeal of his wife; but if he thought proper either to defend himself, or to remonstrate with her, he chose another occasion. When the passions are inflamed, the judgment is seldom sufficiently unbiassed to listen to reason or to consult propriety. It has been questioned, however, whether in this instance he was not too submissive. The Egyptian maid seemed entitled to protection; and, instead of yielding to the rage of Sarah, he should have interposed his *meditation*, and if necessary, his *authority*, to restore peace.

Incapable of resisting the combined assaults of jealousy, rage, and revenge, the poor foreigner is driven from the roof of Abraham. She fled into the wilderness with the view of returning to her native country, but was suddenly arrested in her flight by an angelic messenger, who admonished her to return to her mistress, and pacify her by ready and unconditional submission. He also predicted the character and habits of her future offspring, mentioning the name by which he was to be called, and consoling her in this season of tribulation by an assurance that "the Lord had heard her affliction." She instantly retracted her steps; and, as no intimation is given to the contrary, we may infer that the fugitive was restored to her situation in the family. She was humble, and Sarah conciliated: and as we hear nothing of her for some years, they probably lived in tolerable harmony. It was a merciful interposition to send her back to the family of Abraham; for a connexion with the people of God, whatever may be their faults, is far more desirable than the richest inheritance, or the noblest alliance, where religion is discarded or unknown.

[Sidenote: Years before Christ 1898]

As the birth of the Egyptian's son was attended by no divine congratulations, Abraham is still permitted to pass thirteen years more in a state of suspense respecting the promised child; when at the age of ninety-nine, the covenant is renewed by another revelation. On this remarkable occasion his wife received the name by which we have uniformly called her, Abraham being distinctly assured of her predestined privilege as the mother of the promised seed. A similar change of name was conferred upon the patriarch. Hitherto he had been called *Abram*, a "high," or "eminent father;" now he is to be *Abraham*, "the father of a great multitude." His beloved wife, who had been called *Sarai*, "my princess," was in future to be distinguished by the name of *Sarah*, "a princess," denoting a more extensive honour. If he were to become the *Father*, she was to be the *Mother*, of "many nations."

Having already witnessed the misconduct of Abraham's wife on two memorable occasions, it would be highly gratifying to hear, in the next circumstance of her history, that she acted worthy of her connexion with so illustrious a husband, But alas! we are still necessitated to derive instruction rather from a record of her faults than of her excellencies. We must expect to witness a variety of these in every human character, combined only with comparatively a small number of shining graces. Indeed we find, in general, but one very distinguishing good quality associated with those of a different complexion; and if the plant of grace spring up and grow in the human character, it is usually in a thicket of inferior principles and unholy propensities. While, therefore, engaged in the cultivation of our hearts, in "keeping them with all diligence," as the wise king of Israel expresses it; one very important duty we owe to ourselves is to watch the appearance of these irregularities, and aim, by unremitting attention, united with fervent prayer, to eradicate them from the moral soil. In Sarah we see as great a luxuriance of evil as can be imagined to blend with real piety, without essentially deteriorating it.

Sitting one day at the door of his tent to enjoy the refreshing shade, [8] Abraham observed three strangers approaching, whom he hastened to meet, that he might offer them any temporary accommodation in his power. This act of hospitality was conformable to the usage of the country; but the peculiar generosity of Abraham seems indicated in his *running* to meet them. The invitation is immediately accepted; and the good old man, with the most obliging readiness, offered water to wash their feet, and bread to satisfy their hunger. He hastened to Sarah, directing her to make some cakes of fine meal, and bake them on the hearth; and then went himself to the herd to choose a tender calf, which he immediately proceeded to dress. Butter and milk, the produce of their own pasture, were of course supplied. The venerable patriarch then took his respectful standing under the branches of a neighbouring tree, which afforded a pleasant screen from the sultry sun. What exquisite simplicity is discernible here! what a subject for the painter! what a theme for the poet! what an example for the good! Three heavenly messengers at the humble table of one of the greatest men that ever inhabited this world--a patriarch--a prince--the father of the faithful--the friend of God--venerable for age--distinguished by his hospitality--still more eminent for faith!--their canopy the overarching sky--their shelter, the wide-spreading tree--flocks and herds grazing around, the indications of an industry which Providence had blessed with remarkable success--and the plain of Mamre spreading its luxuriance before their eyes!--

But we must hasten to the remarkable subject of their conversation. At present the patriarch did not suspect the real character of his visiters; who introduced their intended communication by asking, "Where is Sarah thy wife?" This must have excited great surprise; for how could strangers know the affairs of his family, and the particular name of his wife, which had been so recently changed? He informed them, however, that she was in the tent, where, according to the prevailing custom of the times, she had her separate table. One of the angels, immediately personating Jehovah himself, if he were not, as appears probable, the very "Angel of the Covenant," gave this solemn assurance: "I will certainly return unto thee according to the time of life; and, lo, Sarah thy wife shall have a son!" Sarah, whom curiosity had brought to the door of the tent to listen to what passed, overhearing this assurance, and looking upon it as an impossible occurrence at her time of life, laughed in derision. She had long come to the conclusion that she should produce no son to Abraham, and, therefore, that all such expectations were chimerical and ridiculous. This excessive incredulity--excessive, because a distinct assurance of the fact had been already given to Abraham upon the occasion of their change of names--was highly culpable; but while we denounce it with merited severity, let us examine our own hearts. Have *we* never acted in a similar manner? Have *we* never distrusted the providence of God or his promises? Who can plead exemption from a spirit of unbelief? What surmises have agitated our bosoms, when the events of life contradicted our expectations? What despondency have we shown, and what distrust, when the movements Omniscience were incomprehensible to our reason, and opposed to our apparent interest? If but one part only of the divine proceedings seemed incongruous, we have dared to arraign "the whole stupendous plan;" if but "a momentary cloud" arose upon our prospect, we have begun to fancy that order was at an end, that the sun had for ever disappeared, that God had "forgotten to be gracious, and in anger shut up his tender mercies." Let us then aim to correct these irregularities of feeling, and to dismiss these misinterpretations of providence.

Sarah imagined that her contemptuous incredulity was only known to herself: but the heavenly visiter instantly detected it, and appealed to Abraham on its impropriety. Possibly the reason of addressing Abraham, rather than calling the culprit herself to an account, was to inflict the severer reproof. Ah! how vainly do we strive to conceal the secret thoughts of the mind from the knowledge of God! His eyes, which run to and fro through the earth, penetrate through every disguise, and perfectly discern every inward motion as well as every outward action. We live every moment--in the darkest midnight as well as at the brightest noon--in the full blaze of Omniscience. "O Lord, thou hast searched me and known me: thou knowest my down-sitting and mine up-rising; thou understandest my thoughts afar off."

Incapable of enduring this exposure, the criminal now rushes from her concealment, and boldly calls out, "I laughed not." This was a direct falsehood, dictated by apprehension; and it was confronted by the instant retort of him who knew her heart: "Nay, but thou *didst* laugh." It is possible that Sarah had some mental reservation, when she so flatly denied the assertion of the angel: she might persuade herself that she did not absolutely laugh, but only smiled, or felt contempt; but whatever mode she might have adopted to explain away her conscious guilt, it was unavailable, as every such unworthy subterfuge must always prove.

We cannot help remarking the danger of the least deviation from the path of rectitude. One sin prepares the way for the commission of another; one step over the edge and boundary of uprightness may lead us down a precipice, and plunge us into a fatal series of crimes. We have already seen an exemplification of this remark; and it is more strikingly illustrated in the present transaction. Curiosity brought her to the door, where she was soon betrayed into unbelief: detection soon produced a fear of censure; this dread produced a ridiculous attempt at concealment and self-justification; and the pride of her heart issued in exciting her to a deliberate falsehood. Notwithstanding her incredulity, however, Sarah shall bear a son, to be the spring of innumerable blessings to her posterity. Thus infinite goodness overrules the perverseness of his people, as well as the wrath of sinners, ultimately to promote his own designs.

If, on this occasion, the daring transgressor had been smitten to the earth by an instantaneous judgment, it must have been regarded as a proper expression of the divine displeasure. Her repeated provocations merited the severest chastisement, and would undoubtedly have justified such a proceeding. The thoughts of Jehovah, however, are not as our thoughts, nor his ways as our ways. There is nothing vindictive in the character of the blessed God; and if he have on certain occasions launched the thunderbolt upon the guilty heads of sinners, the circumstances have shown that the atrocity of their iniquities has required a signal visitation. How far punishment of this nature may be necessary in any particular case, it is not for beings limited in their views as we are to decide, but simply to rely on the wisdom of him, who, with a due intermixture of severity and mercy, justice and grace, conducts the affairs of the universe.

Overawed by the angelic presence, and mortified by an inward consciousness of her folly and sin, Sarah uttered not another word. She could neither vindicate her incredulity, nor extenuate her false assertion; and though she proceeded to great lengths, we are happy to find that she sufficiently restrained her intemperate passions to retire in silence.

From this moment we trust she assumed another character. Reflection restored her to her right mind. She dismissed her criminal doubts, and resigned herself to the divine disposal. As the predestined period of her giving birth to the child of promise was approaching, her faith produced the liveliest sensations of joy; and both she and Abraham exulted in the prospect of a son. That this was the state of her mind, we are assured from indisputable authority: "Through faith Sarah herself received strength to conceive seed, and was delivered of a child when she was past age, because she judged him faithful who had promised."

Perhaps we may be disposed to say, it was time she *did* believe. After such remarkable manifestations, and such reiterated promises to Abraham, it would have been passing strange had she continued incredulous. Surely there was enough to convince her, that, whatever difficulties nature might present, grace had determined to overcome them, and that every reasonable and every possible evidence of the intended miracle had been given. But is it so unusual for mankind to resist the most convincing arguments, and to disbelieve even the most obvious truth, that the case of Sarah ought to be regarded as so extraordinary? Have we not daily proof of a similar obstinacy and perverseness? If it be observed that Sarah possessed great advantages, being connected with so excellent a man, and so great a favourite of Heaven as Abraham, and being visited by angelic messengers, and instructed by celestial visions; this may be admitted. But do not those who reject the truth of Christianity, or disobey its precepts, act a more criminal as well as unreasonable part, inasmuch as they enjoy all the instruction and all the experience of past ages? And is it not a more outrageous defiance of Heaven to oppose the reality of its manifestations, after successive centuries have demonstrated the truth of predictions once mysterious, evinced the nature of facts once misunderstood, dispersed the typical shadow which once enveloped the sublimest discoveries of infinite wisdom, and poured upon a benighted world the full blaze of evangelical revelations?--Sarah doubted the possibility of an occurrence which was attended with striking difficulties, and evidently miraculous; but what censure do not they deserve who shut their eyes against the clearest light, perplex with sophisms the most intelligible statements, and endeavour, by every exertion of a slanderous tongue and a malignant pen, to subvert the basis of our religious hopes, and to undermine a fabric which has stood the test of ages, giving repose and refreshment to millions of heaven-bound pilgrims on their journey!

To draw the circle of reflection closer.--If *our* inconsistencies were written in a book--if the instances of *our* unbelief amidst evidences, of *our* failures in temper and spirit, of *our* misimprovement of the peculiar advantages of our situation, were recorded for the warning of others--is there any probability that we should acquire much honour by a comparison with the wife of Abraham? We do not indeed justify *her* faults, but let us not overlook *our own*. We have better means, and brighter discoveries. In these last days God hath spoken unto us by his Son. We are, through faith, become the children of Abraham, interested in the new covenant, introduced into the family, and admitted to the friendship of God. We have seen the visions of patriarchal days, the promises and blessings of the ancient dispensation, the memorable and terrific descent of Jehovah on Sinai, the prefigurations of the Mosaic economy, the personal glories, the incarnate love, the agonizing death, the triumphant ascension of the Son of God: we enjoy means of instruction which no other age did or could possess. And wherein consists our superiority to former saints, even those whose imperfections are the most conspicuous? Surely, the observation may be retorted upon many hearers and professors of the gospel, in reference to their too frequent instances of inconsistency--it is time you *did* believe!

The birth of Isaac, the promised seed was attended with great rejoicings. His very name, signifying *laughter*, was expressive of the happy occasion; and Sarah, in the ecstacy of her mind, exclaimed, "God hath made me to laugh, so that all that hear me will laugh with me." The birth of a child is naturally the subject of joy and congratulation; but the introduction of Isaac into the world, who had been so long and repeatedly promised, demanded and excited unusual satisfaction. Sarah, who introduced him with a mother's joy, nursed him herself with a mother's care. She was ignorant of the cruel absurdity which modern refinement has invented, of separating the tender offspring from its proper guardian and provider, and thus not only exposing it to many inconveniences and hardships, but nullifying the wise and kind arrangements of Providence. Alas! nature, reason, and religion, must all be violated in compliance with fashion! Need we feel surprised that barbarity should produce alienation, and that she who refuses to show tenderness, should fail of receiving attachment? Is it at all astonishing, that habits and sentiments foreign to domestic comfort should be acquired; and that, when proper discipline and personal superintendence are neglected, the young plant should shoot into unsightly irregularities of spirit and character?

How soon may the brightest day be overcast with a cloud! How liable are our best enjoyments to interruption! The weaning of Isaac was celebrated with great festivities; upon which occasion this favourite child was recognized as Abraham's heir. This excited the displeasure of Ishmael; which the jealous eye of Sarah observing, she insisted upon the instantaneous expulsion of mother and son from the family. We are sorry to witness any revival of the old spirit; but, in this world, unholy passions cannot be totally eradicated. We should hope, however, there was more reason, as well as religion, in her displeasure on this than on a former occasion. The young man was, probably, ridiculing the whole ceremony, and deriding the parents, the child, and the promise; for passion and prejudice are never very discriminating in their censures. Ishmael was, in fact, of a wild, ungovernable temper; but we have no evidence that the provocation was sufficient to justify the proceeding of Sarah, in peremptorily demanding the expulsion of the mother and her child. Thus did Abraham's concubinage continue to imbitter his domestic peace; and the good old patriarch was again placed in a most difficult and perplexing situation.

Whatever feelings may be supposed to have dictated the resolution of Sarah, it was coincident with the designs of God; and Abraham, who had certainly sought divine direction, was commanded to comply. This would, no doubt, quiet the feverish anxiety of his mind; for a consciousness of doing the will of God, however contrary it may be to our natural inclinations, is sufficient to smooth the roughest path of duty, and to lighten the heaviest burden we may be called to sustain. Abraham, in this, as well as in various other instances, displayed exemplary faith. The bitter draught, however, was somewhat sweetened. It was difficult to parental feelings to concur in so severe a measure; but some gleam of futurity was afforded to enlighten the darksome but appointed path. "And God said unto Abraham, Let it not be grievous in thy sight, because of the lad, and because of thy bond-woman: in all that Sarah hath said unto thee, hearken unto her voice; for in Isaac shall thy seed be called. And also of the son of the bond-woman will I make a nation, because he is thy seed."

Notwithstanding the faults to which we have found it necessary to advert, Sarah was unquestionably a great character. She not only stands recorded in the New Testament amongst those who were illustrious in ancient times for their faith, but is exhibited as a pattern of domestic conduct. Her defects were but occasionally visible, being commonly concealed amidst the brightness of her numerous excellencies. Her obedience to Abraham is specified by the apostle as a laudable singularity, which, in connexion with other virtues, he thus recommends: "Likewise, ye wives, be in subjection to your own husbands; that if any obey not the word, they also may without the word be won by the conversation of the wives; while they behold your chaste conversation coupled with fear.--Whose adorning let it not be that outward adorning of plaiting the hair, and of wearing of gold, or of putting on of apparel; but let it be the hidden man of the heart, in that which is not corruptible, even the ornament of a meek and quiet spirit, which is in the sight of God of great price. For after this manner, in the old time, the holy women also, who trusted in God, adorned themselves, being in subjection unto their own husbands, even as Sarah obeyed Abraham, calling him lord; whose daughters ye are, as long as ye do well, and are not afraid with any amazement."

[Sidenote: Years before Christ, 1859.]

Seven and thirty years after the birth of Isaac and when Sarah had attained the age of one hundred and twenty-seven, we come to the conclusion of her "mortal story." Her death, and the respect paid to her memory, are related with a circumstantial minuteness which is truly honourable to her character. This affecting event occurred at Kirjah-Arba, or Hebron, in the plain of Mamre, where Abraham came to bemoan his loss. Venerable man! thine was no common mourning! Thou didst not merely sit upon the ground, assuming the customary attitude of grief; but thine were genuine sorrows! What big tears of undissembled pain poured down thine aged cheeks! How did affection recal the days, and months, and years of delightful union, which time had strengthened, but death had now dissolved! And yet, while nature demanded this tribute of fond remembrance, religion had taught thee to moderate thy distress, and to elevate thy hopes to a brighter world, where holy friendship, begun on earth, shall be purified and perpetuated through everlasting ages!

The longevity of ancient times, and especially of the antediluvians, naturally excites surprise; but what a dream is human life, even at its most protracted period! How soon do even centuries elapse! How solemn the consideration, that the flood of ages, which has swept from the surface of this globe so many millions of our predecessors, however firm may have been their health, or numerous their years, or eminent their characters, is daily impelling us forward to the "house appointed for all living." *Their* pilgrimage terminated, and so must *ours: their* earthly relations were dissolved, and *their* places in society were vacated; and soon the place which we occupy, shall "know us no more." The stream flows on, and we cannot arrest its course. Happy for us, if it should appear that we are going to join the society of the blessed; if, possessing the faith of Abraham, we have reason to indulge the hope of being eventually transported to his bosom!

Sitting in imagination at the grave of Sarah, and blending our sympathizing tears with those of her honoured husband, what a lesson may we learn respecting the vanity of human life! The flower whose exquisite beauty and attractive sweetness once excited so much desire, is faded, and mingled with common dust! There lies a form, which *was* so lovely and so beloved, to furnish a repast for creeping worms! How bereft of that spirit which once animated it! How altered and defaced by the putrifying touch of mortality! Here the race of life terminates; and to this loathsome dwelling, the proudest, the fairest, the wealthiest, the most celebrated, and the most elevated of our race, must sooner or later descend! "Prepare to meet thy God!"

We may take a momentary glance at another consideration. In order to answer the great end of their being, in order to be furnished with adequate means for the employment of their immortal faculties, and for possessing that plenitude of felicity of which their sanctified natures are capable, the saints of God must be removed out of the present world. Often do they exclaim, "I loath it; I would not live alway:"--"O that I had wings like a dove; for then would I flee away and be at rest!"

This prevailing *wish* accords with the *purpose* of Heaven. Infinite benevolence cannot allow a spiritual and sanctified character always to be imprisoned within the narrow confines of flesh and blood. It could never be satisfied to assign the objects of its affection so mean a portion as the pleasures and the possessions of this inferior state of existence. They must *die* to be perfectly *blest*. This earth *will not do* for a Christian in the *maturity* of his character. It is too vile, and too transitory. Its gold is but dust--its applause, a puff of noisy air--its sparkling pleasures, but polluted cisterns--its richest gifts, but bubbles, which, if they reflect the fairest colours of the rainbow, break when they are grasped, or dissolve as we approach them, into mist and nothingness! "Set your affection on things above:--the things which are *seen* are TEMPORAL; the things which are *not seen* are ETERNAL!"

Hagar Chapter III

The contention between the wife of Abraham and her Egyptian handmaid, has already been the subject of animadversion; but although their histories are considerably blended, some features in the character of the latter, and some affecting circumstances of her life, have been hitherto omitted, which seem to claim a separate notice. That retreat into Egypt, which was in some respects so dishonourable to the integrity, both of Abraham and Sarah, was overruled for good. Pharaoh showed great kindness to the patriarch, on account of his fair companion, who he had been led to suppose was his sister; and according to the custom of the age, and the high station of her admirer, he presented him with "sheep, and oxen, and he-asses, and men-servants, and *maid-servants*, and she-asses, and camels." No doubt it was at this time Hagar was introduced into this pious family, and left her native country to accompany her mistress and master upon their return.

The handmaids were a sort of female slaves. They were considered as the unalienable property of their mistresses, who claimed the produce of their labour, and even the children they bore. [9]

Sarah's impatience for offspring, and the rash policy of her urging Abraham to take this Egyptian servant as a concubine, have been already mentioned, as well as the unhappy differences it occasioned in the family. We have seen the pride of Hagar, the petulance of Sarah, and the consent of Abraham that she should be banished from their dwelling. Let us follow the fugitive into the wilderness, and observe the extraordinary result.

It was the evident intention of Hagar to escape to her native country. She went into the wilderness of Shur, which extended between Canaan and Egypt, where she sat down for refreshment by a spring of water. Whatever degree of blame we may impute to her in this precipitate removal from the house of her pious master, it is impossible not to pity her melancholy situation. Alone, and unbefriended by any human being; surrounded by a thousand perils in the desert which stretched its cheerless solitude before her; expelled from a family where she had so long resided, and where she enjoyed so many advantages; uncertain of her future residence; and in a condition which peculiarly claims our sympathy with the female sufferer; her history cannot but excite inquiry, and produce interest. There was an eye that watched her movements and her tears. In a short time she is addressed by an unknown voice, which proved to be the voice of one of those ministering spirits that are employed to execute the designs of infinite goodness. "Hagar," said he, "Sarah's maid, whence earnest thou? and whither wilt thou go?"

The knowledge of her past history which this question indicated, must have convinced the poor, fugitive that this was some divine visitation; and she immediately answered, "I flee from the face of my mistress Sarah." This was a simple, direct, ingenuous statement. Here was no concealment; no prevarication respecting the whole truth; and how much better was this than any attempt at evasion or dishonesty! We are not, indeed, always obliged to disclose our circumstances to every inquirer; but, if we do, our words ought to be the exact representation of the case: for, sooner or later, integrity will be advantageous both to our character and our real interests.

The reply of Hagar was, moreover, creditable to her *temper*, Sarah and her handmaid had parted under circumstances of mutual provocation; and the latter had, no doubt, suffered very indignant treatment. But she does not avail herself of this unexpected interview to enter upon her own justification, or to produce a long and formal charge against her mistress. The mere fact of her expulsion is stated without any comment. It must indeed be admitted, that her introduction into the family of Abraham placed her in that inferior condition in which Sarah possessed an indisputable right over her person; and it must be also admitted, that she had manifested a very unwarrantable vanity in despising her for barrenness; yet, judging from her dispassionate language to the angel, we should infer that she was naturally of a more patient disposition than her mistress, and is in this view worthy of the imitation of young women whom Providence consigns to the same menial state. How many would have been clamorous and peevish, hasty in censuring their mistress, and forward in vindicating themselves! They would have obtruded the story of the fancied injuries they had sustained upon every occasion, and wearied with the ridiculous recital, every one who might be found willing or unwilling to hear their complaints. But Hagar, simply and without any marks of irritation or resentment, stated the reason of her being alone in the wilderness at the fountain of water.

If our idea be correct, we have here a specimen of a no very unusual case. Some who have no claim to the distinction of religious persons, which at present was the probable character of Hagar, frequently possess a mildness and amiableness of disposition which is peculiarly attractive; while those who undoubtedly belong to the superior class of the pious and devout, exhibit unhappy defects of temper and disposition. The former resemble the flowers of the wilderness, beautiful indeed, and fragrant, but wild; the latter, those of the cultivated garden, blooming like the rose among thorns. The loveliness of those who are otherwise "far from God," excites our admiration, and wins our regard; while the unsightly "temper flaws" of such as generally class with the servants of God are repulsive and disgusting. In consequence of this, the distinction between the two essentially different characters, is not always sufficiently marked, or very perceptible; the excellence of the one elevating them almost to the dignity of saints, and the defects of the other sinking them almost to the meanness of sinners. But we should be cautious in passing our judgment, lest we also be judged. Let us not undervalue the sterling worth of the genuine Christian, because it is blended with some obvious, or even some glaring incongruities. Let us equally beware of attributing undue value to the good qualities of the worldling, and thus annihilate the distinction between the natural and spiritual character.

It was happy for Hagar that the angel was sent to arrest her progress. After her explicit declaration of the reason of her flight, she was directed to return to her mistress, and submit herself. This was, perhaps, a hard saying, and a haughty spirit might easily have raised ingenious and perverse objections; but we have additional evidence of this young woman's good disposition, in her receiving the mandate with a silent obedience of spirit. Her best interests were likely to be more promoted by her returning into a pious family, notwithstanding all its faults, than in going to reside amongst the idolaters of her native country; and thus, when she knew not how to choose for herself, the goodness of God was displayed in appointing the bounds of her habitation. This command would prove to her, and should teach us, that whatever provocations or injuries we may have sustained, these cannot justify a wrong proceeding; and we should hasten to retrieve our error by retracing our steps.

This, however, was only the secondary purpose of the present remarkable manifestation. Words of astonishing import immediately followed. Hagar was promised a numerous offspring, although the Messiah was not to descend from her; and the promise was pronounced in a manner so solemn, so significant, so overwhelming, that her eyes were opened to see it was no other than the patriarch's God that assured her of a participation in the patriarch's blessing. "And the angel of the Lord said unto her, I will multiply thy seed exceedingly, that it shall not be numbered for multitude. And the angel of the Lord said unto her, Behold, thou art with child, and shalt bear a son, and shalt call his name Ishmael; because the Lord hath heard thy affliction. And he will be a wild man; his hand will be against every man, and every man's hand against him; and he shall dwell in the presence of all his brethren." Similar promises were afterward reiterated:

"Behold, I have blessed him, (Ishmael) and will make him fruitful, and will multiply him exceedingly; twelve princes shall he beget, and I will make him a great nation."--"And also of the son of the bond-woman will I make a nation, because he is thy seed."--"I will make him a great nation."

These predictions have been minutely accomplished. The posterity of Ishmael may be traced in the Ishmaelites, the Hagarenes, the Itureans, and Arabs; especially the Scenites and Saracens, the latter of whom erected one of the largest empires in the world. To this day the Arabs are not only a distinct people, but possess the original character of their father, fierce and unsettled, living in a state of perpetual hostility against the rest of the world. Every attempt to subdue or extirpate them, has proved abortive. The Egyptians and Assyrians were equally unsuccessful, and whatever partial dominion Cyrus and the Persians might obtain, they could never penetrate the interior of the country, or reduce them to tributary subjection. In vain did Alexander plan their destruction; the hand of Providence interposed to prevent it by his death. The Romans could never conquer Arabia; and they continued to molest their neighbours by incessant incursions. Under Mohammed they became a mighty empire, and though it was ultimately dissolved, they still maintained their liberty in defiance of the Tartars, Mamelukes, and Turks.

"Who," inquires a great writer, "can fairly consider and lay all these particulars together, and not perceive the hand of God in this whole affair, from the beginning to the end? The sacred historian saith, that these prophecies concerning Ishmael were delivered partly by the angel of the Lord, and partly by God himself: and indeed, who but God, or one raised and commissioned by him, could describe so particularly the genius and manners, not only of a single person before he was born, but of a whole race of people, from the first founder of the race to the present time? It was somewhat wonderful, and not to be foreseen by human sagacity or prudence, that a man's whole posterity should so nearly resemble him, and retain the same inclinations, the same habits, the same customs throughout all ages. The waters of the purest spring or fountain are soon changed and polluted in their course, and the farther still they flow, the more they are incorporated and lost in other waters. How have the modern Italians degenerated from the courage and virtues of the old Romans? How are the French and English polished and refined from the barbarianism of the ancient Gauls and Britons? Men and manners change with times; but in all changes and revolutions, the Arabs have still continued the same with little or no alteration. And yet it cannot be said of them, as some barbarous nations, that they have had no commerce or intercourse with the rest of mankind; for by their conquests they overran a great part of the earth, and for some centuries were masters of most of the learning that was then in the world; but, however, they remained, and still remain the same fierce, savage, intractable people, like their great ancestor in every thing, and different from most of the world besides. Ishmael was circumcised, and so are his posterity to this day; and as Ishmael was circumcised when he was thirteen years old, so were the Arabs at the same age, according to Josephus. He was born of Hagar, who was a concubine; and they still indulge themselves in the use of mercenary wives and concubines. He lived in tents in the wilderness, shifting from place to place; and so do his descendants, particularly those therefore called Scenites formerly, and those called Bedoweens at this day. He was an archer in the wilderness, and so are they. He was to be the father of twelve princes, or heads of tribes; and they live in clans or tribes at this day. He was a wild man, his hand against every man, and every man's hand against him; and they live in the same state of war, their hand against every man, and every man's hand against them.

"This, I say, is somewhat wonderful, that the same people should retain the same dispositions for so many ages: but it is still more wonderful, that with these dispositions and this enmity to the whole world, they should still subsist, in spite of the world, an independent and free people. It cannot be pretended, that no probable attempts were ever made to conquer them; for the greatest conquerors in the world have almost all, in their turns, attempted it. It cannot be pretended, that the dryness or inaccessibleness of their country hath been their preservation; for their country hath been often penetrated, though never entirely subdued. I know that Diodorus Siculus accounts for their preservation from the dryness of their country; that they have wells digged in proper places known only to themselves, and their enemies and invaders, through ignorance of these places, perish for want of water; but this account is far from being an adequate and just representation of the case. Large armies have found the means of subsistence in their country; none of their powerful invaders ever desisted on this account; and therefore, that they have not been conquered, we must impute to some other cause. When, in all human probability, they were upon the brink of ruin, then they were signally and providentially delivered. Alexander was preparing an expedition against them, when an inflammatory fever cut him off in the flower of his age. Pompey was in the career of his conquests, when urgent affairs called him elsewhere. Ælius Gallus had penetrated far into the country, when a fatal disease destroyed great numbers of his men, and obliged him to return. Trajan besieged their capital city, but was defeated by thunder and lightning, whirlwinds, and other prodigies, and that as often as he renewed his assaults. Severus besieged the same city twice, and was twice repelled from before it; and the historian, Dion, a man of rank and character, though a heathen, plainly ascribes the defeat of the two emperors to the interposition of a Divine Power. We who know the prophecies, may be more assured of the reality of a divine interposition; and, indeed, otherwise how could a single nation stand out against the enmity of the whole world for any length of time, and much more for near 4000 years together; the great empires round them have all in their turn fallen to ruin, while they have continued the same from the beginning, and are likely to continue the same to the end: and this, in the natural course of human affairs, was so highly improbable, if not altogether impossible, that as nothing but a Divine Prescience could have foreseen it, so nothing but a Divine Power could have accomplished it." [10]

To return to Hagar. The effect of this angelic visitation was her conversion to the knowledge and love of God. The advantages of her former situation in the family of Abraham, do not seem to have produced any remarkable change of character; but in this the day of her affliction, in this the sad hour of her retreat and solitude, she is taught to pray. So true is it, that "thy people shall be *willing* in the day of *thy power!*" How often have those means which to human apprehension seemed best calculated to produce a renovation of heart utterly failed, while the Spirit of God has successfully operated by methods and in situations the least expected to avail! Happy solitude that brings us into the society of God! Welcome affliction that subdues us to his will!

In the transports of holy affection, Hagar addressed Jehovah by a phrase, importing "Thou, God, seest me;" and intimated the unexpected but welcome nature of the discoveries she had made, and of that influence which drew her after God in faith, and hope, and love:--"Have I also here looked after him that seeth me?" As a memento of this wonderful interposition, she named the spring of water by which she was sitting, "Beer-lahai-roi," that is, "The well of him that liveth and seeth me."

Hagar, in adopting this language, expressed her *grateful sense of the divine interposition.* She felt conscious that in her present circumstances she might have perished alone and unpitied; or, if she had survived, and taken up her residence in Egypt she would have remained destitute of the religious instruction already received, and the future advantages of pious intercourse. Her gratitude was blended with a feeling of humility, a consciousness of unworthiness. What could be more surprising, than that an angel should descend from the splendour of the divine presence, to converse with a poor wanderer in the wilderness of Shur, and console her by such wonderful promises? These benevolent spirits appear to have maintained a frequent intercourse with the best inhabitants of our globe in former ages, and to have been intrusted with the holy ministration of attending the Son of God in his incarnate state. If, since the completion of the canon of Scripture, the necessity of angelic visits be superseded, we ought nevertheless to record the goodness of a superintending Providence. He who forms a just estimate of his mercies, may surely fill the diary of every day with grateful notices, and cannot take even a cursory retrospect of the years of past existence, without recollecting some striking interpositions which should often renew his praise and thanksgiving. Have we not been sustained in weakness, guided in perplexity, healed in sickness, supplied in poverty, or defended in danger? Let not insensibility and forgetfulness add to the already large accumulations of our guilt.

The words of Hagar ought also to be regarded as indicative of *pious resignation of spirit* amidst the adversities of life. It is common in calamitous circumstances, or in afflictions which seem immediately occasioned by others upon whom we may have been dependent, or with whom we have been in any way connected, to exclaim against the cruelty of our enemy, or the malice of such as have been instrumental in producing our unhappiness; but Hagar utters no complaints against Sarah, who had driven her into the wilderness, where she and her infant offspring might have perished.

This is instructive. Admitting that we are not mistaken in our views, and that others may be really cruel; if we consider affliction aright, we shall leave the instrument to the judgment of God, and be solicitous only of glorifying him, by possessing our souls in patience. Joseph afterward was an illustrious specimen of this disposition. "Now, therefore," said he to his brethren, "be not grieved nor angry with yourselves that ye sold me hither; for God did send me before you to preserve life."

All second causes constitute but the machinery on which the great First Cause operates. If we look merely to *them*, we shall find an endless source of disquietude: if to *him*, who regulates the whole system of means, we cannot fail of obtaining satisfaction and peace of mind. Resignation is to be distinguished from a stoical indifference, or a sullen insensibility, occasioned by the conviction that, as afflictions could not be avoided, they must be borne; that it is in vain to struggle or resist; and that our weakness renders endurance necessary, however irksome. It consists rather in a pious acquiescence in the will of Heaven, arising from a persuasion that God knows what is really best for us; and that his dispensations, however painful or opposite to our wishes, will prove conducive to our real benefit. He uses the corrective rod, not the destroying sword. If he amputate the disordered member, it is to save the life.

Cheerful hope for the future seems also to breathe through the expressions of Hagar, in which she is worthy of our imitation. Past interpositions form a solid foundation for future confidence. "Surely," said David, "goodness and mercy shall follow me all the days of my life." Disconsolate believer, be assured that the pillar of cloud, which has hitherto directed thy path, shall accompany thee to the very borders of Canaan! "Fear not," says Jehovah, "for I am with thee; be not dismayed, for I am thy God: I will strengthen thee; yea, I will help thee; yea, I will uphold thee with the right hand of my righteousness--I will never leave thee, nor forsake thee."

It is natural to wish to pry into futurity. We are impatient to penetrate the clouds that envelope us, and to discern the distant course which Providence has prescribed for our feet. Curiosity combines with self-interest to urge this inquiry; but the reproof which Peter received is justly merited by ourselves: "What is that to thee? Follow thou me." If we follow Christ, we have nothing to dread; if we desert him, we have nothing to hope. Futurity can be no source of alarm to him who is conscious of acting right. It is filled with no "Gorgons, and hydras, and chimeras dire," but to the distempered imagination of the guilty spirit; and, therefore, if we would escape *misery*, we must resist *sin*.

The language in question may be considered as expressive of *self-dedication*. "Thou, God, seest me," my wants, my wishes, my entire situation! I have no will but thine; no desire but what I readily submit that thou shalt gratify or disappoint according to thy pleasure. If thou inflict chastisement, I will cheerfully sustain it; if thou afford prosperity, I will humbly enjoy and improve it. I will no longer live to myself; I am not my own. I agree to the transfer of all my powers, talents, and possessions to thy service. My whole being shall henceforth be at thy disposal; it shall become thy absolute and inalienable property: this is a "living sacrifice" which I admit to be "reasonable," which I rejoice to believe is "holy and acceptable." In time past I have "sown to the flesh;" let this suffice--another principle influences me--another motive shall evermore predominate.

A resolution of this nature must be dictated by the lowest opinion of ourselves, and the highest idea of God: and what is our proper situation, but in the dust? and where should we place God, but on the throne? To acknowledge this in theory, and to abandon it in practice, is to trifle both with ourselves and with him.

Entire dedication to God is by no means incompatible with the duties of life. It is possible to be "diligent in business," but "fervent in spirit, serving the Lord." We contend not for a voluntary seclusion from society, seeking the retirements of the cloister or the retreats of the wilderness: but we plead with you, whatever situation you occupy, to set God always before your eyes, to act as in his sight, and daily to realize the true character of saints as "strangers and pilgrims on earth." Religion, that flower of paradise, was never intended to "waste its sweetness on the desert air;" but to flourish in society, and to diffuse its sacred perfumes in every walk of life.

This elevation of piety, so far from poisoning the springs of human joy, so far from imbittering the cordials of our cup, will refine every enjoyment and purify every pleasure. It will blunt the keen edge of sorrow, and smooth the asperities of adversity. It will bring down heaven to earth, and render death itself a desirable passage to everlasting life. Let us accustom ourselves to contemplate the most eminent examples of this spirit, that, by daily imitating them, we may, through grace, be progressively "meetening" for the participation of their inheritance.

If it were not Hagar's immediate intention, her language may at least be adopted to express a *constant sense of the divine omniscience.* No idea is so calculated to animate us in the discharge of duty, or to sustain us in submission to evil. In the ancient Olympic games, how must the consciousness of twenty or thirty thousand witnesses of their efforts have stimulated the Grecian combatants, ranged as they were around them in an amphitheatre, and consisting of the first magistrates of the kingdom! But how much more impressive and awful is the persuasion that the great eye of the universe is upon us in our Christian race; that the "King eternal, immortal, invisible," watches every movement, and beholds with approbation or kindles into wrath, as we persevere or draw back to perdition! He sees in solitude and in society, in the crowded city and the distant wilderness. On the one hand, he witnesses the aversion and rebellion of the wicked; on the other, he gathers the tears of penitence into his bottle, records the petitions of faith in his book, and amidst the music of angels, bends his listening ear to the sighs of the sorrowful.

Let Christians remember that they have a mighty struggle to sustain, but their resources are inexhaustible. They have to contend with the powers of darkness and the corruptions of nature. In the issue of this contest heaven and hell are interested; the one, that you should fail; the other, that you should come off "more than conquerors." Angels are waiting on the shores of immortality to see the final result, and are already tuning their harps to sound your victory through the universe. The ascended Saviour addresses you from the skies: "Be thou faithful unto death, and I will give thee a crown of life."

In the preceding chapter, the occasion of Hagar's second banishment from the family of Abraham was related. During the festivities which were observed at the weaning of Isaac, her son indulged himself in profane mockery; the consequence of which was, that Sarah insisted upon the instant expulsion of mother and child. Notwithstanding Abraham's repugnance to this proceeding, he was induced to it by divine a command. Early in the morning he dismissed Hagar and her son, with a bottle of water and some bread, with which she hastened away into the wilderness of Beersheba. This scanty supply was soon exhausted, and the unhappy fugitives became reduced to the greatest distress. What could an unprotected female do in such melancholy circumstances, but simply commit herself to the guidance of Providence, and pursue, though she knew not whither, her adventurous way? Past deliverances ought to inspire confidence in every season of suffering; and we cannot but hope that her mind was long consoled, by the recollection of the heavenly interposition which she had enjoyed sixteen years ago, in her first banishment. No resentful feelings, no irritating language is recorded; and doubtless Abraham dismissed her with as much kindness as the peculiarity of the circumstances admitted.

But behold a most tragical scene. In a few days the water is spent in the bottle. Poor Hagar pants along the solitary desert, turning hither and thither in search of some scanty supply. Not a drop of refreshment is to be found; till at length, arriving at some shrubs, she sat down with her exhausted-- and, as she imagined, her *dying* child, beneath the welcome shade. Nothing but silence and solitude reigned around her. The burning sun had scorched up every sign of vegetation. She was driven from a pious family; but she had no home, no friend, no helper! Officious kindness, which often soothes the agonies of death, was denied her. None were at hand to soothe her mind, or wipe away her tears; and her maternal heart was rent by the distracting expectation of her son's dissolution. At the very point of despair, she left Ishmael under a shrub, and retired to some distance to avoid the sight of his expiring agonies.

Who can imagine the pain of this excruciating moment, or the bitterness of the tears she shed! O what lamentations did she utter, and perhaps what self-reproaches for her undervaluation of past mercies! What regrets that she encouraged, or probably did not suppress and correct, the perverse spirit of her son!

While we pity her desperate condition, we must not apologize for her sins. After the remarkable assurances which the angel had given her on a former occasion, it was criminal unbelief in Hagar to sit down in despondency, and conclude that she and her son must inevitably perish: and yet this is but a specimen of the distrust which is too frequently manifested, even by those who profess to rely upon the promises of God. Happy for us, if, in cases of far less extremity, we have not been tempted to forget our mercies and relinquish our confidence!

The sighs of the lad were heard. An angel again appeared to his desponding mother--"What aileth thee, Hagar? Fear not, for God hath heard the voice of the lad where he is: arise, and lift up the lad, and hold him in thine hand; for I will make him a great nation." At the instant of this address, God is said to have opened her eyes, and she saw a well of water, whence she replenished the bottle, and supplied her fainting son. He revived, and afterward settled in the wilderness of Paran with his mother, and probably maintained her by the use of the bow. So wonderfully does the providence of God accomplish its predestined purposes!

This distressing circumstance in the life of Hagar was a link in a great chain of events, which were connected together by an invisible agency, and held in the divine hands. A superficial observer might see nothing in all that transpired but a curious concurrence of ordinary events. The insolence of Ishmael irritated the temper of Sarah; she procured his expulsion, and that of his mother from her household; retiring in disgrace, she narrowly escaped destruction in the wilderness, and afterward took up a casual residence in the vicinity. But if we pay a proper attention to these events, we shall view them with another eye. Every circumstance was connected with a vast providential plan, and tended to illustrate the power and sovereignty of God in the accomplishment of his designs. The folly of Ishmael, the conduct of Sarah, the compliance of Abraham, the various occurrences connected with the settlement in Paran, concurred to *fulfil a divine prediction*, and thus to evince the superintendence of God over all human affairs. "Surely the wrath of man shall praise thee, and the remainder of wrath wilt thou restrain."

Lot's Wife Chapter IV

"Judge not," said our Saviour, "according to the appearance, but judge righteous judgment." This is a maxim which, though originally uttered in vindication of his character against the reproaches of the Jews, is capable of a more extensive application.

Captivated by the fascinating exterior of the world, the prospect of temporal advantage, and diversified enjoyment, how many neglect to regulate their desires by those superior principles which Revelation inculcates, and which alone can secure substantial happiness! The young, especially suffer by this delusion. Lively in imagination, but immature in judgment; easily, and therefore frequently deceived; they are hurried into those premature determinations which cannot be corrected when they come to discover their mistakes. It is to be deeply deplored, when young persons, through refusing to listen to the dictates of wisdom or the suggestions of experienced age, precipitate themselves into misery, and sacrifice to the fleeting possessions and pleasures of this life, the higher interests of another existence. Deeming themselves privileged to disregard, if not to ridicule religion, by virtue of their age, rank, or talents; and living as though they held their present being by no precarious tenure, they trifle away their time in criminal indulgences, and "lose their own souls" by a guilty procrastination. To persons of this class, Solomon suggests a most important truth, in the form of a sarcastic appeal--"Rejoice, O young man in thy youth, and let thy heart cheer thee in the days of thy youth; and walk in the ways of thine heart, and in the sight of thine eyes; but know thou, that for all these things God will bring thee into judgment."

There are also young persons of another description, who, though partially influenced by such motives, possess upon the whole a different character. Their inconsistencies, although highly detrimental, result rather from temporary illusion than from radical depravity. The passions which through grace are habitually subjugated to the yoke of reason and religion, acquire, on some occasions, a momentary ascendency; and, as the apostle describes it, "they do" that which they "allow not," and that which they "would," they "do not." They are, for a time, inveigled by their senses-- their eyes are dazzled, and their minds perverted. Their mistakes both of judgment and of feeling, connect themselves, perhaps, with a long series of disasters, neither to be foreseen nor prevented. Sometimes the individual himself does not discover his error for a lapse of years; continuing under the deception, till the course of providential events awakens him from the dream of enjoyment, and successive afflictions restore him to his "right mind."

If at that unhappy moment, when Lot, regarding temporal advantages only, and forgetting his religious dangers, "lifted up his eyes and beheld all the plain of Jordan, that it was well watered every where, before the Lord destroyed Sodom and Gomorrah, even as the garden of the Lord, like the land of Egypt, as thou comest unto Zoar"--if he could have anticipated the melancholy consequences of one false step, surely he would not have chosen the plain of Jordan for a residence, or pitched his tent towards the city of Sodom! Infinitely better had it been for him to have accompanied Abraham to Mamre, or even to have lived in a retired and desolate wilderness.

The most exalted piety does not necessarily exempt the individual who possesses it from the trials of life; but it prepares the mind for enduring and improving them. In some instances, it obviates those external calamities which befall an ungodly world, supplying the means of escaping from many of the punishments and penalties which the wicked suffer; but, in all cases, it prevents that anguish which arises from the secret conviction, that the afflictions of life are the consequences of personal guilt and misconduct-- sent, it is true, for their ultimate benefit; but sent in judgment, and expressive of displeasure. Sin is always pernicious. It not only involves the impenitent in present sufferings and future wo, but inflicts even on the people of God, in proportion to the degree in which it prevails, embarrassments and calamities.

If we direct our course by mere worldly considerations, however fair the prospect may seem, the luxuriant plain is likely to become overspread with confusion, and deluged with misery. In consequence of the fatal choice of Lot, he soon became a captive, then a fugitive. He lost his liberty, his peace, his possessions, and finally his dearest connexion in life, by one of those awful dispensations in which the hand of God is so visible, the punishment of sin so striking, and the lessons of divine justice so terrible. We are admonished to "remember Lot's wife;" and truly, her *advantages*, her *deliverance*, her *guilt*, and her *doom*, furnish so many subjects of instructive reflection.

The ADVANTAGES of Lot's wife were considerable. She was the nearest connection of a "just or pious man;" who though he dwelt in Sodom, the very rendezvous of all the vices, "vexed his righteous soul from day to day," with the "unlawful deeds," and "filthy conversation" of its wicked inhabitants.

Obvious and lamentable as were the defects in the character of Lot, it must, nevertheless, be admitted that he was a man of eminent piety--a piety the more conspicuous, from the circumstances in which he was placed. His fellow citizens were inexpressibly depraved; so much so, that in all the annals of sacred and profane history, we find no parallel example. Sodom was, in fact, one mass of pollution. High and low, rich and poor, seem to have been infected with moral contamination; and every day their excessive immoralities dared the vengeance of Heaven. Lot stood alone and unsupported, struggling against the torrent of iniquity that flowed down every street, and inundated with its filthiness the adjacent cities of the plain.

Society animates the desponding spirit amidst discouragements. It inspires diligence, quickens zeal, and strengthens against resistance. The example of the multitude often operates with pernicious influence in situations where the pious experience considerable co-operation; and considering the weakness of human nature, the force of temptation, the numerous instances of defection which occur even within the pale of the Christian church, continuance in well doing is a just cause of congratulation under any circumstances. But that this holy man should have remained steadfast and immoveable amidst the abominations of Sodom, is a proof of the confirmed stability and superior excellence of his religion. Neither promises nor threatenings, neither ridicule nor flattery could divert him from his course. He was neither to be cajoled nor coerced; but set his face like a flint, and pursued the narrow path of obedience to God with undeviating perseverance. Piety had, in fact, exalted him to a higher sphere, and, like the sun, that pursues his circuit alike through the calm or the stormy day, the obstructions which impiety seemed to throw in his path, proved nothing but cloud and vapour before his resistless progress.

It must have been a singular privilege to have sustained the intimate relationship of a *wife* to one so excellent, and at a period, not only when immorality had acquired such an odious ascendency in the particular place of their residence, but when there was little religion in the world. His favoured partner had every opportunity of knowing his views upon the most important religious topics, and especially of being informed or reminded of the great designs of eternal Providence respecting the future mission of our Saviour; to which bright consummation of human happiness the saints of God, in the remotest ages, look forward with confident anticipation.

She had, besides, the best means of observing the influence of true religion upon the character. She saw him in every position, and witnessed his conduct every day. If she were no stranger to many of his imperfections, and these attach more or less to every one in the present state, she could not fail of perceiving a mighty contrast between his general deportment and spirit, and that of the guilty inhabitants of Sodom. He was not only unseduced by their example, but detested their practices; and bore a decided, if it were an unavailing, testimony against them. She must have seen that his passions were under the regulation of principles to which *they* were perfect strangers; and that his whole character was cast in a different mould. His fellow-citizens, indeed, possessed the advantage of his public example and judicious reproofs, although they were too base to receive any impression; but *she* saw him at home, and had the privilege of domestic intercourse. There he presented his private and frequent devotions--there, no doubt, he erected the family altar, and day by day offered the solemn sacrifices of prayer and praise. Upon that house the eye of God was fixed, and there his blessing descended. One voice in Sodom, discordant to the universal chorus of imprecation and blasphemy was harmonious in the ear of Heaven--one hallowed flame ascended amidst the fires of lust--one drop of purity mingled with an ocean of wickedness!

Whether the wife of Lot were benefited by his example, or properly observant of his actions, or whether she were infected by the general contagion, it is not possible to ascertain with certainty: her subsequent conduct renders us suspicious of her having been, if not a practitioner of atrocious crimes, at least in love with the world, and destitute of real religion.

Some of the best of men have suffered this severe affliction. The chosen companions of their pilgrimage have been strangers to their religious feelings, and could cherish no kindred sympathies. Instead of proving help meets, they have been hinderances; instead of assisting, they have retarded their journey. In some cases, this must be imputed to themselves, as their *own fault*. They have been misled by their passions; and, in consequence of "entering into temptation," they have plunged themselves into inevitable wretchedness. This is a sin which, we should hope, is not often committed; and, as a means of prevention, we would enforce a contrary conduct by all the authority which can attach to the language of an inspired adviser. Paul exhorts us to marry "only in the Lord;" and he sustains his admonitions by irresistible argument: "Be ye not unequally yoked together with unbelievers; for what fellowship hath righteousness with unrighteousness? and what communion hath light with darkness? and what concord hath Christ with Belial? or what part hath he that believeth with an infidel?"

There is one case, in which we must rather pity than censure this incongruous association. Previous to that essential change of character which is introductory to the kingdom of heaven, and which the New Testament represents as being "brought out of darkness into marvellous light," the woman and the man have, perhaps, become "equally yoked" in unbelief. At the period of their early matrimonial connection, no dissimilarity in point of religious principle existed. Both were "lovers of pleasure more than lovers of God;" and unhappily, neither of them felt the importance of securing permanent and solid enjoyment, by constructing it on the basis of genuine religion. Resembling others in the same period of youth and illusion, they embarked on the smooth and inviting surface, unaware of what storms awaited them, or what dangers lurked in the perilous sea of life. It was, morning--the scene was new--the prospect gay--and their fair horizon seemed to encircle an earthly paradise! They knew not it was a *painted* landscape, and that "pure and undefiled religion" alone could effectually prepare them for the disappointment.

Since that period, one of this happy pair has become "a follower of God," the other remains "a servant of sin"--the one has discovered the paramount importance of the interest of eternity, the other has not yet learned the necessity of salvation, or the value of the soul. Now is fulfilled the prediction of Christ, "I came not to send peace, but a sword. For I am come to set a man at variance against his father, and the daughter against her mother, and the daughter-in-law against her mother-in-law; and a man's foes shall be those of *his own household*."

Let those who are thus united together by the conjugal tie, although dissimilar in character, be excited to a consideration of their respective duties. The religious party should pursue a system of conciliation and kindness, as best calculated to exemplify the excellence of religion, and *win* the disobedient yoke-fellow; and the irreligious husband or wife should study the virtuous peculiarities, and worthy example, of the pious partner: the one being anxious to exhibit the genuine effect of religion--the other to examine with impartiality, and an unprejudiced attention, the operation of grace.

Another circumstance to which our attention is directed, in the history of Lot's wife, is her DELIVERANCE from the miraculous conflagration of Sodom. The angelic messengers who were sent to Lot, conducted him and his family from the scene of danger. They first distinctly predicted the destruction of the city, on account of its extreme iniquity, and intimated that they were commissioned to execute this awful purpose of eternal justice. They then inquired about his relations, commanding him to bring them out of the place; but, with a spirit of infatuation too common to the impenitent, the earnest solicitations of Lot were utterly rejected, and even ridiculed.

"Up," said he, "get you out of this place, for the Lord will destroy this city! But he seemed as one that mocked unto his sons-in-law."

On the ensuing morning, at a very early hour, the two commissioned angels urged Lot to use all possible despatch in his departure, and to take with him his wife and daughters. The predestined moment was at hand; the windows of heaven were opening, and the burning tempest ready to descend. "And while he lingered, the men laid hold upon his hand, and upon the hand of his wife, and upon the hand of his two daughters; the Lord being merciful unto him; and they brought him forth, and set him without the city. And it came to pass, when they had brought them forth abroad, that he said, Escape for thy life; look not behind thee, neither stay thou in all the plain; escape to the mountain, lest thou be consumed."

This narrative intimates with sufficient plainness that Lot's wife and daughters were spared for *his sake*; and that it was nothing but the impenitent obstinacy of his other family connexions, that prevented their escape. They would not listen, even though he "lingered," probably, to persuade them to accompany his flight; they must, therefore, perish. It appears that his wife and daughters also were reluctant, as the angels were obliged to take them each by the hand, and conduct them into the plain; but, *for the sake of Lot*, they were happily compelled to flee. If this woman had not been the wife, and these the daughters of a *good man*, they would have shared the tremendous fate of the other inhabitants of the city; their near connection with him, unquestionably saved their otherwise unprotected lives.

Humiliating as the sentiment may be to the enemies of religion, it is clearly deducible from this affecting narrative, and strikingly confirmed by other scriptural accounts, that righteous persons are the salt of the earth; the means, not only of preserving it from becoming an entire mass of corruption, but of averting the judgments of Heaven from others; and especially of preserving those from awful calamity, who are more immediately connected with them by the ties of consanguinity or friendship.

The escape of Lot's wife and daughters, on this disastrous occasion, was an illustration of the promise which had but a short time before been made to Abraham, when he was permitted to commune with Jehovah respecting the destruction of this city. Having been informed of the divine determinations, Abraham, deeply affected with the condition of his wicked neighbours, but feeling a peculiar concern for his nephew, drew near with holy boldness to inquire whether the righteous and the wicked were to be involved in the same common catastrophe; and whether, if fifty righteous persons could be found, the city might not be spared? To this he obtained full consent: upon which he ventured to limit the pious number, for whose sake all the inhabitants should be spared, to forty-five--then to forty--to thirty--to twenty--and to ten; "And the Lord said, I will not destroy it for ten's sake."

Here it is observable, that the patriarch did not request the preservation of the wicked for *their own sake*, or because of any supposed severity in the predicted punishment, but solely for the sake of the *righteous* who might be discovered in the place. Value your connexion, then, with the people of God. To be born of pious parents, or to be situated amidst religious advantages, is an unspeakable favour. The church of Christ, especially, is a privileged spot--there celestial mercy takes her favourite walks--thither she conveys her choicest blessings--and to that sacred enclosure from the world, she extends her most powerful protection. How many families, besides the house of Obed-edom, have been blessed "because of the ark of God!"

[Sidenote: Years before Christ, 1897.] The inspired history, in the next place, particularly points out the GUILT of Lot's wife. As soon as this favoured family had reached the suburbs, and at a moment when the rising sun shed his unclouded radiance over the devoted scene, and, consequently, indicated no approaching storm, the mighty tragedy commenced. Down came the burning sulphureous deluge upon Sodom, Gomorrah, Admah, and Zeboim; which, mingling with the bituminous soil of the valley, and blazing with inconceivable intensity, spread sudden, awful, and universal desolation. From this horrible moment, the site of these ancient cities became converted into a lake, which, from its bituminous quality, is termed the lake *Asphaltites*, and sometimes the *Dead Sea*, from the idea that no creature can exist in its waters. [11]

During this miraculous tempest, the wife of Lot, who was now flying to Zoar, "LOOKED BACK FROM BEHIND HIM;" and in consequence, suffered an instantaneous judgment, which we shall presently have occasion to notice.

And was this the whole amount of her criminality? Was it a mere glance of the eye, for which she is become an object of execration, and a warning to all ages? Was this the single action for which she suffered?--Have we not been led to suppose, that apostacy is rather a *course of conduct*, than the perpetration of any particular crime, however atrocious? And yet does not the wife of Lot appear to have been punished as an apostate?

Beware of forming a hasty judgment, and recollect that, in some cases, a single action is an infallible criterion of a most impious character. It is the *last in a series of crimes*, although, perhaps, the only *discovered* iniquity. The rest have been concealed by circumstances, or by artifice; and, like the apex and point of a rock piercing the surface of the deep, which indicates its immense magnitude and elevation above the bottom of the ocean, *one* considerable act of baseness indicates the real existence of an immense accumulation of secret iniquity. Such was the character of *Judas,* and probably of *Lot's wife.*

The recorded action in question indicated, in fact, a very complicated crime. It was a direct disobedience to an express and solemn command; and whether the command respected a mere look, or a mighty undertaking, the *principle* which influenced the conduct, was equally censurable. We must abstain from *whatever* is interdicted, whether it respect the tasting of fruit, as in the case of Eve, or the looking back to relinquished possessions, as in the example of Lot's wife. Unbelief was also a probable concomitant in this transgression. She might doubt the reality of the threatened destruction, or be influenced by a spirit of unhallowed curiosity: or, if she heard the descending tempest, some dread of being overtaken by it might induce her to look back. But, above all, our Lord, in commenting upon her conduct, intimates that her *heart* lingered after the possessions she had left, and her look implied a *wish* to return to their enjoyment.

The case of this woman is peculiarly affecting, from other considerations. It has been already stated, she had peculiar advantages, being the wife of a righteous man--she had thus far escaped the pollutions of Sodom, and avoided its destiny--she had obeyed the voice of the celestial messenger, and was led forth under a heavenly ministration--she was in the company of the pious--participated the deliverance of her husband, and was on the point of having completely escaped--Sodom was left behind--Zoar was at hand--the raging storm was desolating the devoted cities, while the bright sun of the morning lighted the fugitives on their way. Before, all was smiling! Behind, all was tempestuous!--Salvation, if they persevered! Perdition, if they retreated or looked back!--It is written in the book of God--may it be written indelibly on every heart--"If any man draw back, my soul shall have no pleasure in him."

It will conduce to the purposes of instruction, if we generalize this subject, by briefly stating a few of the most usual causes of apostacy from God; some of which are strictly applicable to the history of Lot's wife.

Sometimes it originates in *fear;* and though every period could furnish instances, we must expect to find them principally in times of persecution. Many, under the awful apprehension of excruciating torments, and some even from very inferior reasons of alarm, have signed their recantation of principles which they had long professed to venerate; but few have imitated the noble heroism of a CRANMER, who publicly denounced his own recantation, and resolutely thrust the hand that signed it first into the fire, on the day of his martyrdom, calling it, "this unworthy right hand!"

But in all ages a *love of the world* may be justly considered as a much more prevalent occasion of apostacy than fear. Demas, and the wife of Lot, live again in a thousand wretched examples. It may be acknowledged difficult to point out in all cases with perfect exactitude, the precise line of demarkation between a proper and an inordinate pursuit of worldly good, and thus to detect the first commencement of an avaricious temper, the embryo germ of an apostate disposition; but at least no difficulty should remain with *the individual himself* in deciding upon his own actual state, even though he be not guilty of flagrant immoralities, if conscious that his heart is in his covetousness--if the love of gain have usurped the dominion of his soul, and dethroned the love of God--if he gladly embrace every opportunity of promoting his worldly interest, and obey but slowly and reluctantly the calls of duty. Let him apprehend that he is drifting along to ruin--let him fear, and fear justly, that the pleasant gale of success to which he has expanded all his powers, is only bearing him upon the rocks of eternal destruction. Be not deceived, though they appear covered with flowers of surpassing beauty, and exquisite fragrance. "Love not the world, neither the things that are in the world. If any man love the world, the love of the Father is not in him."

Levity of mind is a frequent occasion of apostacy. It predisposes the unhappy individual to the ruinous influence of vicious society and injurious publications. These, most fatally adapted to their purpose, soon induce the unwary to neglect, and finally to despise all religious institutions. The apostle Paul intimates that some are "tossed to and fro, and carried about with every wind of doctrine," like clouds which, possessing no solidity, are driven in every direction through the atmosphere. Persons of this description are easily persuaded by a plausible reasoner, that his opinions are true, and with equal facility submit to the next artful sophist, who avows even contrary sentiments. The natural effect of this inconstancy will be, a disregard of ALL truth, and a ready admission of every sceptical principle. When the mind is in such a state of fluctuation and uncertainty, or rather the willing slave of every tyrant, it is well prepared for vice: it will admit a criminal thought, as well as a sentimental error, and the same plausibility which could successfully insinuate a sceptical principle, can excite to an immoral practice. In the circles of gay dissipation, every remaining scruple is easily dissipated; the poison of "evil communications" is voraciously swallowed, and "good morals are corrupted."

Such a disposition is closely allied to *pride*, which often "goes before, destruction, and a haughty spirit before a fall." Praised by their companions as persons of distinguished genius, or admired for a natural wit, they sacrifice every thing to flattery. They have been stimulated to believe that the possession of religion is a decisive proof of intellectual inferiority; or at least, that a punctilious observance of its practices, or a fervent attachment to its peculiar doctrines, is enthusiastic. They listen to the artful seducer, who assures them that their principles are too evidently drawn from the lessons of the nursery, and that it is time to shake off--their own penetration, indeed, will lead them to discard--the mere prejudices of an illiberal education. It is not improbable they may meet with some advocate of deistical principles or libertine conduct, who zealously instils into them the maxim of the well-known Earl of Shaftesbury, that "whoever is searching for truth, should examine if they cannot find out something that may be justly laughed at;" and if they can be persuaded as he was, "not to think on the subject of religion, without endeavouring to put himself in as good a humour as possible," it is not unlikely they may adopt what he calls a *natural suspicion*, that "the holy records themselves were no other than the pure invention and artificial compliment of an interested party, in behalf of the richest corporation and most profitable monopoly which could be erected in the world."

In the scriptural statement of the fall of man, it appears that pride and sensuality were the first dispositions which polluted the human mind in paradise, and their contaminating influence has descended upon the whole human race. From these two springs the torrent of corruption originated, and has never ceased to pursue its course and widen its channel through the successive ages of time. "When the woman saw that the tree was good for food, and that it was pleasant to the eyes, and a tree to be desired to make one wise, she took of the fruit thereof, and did eat; and gave also unto her husband with her, and he did eat."

The DOOM of Lot's wife is one of the most memorable in the records of either profane or sacred history. It is said, that "she became a pillar of salt," or a nitro-sulphureous pillar; the singularity and severity of her punishment being thus proportioned to the atrocity of her crime. When we recollect that Jehovah afterward proclaimed himself to Moses as "the Lord, the Lord God, merciful and gracious, long-suffering, and abundant in goodness and truth; keeping mercy for thousands, forgiving iniquity, and transgression, and sin;" that he is frequently celebrated by the inspired writers, as "ready to pardon, slow to anger, of great kindness, plenteous in mercy, full of compassion;" that he is represented by the apostle John as "love" itself; and that infinite benignity is essential to his nature, and characteristic of his dispensations--we cannot but tremble at the sight of such a visitation.

Inexpressibly awful as the overthrow of Sodom, Gomorrah, Admah, and Zeboim appears, there is an additional feature of horror in the destruction of this woman. Our imagination is bewildered amidst the general ruin of multitudes; while, by the contemplation of an individual instance, appointed to a separate and peculiar punishment, we become excited to deeper feeling. From the very constitution of our nature, we view the doom of numbers with a diminished impression; we have not time to select and meditate upon the peculiarities of individual agonies, and regard them only in one vast heterogeneous mass, consigned to one common portion of suffering: but the emotion is widely different, and incalculably more poignant, when a solitary example is presented to us, alike distinguished for guilt and for punishment. In the present case, too, the degree of sensibility excited into action is necessarily more acute, from the very circumstance forbidding us to pity, and demanding an unmingled overwhelming sense of omnipotent justice. Nor is this a censurable, but a necessary feeling, indicative of a proper coincidence of mind with the perfect will of Heaven: it is allied to the sentiments attributed to purer spirits, who, when they witness the seven angels distributing the seven last plagues in which is filled up the wrath of God, are represented as standing on the sea of glass, having the harps of God.--"And they sing the song of Moses the servant of God, and the song of the Lamb, saying, great and marvellous are thy works, Lord God Almighty; just and true are thy ways, thou King of saints. Who shall not fear thee, O Lord, and glorify thy name? for thou only art holy, for all nations shall come and worship before thee: for thy JUDGMENTS are made manifest." In the same spirit, the heavens, the holy apostles and prophets, are called upon to rejoice over Babylon in the hour of her destruction; and a great voice of much people is heard in heaven, saying, "Alleluia; salvation and glory, and honour, and power, unto the Lord our God; for true and righteous are his JUDGMENTS." "And again they said, Alleluia. And her smoke rose up for ever and ever."

The justice of God displayed even in the awful form which it assumes in the punishment of the wife of Lot, is, in fact, only a modification of goodness, and therefore a proper reason both for angelic and human celebration. The love of order is no less essential to a holy being than the love of mercy; and therefore it is compatible with the most perfect goodness, in its association with justice, to punish transgressors either on their own account or for the sake of others--either for the purpose of individual correction or of general warning. It would be a far less display of goodness to suffer men to persevere in sin without any control, than to arrest them by some powerful stroke. In the former case, they not only plunge into ruin themselves, but draw others, by their fatal and malignant attraction, into perdition: in the latter, a salutary precaution is given to such as lie within the reach of their mischievous influence. Whatever has a tendency to prevent sin is a benevolent exercise of power; because sin is the source of individual and universal misery: if it had never entered into this world, man would still have been happy; and when, in the merciful appointments of Heaven, the guilt which now stains the moral creation shall be purified away by the efficacy of the blood of Christ, paradise will be restored, and the long-renowned tabernacle of God again descend to be with men. To this glorious consummation of human felicity, all the dispensations of Providence point; and to produce it, all his judgments are inflicted: the promises and the threatenings have each a similar design, and will ultimately promote the same general object. The tempest and the tornado have their peculiar uses, as well as the small rain that descends upon the tender herb. "Mercy and truth meet together-- righteousness and peace kiss each other."

In turning our eyes, then, towards the plain of Sodom, we must combine a sentiment of holy reverence with trembling horror. The destiny of the atrocious sinner was intended to produce salutary apprehensions in her surviving relatives, and in all her posterity. Upon that accursed plain Eternal Justice erected a monument of infinite displeasure; but the hand which raised the pillar of salt, at the same time inscribed upon it, in characters too large and legible to be mistaken, "FEAR GOD, AND KEEP HIS COMMANDMENTS."

The terrific nature of this judgment was enhanced by the *instantaneous* manner in which it occurred. No sooner did the wife of Lot look back, than she was converted into a pillar of salt, [12]--*this moment* in the midst of life, and apparently escaping from the scene of danger--*the next*, a monument of wrath! What a transition from happiness to misery! What a descent from the summit of hope to the depths of despair! Mercy had almost conducted her to Zoar--Guilt transported her to the abyss of wo! She had even tasted the cup of blessing; but, dashing it from her lips in the spirit of daring rebellion, she was made to drink "the wine-cup of fury."

It elucidates the divine condescension and forbearance, when the wicked, instead of being withered at a touch, are allowed time for reflection.-- The ordinary dispensations of Providence are characterized by a merciful tardiness: the daring transgressor is addressed by reiterated appeals, and perhaps placed under a course of moral discipline: he is not smit by the thunder, or blasted by the lightning; but a series of smaller precursory punishments precedes a great catastrophe: his way is hedged up; reproofs, remonstrances, losses, afflictions, bereavements, constitute so many obstructions thrown across the path to perdition; and if he perish, it is necessary to force his way through them with a daring and infatuated heroism: voices from heaven and earth precede the infliction of merited vengeance, saying with loud and harmonious exclamations, "Let the wicked forsake his way, and the unrighteous man his thoughts; and let him return unto the Lord, and he will have mercy upon him; and to our God, for he will abundantly pardon."

But in the present melancholy instance, the wife of Lot was cut off as in a moment: she was ripe for the sickle, and justice delayed not to gather her into the storehouse of wrath; she cumbered the ground by her impieties, and was worthy of no additional cultivation. Here we behold an awful specimen of the obstinacy of sinners, the effect of disobedience, and the determination of God, in a visible and striking manner, to vindicate his holy name.

Reader! flatter not yourself that the circumstance of having hitherto escaped remarkable judgment is any real indemnification against future punishment: do not imagine that the supreme God is unobservant, because he is not vindictive; that it is possible to elude his eye, because you have not yet been slain by his sword. The delay, which is intended as a benefit, may, and often does, by perversion, aggravate the sinner's doom: and indeed it is one of the most lamentable proofs of human degeneracy, that the very circumstance in which the goodness of God is singularly apparent, and which ought to lead to repentance, is made the occasion of more atrocious crime and more resolute perseverance.

But delay is no evidence of indifference; and if justice have hitherto slept, it is to be apprehended it will rise with recruited vigour. While you go on still in your trespasses, be assured the glittering sword is drawing from its scabbard--it is even whetting to the final stroke!

Rebekah Chapter V

Section I

Rapid, irresistible, and certain is the progress of time. The few incidents of which human life consists, transpire in quick succession; the few years of which it is composed, even in cases of the greatest longevity, soon elapse: the cradle and the grave seem placed very near each other; and scarcely does the voice of congratulation cease at our birth, before it is succeeded by the lamentations of sorrow at our funeral.

There is a wide difference, however, in the actual impression, between passing through the details of existence in daily and hourly engagements, which, from their variety, produce an illusion of slowness and a vague idea of almost interminable continuance, and looking at expended years *after their termination*, or at successive lives in the perspective of history. In the latter case, events appear crowded together, the intervening spaces are riot distinctly perceptible, and the distance is diminished. If the life of an Abraham, an Isaac, or a Jacob, had been presented to us in the form of a daily journal of occurrences, how easily might it have been expanded into a volume equal in dimensions to the whole inspired record; and how distant would each eventful period of their respective lives have appeared! how vast would have seemed the space between them if minuter circumstances had been formally detailed in the order of months, and days, and hours! Even a single year assumes a considerable magnitude when viewed as three hundred and sixty-five days, each day and night as four-and-twenty hours, each hour as sixty successive minutes, and each minute or hour as occupied with its appropriate and necessary engagements: but when we ascend that elevated spot to which history conducts us, and look back upon the long track of time, and through the course of revolving centuries, we reflect at once on those images of Scripture with which our imagination has been so often arrested, and see that the motion of the "weaver's shuttle" scarcely represents the "swiftness" of our days; the passing shadows that fly across the plain, imperfectly display the nothingness of fleeting years; "the little time" in which the "vapour appeareth," is but faintly expressive of the manner in which life "vanisheth away." It is almost impossible to observe the small number of pages which relate all that is really worth recording, of hundreds and even thousands of years, without being deeply affected. A few chapters suffice to state the principal circumstances relating to the creation, destruction, and renewal of the world; and a single book contains, in addition to this information, the lives of patriarchs the most distinguished, and the account of ages the most eventful and extraordinary. Solemn consideration--"one generation passeth away, and another cometh!"

We have been led into these reflections chiefly by observing how rapidly the inspired writer passes from one event to another in the life of Abraham, though many years intervened; and especially by noticing the *immediate* connexion in which the death and burial of Sarah are placed with the marriage of Isaac: so nearly allied, so few are the intermediate steps between the most joyful and the most painful events of human existence! A marriage to-day--a funeral to-morrow! This hour congratulated--the next lamented! "Great and marvellous are thy works, O Lord God Almighty: just and true are thy ways, thou King of saints."

The family histories of the patriarchs are rendered peculiarly attractive by the simplicity of their manners, and their pastoral mode of living. We are transported into ages, around which antiquity throws a powerful charm, and revelation an extraordinary lustre. What are scenes of blood, and acclamations of triumph, in comparison with the private history of a man of peace, and a man of piety? what are heroic deeds to virtuous achievements? and what the most splendid page of secular history to the beautiful and interesting account of the various transactions relating to the union of Isaac and Rebekah?

These are so intimately blended together, that the present chapter must embrace at least a brief notice of them, in order to form an adequate idea of the heroine of this inimitable Scripture narrative.

[Sidenote: Years before Christ, 1856]

Abraham had now attained the venerable age of one hundred and forty years; his beloved Sarah was no more; and after weeping over her grave, and negociating for the entire possession of the field of Ephron in Machpelah, where she was interred, as a family burying-place, his thoughts were forcibly attracted towards the day of his own dissolution. "The Lord had blessed him in all things," but his affections were detached from earthly possessions, and permanently fixed upon his unchangeable inheritance in the skies. He "desired a better country, that is, a heavenly; wherefore God was not ashamed to be called his God, for he had prepared for him a city."

Previous to his departure, Abraham felt solicitous respecting the adjustment of his temporal affairs, and particularly the settlement and marriage of his beloved son. Actuated not merely by the common anxiety of a parent, who knows that the credit and happiness of his family depend on the propriety of the connection which he may form; but contemplating with the eye of faith his future posterity, the patriarch called his eldest and confidential servant. This was Eliezer of Damascus, the steward of his house; and, in case of his death, the manager of his affairs. He was, unquestionably, under that divine direction, which in this as in every other concern of life, he anxiously sought. It is pleasing to witness the result which was so evidently connected with the prudence and piety of his proceedings, and which points us to the never-failing promise, "In all thy ways acknowledge him, and lie shall direct thy paths," Isaac is not, indeed, distinctly mentioned, but he was no stranger to prayer; and having attained his fortieth year, he had doubtless felt a laudable anxiety to enter into the honourable state of matrimony, expressed his desires to God, and after concerting the proper measures with his father, patiently waited the will of Providence.

Abraham explained his views to Eliezer, and exacted a solemn oath respecting the punctual fulfilment of his commission, in which some of the characteristic principles of this illustrious saint were conspicuous. In the selection of a wife for his son, he seems uninfluenced by worldly policy. He wishes him to connect him with virtue rather than wealth; knowing that the latter is not only uncertain, but unnecessary to the purposes of real happiness.

It has been often said, there are "few happy matches;" but the cause of this fact is seldom traced or regarded. If our calculations be founded solely upon a reference to temporal interests, if the importance of a connexion be measured merely by the probable amount of gold it may produce, or the degree of worldly influence it is likely to confer, we may add another item to the sum of probabilities--that of *disappointment*. The inconsistencies into which this strange match-making infatuation has betrayed some of the greatest and best of men, is truly deplorable; and if it do not incur immediate calamity, it certainly excites the divine displeasure. God requires to be honoured in this, no less than in every other transaction.

Abraham also evinced his characteristic aversion of idolatry. He desired his servant not to seek a wife for Isaac in Chaldea, but to proceed to Haran in Mesopotamia, to the house of Nahor his brother. He was particular in requiring him to swear by the Lord, the God of heaven and the God of the earth, that he would not take his son a wife of the daughters of the Canaanites, among whom he resided. The danger of his posterity becoming blended with idolaters, and contracting their habits, induced him to use this solemn precaution; although his faith realized the peopling of this country, by his descendants. His servant put his hand upon his thigh, in confirmation of the agreement, [13] and immediately prepared for his journey. The distance from Hebron, the present residence of Abraham, to Haran, was about seventeen days' journey; and the servant must have travelled about four hundred and sixty miles.

Servants may learn, from this example, the kind of conduct which adorns their station. They should be punctual in the discharge of their duties, and readily comply with the directions they receive. Eliezer felt himself bound to comply with his master's injunctions, and not only proceeded on his distant expedition without reluctance and murmuring, but with that despatch which proves his whole heart was engaged in his duty. If any should plead, that it was, no doubt, a privilege to have such a master, and any one would have been happy in such a situation, let them be reminded that this is a very questionable position; for it is common for servants to disregard the authority, or undervalue the character of the best masters and mistresses; but their duty is not to be measured by the virtue or even the kindness, of their domestic superiors, the apostle expressly ordaining obedience "not only to the good and gentle, but also to the froward."

Upon Eliezer's arrival in the vicinity of the city of Nahor, he made his camels kneel down by a well, intending to supply them as soon as possible with water. The whole retinue was, no doubt, sufficiently weary with the journey. It was evening, and about the customary hour when the women of the country came out to fetch a supply of water. This faithful and pious servant was aware of this circumstance, but, previous to the arrival of any of these strangers, he betook himself to solemn and effectual prayer. His words are remarkable: "O Lord God of my master Abraham, I pray thee send me good speed this day, and show kindness unto my master Abraham. Behold, I stand here by the well of water, and the daughters of the men of the city come out to draw water: and let it come to pass, that the damsel to whom I shall say, Let down thy pitcher I pray thee, that I may drink; and she shall say, Drink, and I will give thy camels drink also; let the same be she that thou hast appointed for thy servant Isaac; and thereby shall I know that thou hast showed kindness unto my master!"

While the words of supplication were still upon the tongue of this worthy servant, behold a damsel of singular beauty approaches the well! It is, in fact, Rebekah, who was born to Bethuel, son of Milcah, the wife of Nahor; and whom an invisible but all-wise Providence had sent at this precise moment, and by this happy concurrence of circumstances, introduced to the travelling stranger. Beautiful, young, and artless; bearing a pitcher upon her shoulder, which she hastened to the well to fill for the necessary supply of the family; we cannot imagine a more finished picture of loveliness, or one to which the Miltonian description of Eve, as first beheld by her admiring partner, is more justly applicable:

"Adorn'd
With what all earth or heaven could bestow
To make her amiable; on she came
Led by her heav'nly Maker, though unseen.

"Grace was in all her steps, heav'n in her eye,
In every gesture, dignity and love."

She speedily descended to the reservoir of water, and filled her pitcher.
[14] The servant was attracted by her remarkable appearance, for she seemed
"like the lily among thorns;" but, at present, remained silent. Intent upon
her proper business, she did not indulge an idle curiosity, and waste her
time, by stopping to make inquiries respecting the stranger, and his train
of camels, which were reclining near the well; nor would she have been
detained a moment, had not a motive of kindness prompted her to listen to
his solicitations for help. He, at length, hastened to meet her, and requested
to drink a little of the water with which she had just replenished her pitcher.
This was granted with the utmost readiness; she let down the vessel from
her shoulder, and desired him to take whatever he pleased. After this, she
kindly offered to supply all his train of camels; and, regardless of the trouble
which such officious hospitality occasioned, she did not even wait for a
reply, but ran to fill the trough, by repeated draughts of water.

All this time, the man, who, by the way might have rendered this
lovely young woman some assistance, stood gazing in silent astonishment.
There was so striking a coincidence between her conduct, and the wishes
he had been expressing, that he could not help connecting them together.
"Wondering at her, he held his peace, to wit whether the Lord had made his
journey prosperous or not." It seems strange that he should have felt even
a momentary hesitation upon the subject, but it exemplifies the frequent
state of our minds respecting anticipated blessings. We seek them with
an importunity which procures their communication, but, when actually
bestowed, we scarcely believe them to be in our possession, and are too
reluctant to recognize the divine bounty. But what has been sought with
eagerness ought to be acknowledged with promptitude.

As soon as the camels had been supplied, the good man presented
Rebekah with a suitable token of his thankfulness. It consisted of a golden
ear-ring, of half a shekel weight, and two bracelets for her hands, of ten
shekels weight of gold. These were, probably, the costly ornaments which
Abraham had commissioned his servant to bestow upon the future wife of
his son; and which, as he had now seen the accomplishment of his prayer,
he no longer hesitated to give this interesting young woman.

Availing himself of the present favourable opportunity of entering into some conversation with her, he inquired whose daughter she might be, and whether she thought her father could afford him and his attendants; and camels, sufficient accommodation? In the east this was so common an act of hospitality, that the question did not appear strange, or the request obtrusive. It was, besides, dictated by a strong suspicion, if not a full assurance, that he had attained the object of his journey. She gave a prompt and kind answer: "I am the daughter of Bethuel, the son of Milcah, which she bare unto Naoh. She said, moreover, unto him, we have both straw and provender enough, and room to lodge in," The man bowed in thankfulness to *her*, but in more expressive praise and gratitude to GOD. His heart was full, and his tongue could no longer remain silent. "Blessed," said he, "be the Lord God of my master Abraham, who hath not left destitute my master of his mercy and his truth. I, being in the way, the Lord led me to the house of my master's brethren." This was the language of *faith*--he recognizes the divine "mercy and truth" which had promised to multiply and extend the family of Abraham. It was the voice of *gratitude*--for he remembers the way in which God had conducted him, and sees the concurrence of Providence in all that had transpired. It contained also a delicate intimation to the young women, not only that he came from her venerable relative, but had some important business with her family. Rebekah made all possible haste back, and soon circulated through the family the joyful intelligence of this arrival.

In reviewing what has been hitherto related of this charming story, and the circumstances of the first interview between the servant of Abraham and the future wife of Isaac, we beg to present to our young female readers, a more distinct statement and recommendation of the good qualities discoverable in Rebekah.

1. Observe her *industrious and domesticated habits*. She was high-born, and had great connections--she possessed a commanding beauty of person and fascination of manners--but yet she did not indulge in indolence, or in frivolous pursuits. At that period luxury and refinement had not corrupted simplicity of manners, the affairs of a family were usually under the more direct inspection and management of its principal members, and custom did not prescribe an avoidance of all careful, nor even of all laborious, interference in domestic concerns. But there was a cheerfulness and an assiduity in the whole deportment of Rebekah, that proved it not merely custom, but a sense of duty that influenced her. She was attentive to her proper business, neither omitting nor performing it negligently. It is very unbecoming to see young persons resisting the wishes of their kind parents, who having had a better experience than themselves, are desirous of training them to domestic usefulness. Ill do they requite parental affection,

which has devoted, perhaps, a considerable portion of hard-earned profits to their education in useful branches of knowledge, or to their acquirement of polite accomplishments: by refusing to assist in family arrangements, or to submit to that wise after-discipline, by which they may be prepared to occupy important situations in future life. It is not the proper business of a woman to *shine*, to court admiration, or to display superficial acquirements; nor, on the other hand, does either reason or religion reduce her to the inferior situation of a domestic drudge; but her education is ill bestowed, and perversely misapplied, if it unfit her for the appropriate duties of her station, if it make her proud and petulent, if it raise her above her sphere, and if it indispose her to a proper "care for the things of the world, how she may please her husband."

In modern times it would be unjust to impute the entire blame to the young women themselves; much is attributable to the *system* which has been adopted in their education. Nothing indeed can justify, and few things can be said in extenuation of the guilt of an arrogant disposition, unyielding to the wishes of tender though perhaps less educated parents; but it is to be regretted, that the useful is often far less regarded in public seminaries than the ornamental; and that, while the exterior is polished, the mind remains comparatively uncultivated. We shall not be understood to require a total exclusion of elegant instruction, or polite accomplishments; but let the understanding be well directed, the memory amply stored, the judgment constantly exercised, the hands usefully employed, the temper carefully watched and disciplined--above all, let religion and the fear of God be the basis of the whole fabric, that "our daughters may be as corner-stones, polished after the similitude of a palace."--"By daughters families are united and connected to their mutual strength, as the part of a building are by the corner-stones; and when they are graceful and beautiful, both in *body* and *mind*, they are then *polished* after the similitude of a nice and curious structure. When we see our daughters well established, and stayed with wisdom and discretion, as corner-stones are fastened in the building; when we see them by faith united to Christ as the chief corner-stone, adorned with the graces of God's Spirit, which are the polishing of that which is naturally rough, and become *women professing godliness*; when we see them purified and consecrated to God as living *temples*, we think ourselves happy in them." [15]

2. We see in Rebekah's interview with the servant of Abraham, a pattern of *unaffected simplicity*. It is this which throws an inexpressible charm over the narrative. We see nothing but *nature*; not a particle of false delicacy or finesse. There is no study, no aim to please, no acting a part to court esteem, no suspicions about her, and no concealments; but, in every word and

motion, the most perfect artlessness. "When unadorned" she approaches the well to draw the evening supply of water, she seems "adorned the most."

Let young ladies beware of affectation. It is one of the most disgusting qualities that can attach to female character. It will never win esteem, but will excite ridicule. There is reason to believe that it is frequently produced in a gradual and almost imperceptible manner, but it takes the deeper root, and extends the wider influence in consequence of a slow growth. It is not always easy to make the individual herself sensible of possessing it, but the surest way of preventing its baneful influence, is to guard against whatever has a tendency to produce it. Be yourself--simple and natural. The art of pleasing is--to please without art. Aim not to shine in borrowed feathers, or to acquire the peculiarities of another, especially when they are obviously incongruous with your own native character; and avoid thinking of yourself as of a person of great consequence in every circle, for this is a most infallible means of really becoming of no consequence at all.

The only sufficient security against affectation of every kind, is Christian humility. An inspired writer admonishes us to be clothed with it; and, where this is wanting, every attempt to conceal deformities of character will resemble only the thinnest veil, which may be seen through by the most careless observer. This recommendation may possibly appear to some rather antiquated and obsolete; we shall, nevertheless, persist in it, as of essential importance; and support it by quoting the reference of the apostle to him who has best exemplified the principle, and whose Spirit alone can effectually impress it upon the heart: "Let nothing be done through strife or *vain glory*, but in *lowliness of mind*, let each esteem other better than themselves. Look not every man on his own things, but every man also on the things of others. Let this mind be in you which was also in Christ Jesus; who, being in the form of God, thought it not robbery to be equal with God; but made himself of no reputation, and took upon him the form of a servant, and was made in the likeness of men; and being found in fashion as a man, he *humbled himself*, and became obedient unto death, even the death of the cross."

3. The *modesty* of Rebekah was conspicuous. Vain is the effort to obtain admiration, without this quality. Confining the term to the general behaviour of females in society, which is its most common application, it may be considered as opposed to obstrusiveness, and as contradistinguished from bashfulness. Rebekah waited till the servant of Abraham addressed her, before she paid any attention to him; and when he put the questions which have been related, she readily gave him an answer.

Forwardness is so unbecoming the female character, so opposite to all real delicacy of mind, that no intermixture of other qualities can render it tolerable. If it be associated with rare and brilliant powers, or very eminent acquirements, it is calculated to excite envy and hatred, because it never fails to produce an overbearing conduct. But whatever another's consciousness of mental inferiority may be, this unhallowed temper will produce determined resistance. The very worm that crawls upon the earth will resent the giant's tread. If, on the contrary, it be united to shallowness of capacity, it will render its unhappy possessor utterly contemptible notwithstanding other exterior attractions which might otherwise command attention. It is, in this case, the effect of egregious ignorance; and so far from extorting respect, it only serves to expose that imbecility, which, but for this strange mode of attempt at concealment, might have remained, in a considerable measure, undetected.

Genuine modesty is also distinguishable from extreme bashfulness. As the usages of civilized society do, by no means, banish females from social intercourse, it is requisite in avoiding forwardness to retain a certain degree of self-possession. Boldness and excessive timidity are the two extremes to be avoided. The latter is irksome, both to the individual herself, and to others with whom she may be called to associate. It produces an unnatural character, and, perhaps, may be classed with affectation. It is to be feared, that many who blush at the merest trifles, and are confounded at maintaining the least interchange of sentiment, are too little ashamed of sin, and too unacquainted with the state of their own hearts. The young need not be mortified at any deformity but vice, nor afraid even of confessing ignorance, or making inquiries, so long as they show a proper solicitude for improvement. It is, in fact, a consciousness of ignorance that leads to the acquisition of knowledge. It inspires the desire of information, and stimulates to the use of every means of acquiring it; but a vain and conceited mind is really ignorant, and is likely to remain so, while it presumes upon wisdom.

4. *Courtesy* was another conspicuous feature in the character of Rebekah. The stranger had no sooner requested a little supply of water, than she lets down the pitcher from her shoulder, and manifests the most obliging disposition to render him service. Her whole proceeding evinces good humour and affability in the highest degree, and the "law of kindness is in her tongue." Josephus relates that there were other young females with her, who were asked for water, but refused; and that Rebekah reproved them for their churlishness. Her civilities were connected essentially with her promotion, though she had no selfish purpose in view: they resulted solely from a pure and disinterested generosity of spirit.

Let young women remember that an unfeeling and disobliging temper is unworthy of their character, and opposite to their real interest. It is at once a neglect of duty, and a certain forfeiture of esteem. Courteousness is peculiarly suited to their age and sex, and particularly expected of them. Nor should the exercise of this disposition be restricted merely to their superiors or equals; it ought to characterize their behaviour to their dependents and inferiors. If young people display affability only when in company with others, who move in the same, or in a more elevated sphere of life than themselves, but assume consequence, and betray an arrogant spirit amongst their servants; we cannot but suspect that their good qualities are only apparent, and their motives selfish. The true character of every person is to be learned at home, and at times when no exterior influences operate to make persons different from themselves. Then the mask is taken off, meretricious ornaments are dispensed with, and consequently native qualities appear. Tyrannical conduct may compel obedience, but an amiable spirit alone can command affection, and render servitude pleasant. There are, indeed, great constitutional differences; but it is no apology for petulance to say, it is natural to us, or that we were born irritable. Our constitutional imperfections ought to be carefully watched, and resolutely corrected. Irregularities of temper are capable of being subdued by the vigorous efforts of religious principle. It is possible, by careful and constant discipline, to subdue the most untamed spirit; and is equally politic, because it renders its possessor disagreeable to others, and miserable in herself.

It is on many accounts not only wicked, but foolish, to conduct yourselves with provoking superciliousness towards inferiors. Courtesy is easily practised, and the reverse dangerous to your own peace and comfort. Besides, it is scarcely possible to think of a human being so utterly contemptible, that his esteem is not worth possessing, or so morose that he may not be conciliated by kindness: and in a world in which we are liable to such reverses, and exposed to such reproaches, the friendship of the meanest person may be advantageous. Hence, it is well remarked by Dr. Barrow, "the great Pompey, the glorious triumpher over nations, and admired darling of fortune, was at last beholden to a slave for the composing his ashes, and celebrating his funeral obsequies. The honour of the greatest men depends on the estimation of the least: and the good-will of the meanest peasant is a brighter ornament to the fortune, a greater accession to the grandeur of a prince, than the most radiant gem in his royal diadem. However, the spite and enmity of one (and him the most weak otherwise and contemptible) person, may happen to spoil the content of our whole life, and deprive us of the most comfortable enjoyments thereof; may divert our thoughts from our delightful employments, to a solicitous care of self-preservation and defence; may discompose our minds with vexatious passions; may, by false reports, odious suggestions, and slanderous defamations, blast our credit, raise a storm of general hatred, and conjure up thousands of enemies against us; may, by insidious practices, supplant and undermine us, prejudice our welfare, endanger our estate, and involve us in a bottomless gulf of trouble."

5. We may take occasion, from Rebekah's kindness, to commend another quality for which she was distinguished--*humanity to animals*. Abraham's servant merely requested some water to quench his own thirst; but she felt for the dumb creatures that attended him, who could only express their wants by signs. She offered to supply his camels, and hastened to fill the troughs, that they might drink. How kind, how considerate was this! There are few persons of a really amiable temper, who do not cherish an attachment to animals; still we should distinguish between a proper attention to their necessities and comforts, and that excessive caressing fondness which is unbecoming a rational being.

But in what language shall we sufficiently denounce *cruelty* to animals? Are they not the creatures of God; and endowed with capacities both of pain and pleasure? Why should we inflict unnecessary pain, even upon the meanest reptile? Who has given us authority to do so? By what argument, or by what sophistry, shall we seek a justification of such conduct? Why should we abridge the short span of existence allotted to the inferior creation, especially when we recollect that "the spirit of a beast goeth downward;" and that, being destitute of immortality, the whole period of their enjoyment is limited to the short date of their life on earth? It is the mark of a debased mind to seek amusement from the writhings of defenceless creatures, to sport even with the agonies of a fly. Parents and guardians of youth should particularly guard against the encouragement of a principle of cruelty, by allowing this practice. Children should not be suffered to indulge in such abuses, but should rather be taught to set a proper value upon the life and liberty of an animal. The subsequent maltreatment of the lower creation, many of the outrageous passions that in maturer life disgrace the uneducated part of society, and even the cold insensibility to the necessities of others, which so often obtains in the higher circles, may be traced to this early commencement. The future tyrant is formed in the hours of sportive cruelty; and he who in infancy practices on a fly, may in maturity domineer over an empire. It is important to trace evil passions and principles to their origin, to watch their developement and first operations, and, at the earliest possible period, to implant corrective sentiments in the youthful mind.

Solomon represents it as characteristic of "a righteous man," that he is "merciful to his beast;" and if it be censurable to assail the meanest insect which is not positively noxious, how much more to abuse those animals which contribute to our domestic comfort and security? This may be done, not only by beating, goading, and over-driving the laborious ox, or the swift-paced horse, by whom we cultivate our fields, or pursue our commercial concerns; but by stinting them of food, supplying them with insufficient or inferior provender, or leaving them to careless or peculating hands. Jacob was a specimen of kindness to animals--Balaam of brutality. The Mosaic law wisely and mercifully provided for the ox which trod out the corn, an enactment worthy of the supreme legislator, and coincident with the feelings of every humane heart.

Section II

We left the good old servant of Abraham at the well of water--we listened to his grateful acknowledgments to Heaven for prospering his journey--and we saw the interesting daughter of Bethuel run home to inform her friends of the extraordinary circumstance that had occurred. She had met a stranger--he had accepted her assistance, and presented her with costly ornaments--he had requested the customary rites of hospitality--he had been praying like a servant of the most high God--he had even intimated that he was travelling to fulfil some special commission of his master and their relative, the venerable Abraham! Every heart welcomed the tidings, and mutual congratulation circulated through the family.

Laban, the brother of Rebekah, whoso mercenary spirit viewed with peculiar satisfaction the ear-ring and bracelets which had been presented to his sister, hastened immediately to the well, and gave the messenger of Abraham a warm invitation to his home: "Come in," said he, "thou blessed of the Lord; wherefore standest thou without? for I have prepared the house and room for the camels." If we were quite certain that this pious language was dictated by a proportionable purity of motive, we should be highly gratified with it; but, alas! how common is it to use words of customary congratulation without meaning, and to sacrifice sincerity to politeness!

The man accepted the invitation; his camels were soon ungirded and supplied with provender, water was furnished to wash his feet and those of his men, and the table spread with a plentiful supply of provision for their refreshment. We need not be surprised, however, that he refuses to eat till he has introduced the important business upon which he came! the good man's heart is overflowing, and he prefers the discharge of his duty before his "necessary food." O that all our obedience to God were characterized by a similar zeal and fidelity!

"Speak on," said Laban: upon which, with admirable skill and perfect ingenuousness, he recounts a series of simple facts, interweaving his narrative with such touching arguments as proved irresistible: he stated without the vanity of a superior domestic who was actually the steward of the family, that he was "Abraham's servant;" and then proceeds to mention, not his own exploits, or merit, or influence, but the opulence and prosperity of his master; his becoming great and rich in "flocks and herds, and silver and gold, and men-servants and maid-servants, and camels and asses," he devoutly ascribes to "the Lord:" but at the same time gives the fact a prominence in his discourse well calculated to conciliate the persons he addressed, and prepare them for his subsequent statements. He now proceeds to mention Isaac, taking care to intimate the weighty considerations, that he was the son of the illustrious patriarch whom he served, by Sarah his beloved wife; born at an advanced period of their lives, and therefore young, as well as the child of promise, and heir of all the wealth which his master possessed. He then explicitly refers to the solemn oath by which he had been bound to seek a wife for his son; not amongst the idolatrous Canaanites near his own residence, but amongst his kindred in Haran. Dear is the name of *kindred*, especially when families are separated at such distances of time and space from each other, that they scarcely expect to meet again in an unbroken circle, and renew the embraces of friendship. It is then the tenderest sensibilities are excited, the fondest remembrances renewed, and the heart becomes accessible to every endearing impression!

Eliezer, having now gained the ear and won the regard of the listening circle, next adverts to the conversation which had passed previously to the commencement of his journey; in which he exhibits to great advantage the faith of his master Abraham, and the particular direction of his wishes, By repeating the story of his interview with Rebekah at the well, in connexion with the command to seek a wife for Isaac among the kindred of the family, he points at once to the object he had in view, and appeals to their piety in estimating the movements of Providence. They must consider whether all these concurring circumstances were not evidences of a divine interposition, and whether some important consequences were not likely to result from the proposed connexion: "And now, if you will deal kindly and truly with my master, tell me; if not, tell me; that I may turn to the right hand or to the left." In all this the very spirit of his master is conspicuous in the servant; he had not lived with Abraham in vain; a similar fear of God was before his eyes, and the same solicitude to fulfil the duties of his station; he could not eat, he could not drink, till he had disburdened his full heart, and ascertained the probability of success in his important mission.

Every servant may here take a lesson of fidelity to his master on earth, and every servant of Christ especially, who sustains the ministerial character, may see a fine specimen of the ardour, energy, and affection with which it becomes him to execute his high commission. This delicate service upon which Abraham's servant was sent to Nahor, was honourably discharged; but how much more "he that winneth souls is wise!"

What could the friends of Rebekah say to the appeal they had heard? Laban and Bethuel were overwhelmed. There was a mysterious singularity in the whole train of circumstances, calculated to impress the most indifferent and superficial mind, and they bowed to the interposing wisdom of the Supreme Disposer. As soon as the solemn feeling produced by such an extraordinary narrative was sufficiently regulated to permit them to speak, they joined in expressions of devout acknowledgment and submissive consent; "The thing proceedeth from the Lord; we cannot speak unto thee bad or good. Behold, Rebekah is before thee; take her and go, and let her be thy master's son's wife, as the Lord hath spoken."

This was a moment of exquisite satisfaction; but whence did it originate? Not surely so much in worldly as in religious considerations. The period was arrived, that anxious period to the parent, for the marriage of his lovely Rebekah; and now he was satisfied with the disposal of her to a distant relation. A worldly mind would have rejoiced indeed in the outward suitability of the match, but especially in the flattering prospect of great possessions which it presented. These inferior views too generally and too exclusively influence matrimonial alliances; the hearts both of the young and the aged are captivated by the splendours of life, as if they necessarily secured the possession of real happiness, or as if they could compensate for the absence of those mental and moral qualities which can alone constitute the basis of substantial comfort. But in the present instance, whatever pleasure might be lawfully derived from the assurances which were given of the opulence of Abraham, and from the endearing circumstance of the already existing relationship between the two families, it was the perception of a *Providence*, superintending and guiding the whole arrangement, that occasioned these most delightful feelings; it was not an idolatrous, but a pious connexion, and God had given the most striking indications of his will.

Let parents remember, that with whatever temporal prosperities they may connect their beloved daughters, there is no security for permanent happiness without real religion; and let children consider, that if the fear of God do not possess their own breasts, and influence their matrimonial choice, the delirium of pleasure will soon be past, and a sense of inexpressible vacuity be left behind. The world is a gay deceiver, and life a fleeting dream; the mists of illusion which gather over the morning of existence, gradually disappear as the day advances; and this imagined scene of enchantment, this fairy-land of pleasure subsides into the reality of a thorny wilderness.

The only preparation for such a change, is a piety which seeks its happiness on high, and knows that no earthly condition can form a paradise without the presence of the blessed God.

The faithful servant, having adored the divine goodness for thus evidently prospering his way, gave suitable presents to this happy family; jewels of silver, and jewels of gold, and raiment, were presented to the young and beautiful bride elect, and "precious things" to her mother and brother: after this he could eat, necessary food being sweetened by temporal and spiritual blessings.

The next morning, faithful to his commission, and eager to return, he presses for a dismission, to which we need not wonder that the brother and mother object, requiring him to remain at least ten days: still he urges his request, and pleads that the Lord had prospered his way: but how natural is their reluctance to part in a moment from so dear a daughter, never perhaps to see her face again! They at length agree to defer the decision of the affair to herself: Rebekah, with all the frankness so remarkable in her whole deportment, instantly replied, "I will go."

It may appear mysterious, that when her parents pleaded only for a few days, when modesty would even seem to have dictated a little delay; and when filial tenderness must have powerfully resisted so sudden and immediate a departure, that she should express so prompt a compliance, without even stipulating for a single day. Something perhaps may be justly imputed to the times, but far more to the religious state of her own mind; a sense of duty overwhelmed a feeling of reluctance, together with every inferior consideration. She was doubtless in the habit of daily intercourse with God, and in fervent prayer had sought divine direction: she saw an overruling providence--God was in the affair--his finger, visible to the eye of faith, pointed out the way in which she should go, and with unhesitating obedience she confessed her readiness to part with all the felicities of home to seek a distant alliance, at the voice of that sovereign Power to whom she committed her future destiny. Flattering as the scene before her must have appeared to a mere worldly eye, the sacrifices she made at this moment of compliance were certainly most considerable. What could have led to such an answer, when standing between the tears, the tenderness, the entreaties of parental and fraternal affection, and the urgency of a mere stranger, the *servant* too of her future house--but a faith which overcame the world, and dictated her holy resolution? *Heaven* appointed her journey, and *nature* pleaded in vain.

To every reader we recommend the noble principle which actuated this young heroine. Let inclination bow to a sense of duty--let God be obeyed rather than man--let not only authority be resisted, but even the fondest endearments sacrificed to the divine requirements. Apply this principle to a higher occasion, and remember that the Son of God has declared, "If any man come to me, and hate not his father, and mother, and wife, and children, and brethren, and sisters, yea, and his own life also, he cannot be my disciple; and whosoever doth not bear his cross and come after me, cannot be my disciple."

How tender, how affectionate is the parting scene! How the heart speaks in every word! The whole group seems placed before our eyes; and we witness the tears that flow, the sighs that heave each bosom; we seem to hear the faltering yet fond accent, in which the dear forsaken family pronounce the last benediction, "Thou art our sister; be thou the mother of thousands of millions, and let thy seed possess the gate of those which hate them."

Behold Rebekah, quitting the scene of her infancy and youth; Painful was the sacrifice, but pleasant the service: a thousand objects would revive the remembrance of past occupations and occurrences; a thousand circumstances rush into her memory; her susceptible mind would often retrace the scenes once so familiar, now to be abandoned for ever; affection would often recal the names of Bethuel and Laban, and filial tenderness would weep at the thought of maternal anxiety. She was about to commit her happiness to the disposal of another--to form another connexion--to seek another home--the young plant was removed by Providence to take root in a new soil and situation. This is always a moment of trial, and in the usual manner of estimating life, an experiment of doubtful issue; but he who "commits his way to the Lord," and "leans not to his own understanding," but at the call of duty, in the spirit of prayer, dissolves or forms connections, may reasonably hope for the "blessing which maketh rich" in all the essentials of happiness. Young people! venture not upon a single step without a previous application for guidance to the "throne of grace," lest by inconsideration and rashness you forfeit the favours you might have secured by piety. At your eventful period of life the transactions of *one day* are likely to affect the welfare *many succeeding years*; and if you would reap a future harvest of joy, you must sow in present tears and prayers.

No incident of the journey is mentioned till the cavalcade was nearly arrived at Hebron; they then saw a person walking in a thoughtful attitude; and Rebekah, suspecting probably that he might be one of the household establishment of Abraham, inquired of the servant, "What man is this that walketh in the field to meet us?" The servant informed her that it was his young master, the son of Abraham; he was come into the field for the purposes of meditation and prayer. She instantly took a veil and covered herself, alighting from the camel. This was done in compliance with the usages of the times, as a part of the ceremonial belonging to the presentation of a bride to her intended husband: the eastern brides are generally veiled in a particular manner upon such occasions. This custom seems at once expressive of female modesty and subjection.

Isaac appears to have avoided addressing her when he perceives the veil, but taking the servant aside, he learns from his mouth the long and pleasing tale of every circumstance in his journey; he participates the general feeling, and with emotions of gratitude and gladness conducts his Rebekah into the tent of Sarah, whose loss he had so deeply regretted, that now for the first time, he was comforted respecting it. After the customary mode, Rebekah became his wife, and he loved her. [16]

Peace be to that dwelling, the residence of a dutiful son and a tender husband--a kind, generous, open-hearted, pious wife! Dear were the ties of nature which united them, but still dearer the bonds of religion! It was a day they never could forget--it was a friendship that could never be dissolved! What could be wanting to complete their bliss? Approving friends, reciprocal attachment, concurring providences, smiling heaven, sanctioned the proceeding. At present their cup was full to the brim--not a bitter ingredient mingled in the portion. But while we congratulate their situation, let us imitate their example; and if we would participate a similar felicity, cherish a similar spirit: we may be fully assured that real piety will sweeten the pleasures and possessions of life; it may even prevent, and will certainly sanctify, disappointments.

We are, however, easily misled; looking only at the outward appearance, (and in general little more can be known of the history of families,) it is common to fancy the prosperous, and persons of the greatest connections, really possessed of the most abundant share of happiness. In some cases every earthly good seems to be the allotted portion, and we are ready to imagine that sorrow has found no means of access, no door of admission: but a very slight knowledge of the world is sufficient to ascertain that there is a "crook in every lot," and that this world is not the destined abode of unmingled enjoyment. This remark is exemplified in the history of Isaac and Rebekah. Twenty years elapsed, and they had no children: this must have been a severe affliction, not only because at that period a general hope of being connected with the Messiah led all pious persons to be solicitous of a family, but because Isaac was the son of promise, the multiplication of his seed was distinctly recorded, and he had formed his matrimonial connection in the fear of God. As he partook of the trial, he seems to have been endowed with the spirit of his illustrious father; though he lived childless, he did not cherish despondency, but "entreated the Lord for his wife," which was the only effectual means of procuring the blessing.

[Sidenote: Years before Christ, 1836.] His prayer was heard; but this new favour was attended with unusual anxieties, which proved signs of future events. She ultimately bore twins, of which the elder was destined to serve the younger. As names were usually given in reference to the circumstances attending the birth of children, so *Esau* signified *red,* in allusion to his colour, and *Jacob* signified the *supplanter.* Esau, and his posterity the Edomites, were of a sanguinary disposition, and peculiarly hostile to Israel; Jacob supplanted his brother in the birthright; Esau was "a cunning hunter, a man of the field;" Jacob, a "a plain man, dwelling in tents."

From the earliest period of their lives we may trace the existence of those partialities in the two parents which have so frequently disquieted the otherwise most harmonious families. The Scriptures assign a particular cause for the fondness which Isaac cherished for Esau, which seems a most lamentable weakness in so venerable a man: it arose from his eating of his venison; for he was given to the indulgence of his appetite. Surely when we observe how the greatest of men have been guilty of some of the most unaccountable littleness, it should awaken us to holy jealousy over ourselves, and induce us to establish a system of constant, laborious, and impartial self-inspection.

The occasion of Rebekah's partiality is not distinctly recorded; it might possibly have originated in his being more domestic, and attentive to herself. [17] The usual effects resulted from these partialities: Isaac was blind to the sins of his son, who soon pursued a course of conduct that occasioned both his parents the deepest grief; while Rebekah's fondness involved herself and her favourite child in the greatest criminality.

[Sidenote: Years before Christ, 1750.]

Having attained an advanced period of life, and becoming conscious of increasing infirmities, Isaac took measures to convey the patriarchal benediction and the blessings of the covenant to his posterity. With this view he called his eldest son, and in accents of fondness requested him to go and procure him that savoury kind of food to which he was so partial; after which he expressed his intention of pronouncing the blessing, and thus securing for him, as he imagined, the mercies of the Abrahamic covenant. Overhearing this conversation, Rebekah thinks of her favourite son, and instantly devises a plan to supersede his elder brother. This was, indeed, conformable to the determination of Providence; but is no justification of her sinful policy. If it were even her intention to accomplish the divine promises, the plea would not vindicate her doing evil, that good might come.

Her object being to countervail the design of her husband, she instantly commences a system of manoeuvring to carry her point. We must consider her now as under a particular temptation, and evidently acting inconsistently with the natural ingenuousness of her character, no less than with the principles of her religion. The proper course would have been that of persuasion, entreaty, or remonstrance; but under the apprehension that Isaac's extravagant attachment to his darling child would render this unavailable, she deviates at once from the path of rectitude to gain her purpose. It is most unfortunate when the heads of families are influenced by opposite wishes, and refuse a fair, candid exposition of their own views to each other. Confidence is the basis of friendship, and in no case should be cherished with more assiduous care than in domestic life.

Active in the execution of a scheme she had so promptly devised, Rebekah states to Jacob all that had passed between his father and his elder brother; proposing, or rather commanding him to go to the flock with all possible despatch, and fetch two kids of the goats; "and I," says she, "will make them savoury meat for thy father, such as he loveth; and thou shall bring it to thy father, that he may eat, and that he may bless thee before his death." Jacob hesitates--not, however, as we could have wished, at the execution of the plan; but solely because he is apprehensive of its failing, and producing unhappy consequences. Jacob was pacified by his mother's offer to run all hazards, and incur the whole responsibility of the transaction. She reiterates her request with all the fervour that a better cause should have inspired; and has not long to wait in a state of irksome suspense, before the favourite of her excessive affection returns with the kids. Not a moment is to be lost--every thing is put in requisition--the savoury meat is soon prepared. The hunter's speed is outstripped by management and artifice--in vain he toils over the lengthening field. Jacob is introduced, by his mother, into Isaac's apartment, clothed in the goodly raiment of Esau, covered on the more exposed parts of the body with the skins of the kids, to make him resemble his hairy brother; and presents the food with due formality and dissembling eagerness to the blind old patriarch. Some suspicions, however, are awakened--"Who is it?"--"I am Esau, thy first-born."--"How can this be--how quickly thou hast returned?"--The young man blushes and trembles--but he must either confess or persevere--there was no alternative--the mother's eyes probably intimated that he *must* persist in his deception. Awful to relate! he ascribes his good success, personating Esau, to "the Lord." Isaac pursues other measures to obtain satisfaction. His voice appears altered, and he begs to *feel* his son--the falsehood silences, but does not satisfy him. At length, he is persuaded--he blesses him, and eats the venison. Though the dupe of atrocious artifice, Isaac is, nevertheless, under supernatural direction, and was afterwards unable to revoke his benediction.

But what did Rebekah gain by this detestable contrivance? She saw, indeed, her favourite son inheriting the blessing; but this would have descended upon him without her interference, according to the predeterminations of Providence. She saw also a just recrimination upon her deceit on the part of observant Heaven. The original dislike of the two brothers was kindled into a raging flame. Esau burned with indignation at being thus cajoled, and resolved to avail himself of the day of mourning for his father, to satiate his resentment in his brother's blood: and Rebekah, to save both their lives, was obliged to send her guilty, but favourite son, to a distance. Thus were the latter days of both the parents imbittered by their indiscreet and criminal partialities!

After the departure of Jacob, the fond mother becomes not merely solicitous for his safety, but anxious respecting his future conduct. She reflects on the temptation to form an idolatrous alliance to which he might become exposed, unchecked by parental authority, and under circumstances which would naturally induce him to seek a shelter from the storm of adversity in the bosom of conjugal endearment. If the language of Rebekah, upon this occasion, be tinctured with impatience, we cannot but feel gratified to see it founded upon religious sentiment. "And Rebekah said to Isaac, I am weary of my life, because of the daughters of Heth: if Jacob take a wife of the daughters of Heth, such as these which are of the daughters of the land, what good shall my life do to me?"

We are unwilling to part with Rebekah precisely at this point of her history; but here it is that the sacred narrative drops her name. It is written, however, we doubt not, on the imperishable pages of another volume, which is emphatically styled, "the Lamb's book of life."

This abrupt termination suggests, amongst other considerations, the *truth* of the narrative. If it had been the purpose of the writer to exhibit the subject of his story to the admiration of posterity, or to display his own powers, rather than to represent fact or record instructive biography, he would have carefully avoided whatever tended to diminish the interest of the whole, and give it an unfinished appearance. By concealing some of the more unsightly parts of the picture, and by rendering prominent others of a more attractive character, he might have contrived to accomplish an *effect*, though at the expense of truth and reality. But the sentiments and prepossessions of the writer disappear from the narrative of Scripture. There is no effort to conceal any facts which may be supposed to weaken the general impression, or to introduce explanatory or encomiastic statements which may be thought to strengthen and enhance it. In every page, in every sentence, it is apparent that the great object is instruction, and not amusement. The historian has no private views--no partialities--no misconceptions--the pen of inspiration is dipped in the fountain of truth, and "holy men of God spake as they were moved by the Holy Ghost."

Let the sad inconsistencies which disgrace the closing part of Rebekah's history, awaken every reader to a just sense of the importance of a persevering uniformity of character. It is of great consequence, that we adorn the religion we profess, and that our light shine more and more--that we grow in grace as we advance in years, and that we do not resemble the changing wind or the inconstant wave. Let us improve the failure and irregularity of others to the purpose of self-examination; and, while we neither extenuate nor aggravate their faults, aim to avoid them. We have enough to encourage, yet sufficient to caution us, A life of unblemished piety is almost as rare an occurrence, as a day of unclouded brightness; but many such adorn the annals of the church, and the grace of God is fully competent to multiply their number.

Miriam Chapter VI

The family of Amram was distinguished by a very striking peculiarity. All the three younger branches of which it consisted, Aaron, Moses, and Miriam, because eminent in ancient Israel. Their history is considerably intermingled; but the latter, from the design of this work, will claim our chief attention.

[Sidenote: Years before Christ 1571.]

Sixty-four years had elapsed from the death of Joseph, when the "*new king over Egypt*," influenced by an ill-founded jealousy of the Israelites, adopted one of those measures to which weak and wicked princes are sometimes excited by an unhappy combination of bad counsel, and mean-spirited perverseness. Instead of regarding this people, who had been prodigiously multiplied by a series of unexampled prosperities, as the most valuable portion of his subjects, and the best security to his crown; this Pharaoh was jealous of their strength, and determined to weaken it by a course of systematic oppression. This he called "dealing *wisely* with them;" whereas it would have been infinitely wiser, even upon principles of mere political prudence, to say nothing of justice and humanity, to have conciliated by kind treatment, rather than have exasperated by barbarous exactions, six hundred thousand of his subjects!

His plan was, in the first place, to set over them taskmasters, to afflict them with extraordinary burdens; but, to his extreme mortification, "the more they afflicted them, the more they multiplied and grew." Still his obstinacy did not permit the least relaxation of that rigorous discipline he had imposed: although, while he imbittered their lives, he failed of promoting his own interest. Disappointment exasperated his malignity; and he issued orders to certain Hebrew women, of whom Shiphrah and Puah are named as the principal in their office, to destroy every male child that should be born. They ventured, however, to disobey this mandate; the fear of God not allowing them to commit murder, though enjoined to do so by royal authority. The king called them to an account for their disobedience, and "charged all his people, saying, Every son that is born ye shall cast into the river, and every daughter ye shall save alive." When we have such an awful display of the excess of human passions, that fearful band of banditti that is for ever disturbing the peace of society, it should inspire us with holy solicitude to suppress the first emotions of sin in our hearts, and to aspire after the dignity and the bliss of dominion over ourselves. Alas! how many who have been victorious over foreign powers, could never achieve this nobler conquest of internal depravity!

The command of Pharaoh to his too tractable slaves, introduces us to the story of the birth and preservation of Moses. His mother--unenviable name in this sad season of calamity!--his weeping mother, by a thousand schemes, such as maternal fondness and ingenuity would naturally devise to save the little darling of her heart, contrived to conceal this "goodly child" for the space of three months; but finding it impossible to hide him any longer, she took him--and with what feelings, say, ye tender-hearted mothers!--to the river Nile.

--"A dealing parent lives
In many lives; through many a nerve she feels;
From child to child the quick affections spread,
For ever wand'ring, yet for ever fix'd.
Nor does division weaken, nor the force
Of constant operation e'er exhaust
Parental love. All other passions change
With changing circumstances; rise or fall,
Dependent on their object; claim returns;
Live on reciprocation, and expire,
Unfed by hope. A mother's fondness reigns,
Without a rival, and without an end."

H. MORE.

Miriam, an interesting actor upon this occasion, accompanied her mother. Willing to adopt every possible expedient, even at this last extremity, the afflicted parent had prepared a little boat of bulrushes, which grew plentifully on the bank; and, making it water-proof by the use of pitch and tar, she put the child into it, committed it to the uncertain elements, and retired from the heart-rending scene. Poor Miriam, his sister, supposed to be at this time about ten or twelve years of age, was placed at a distance to watch the event. Dear little sentinel! what heart can refuse to pity thy sad employment! who does not sympathize with thy sorrow, and begin to mourn with thee for thy anticipated bereavement! Imagination listens to strains which seem to strike upon the ear of distant ages:

"The flags and sea-weeds will awhile sustain
Their precious load, but it must sink ere long;

Sweet bade, farewell! Yet think not I will leave thee.
No, I will watch thee, till the greedy waves
Devour thy little bark."

The dispensations of Providence are indeed considerably diversified; but at what an early period does affliction familiarize itself, even with the happiest family! Behold Moses, in his cradle of bulrushes, exposed to the waters and the crocodiles of the Nile! Behold his little sister at some distance, participating the cares of her mother, and already at the outset of life deluged with a storm of grief. She had learned to love the babe--she had fondled it, and felt the kindlings of sisterly affection--and at an age just sufficiently advanced to realize something of the nature and extent of her loss, the new-born infant is torn from her heart by the hands of sanguinary violence. It was because he was a Hebrew child. His danger, and the distress of Miriam and her mother, arose from their belonging to the persecuted Israelites; but with all their disadvantages in this unfriendly world, let the children of pious parents rejoice, even amidst their tribulations and reproaches, in being connected with the people of God. It is an honour which, however at present overlooked, will hereafter be fully appreciated, both by those who have desired and those who have despised it!

At this juncture, the daughter of Pharaoh, to whom Josephus has given the name of Thurmutis, came down with her maidens to the river-side; and perceiving the frame of bulrushes, sent her servant to fetch it. Upon opening it the little stranger wept. Her heart was touched with compassion, and she said, "This is one of the Hebrew children."

Miriam, all observant and alert, seized the happy moment, introduced herself, or perhaps she was called by the royal lady; but dexterously contrived to propose her going to call a Hebrew nurse to nourish and rear it as her adopted child. Divinely influenced by him who has all hearts in his hands, and moves them by his secret touch, she consents; and who should the well-instructed young messenger bring, but the babe's own mother! Pharaoh's daughter intrusted the adopted stranger to her care, and pays her for a service which she would willingly have rendered even at the hazard of her life. The child grew, and, from the expression of the sacred historian, appears to have become a favourite with this illustrious princess. "And she called his name Moses; and she said, Because I drew him out of the water." Such is the story, which needs none of the Rabbinical embellishments to make it additionally interesting or wonderful.

Miriam is next introduced to us upon an occasion the most remarkable that ever occurred in the history of the world. Miracle after miracle had been performed by the instrumentality of Moses, ere the infatuated king of Egypt could be persuaded to dismiss the children of Israel; and no sooner had he given his consent to their removal, than taking an immense army he pursued them to their encampment, which was by the sea, beside Pihahiroth, before Baal-Zephon. The terrified fugitives complained to their leader, who presented fervent supplications to Heaven for their deliverance. The ear of mercy heard; he was commanded to take his rod, and stretch it over the waters, upon the assurance that they should instantly divide, and present a dry channel, over which they might safely pass. Awed by a divine [Sidenote: Years before Christ, 1491.] power the retiring waves became a wall of defence on either side, while the pillar of a cloud guided their adventurous march. During the night, the Egyptian and Israelitish armies were kept asunder, in consequence of the cloud affording a miraculous light to the one, and shedding disastrous darkness upon the other. Pharaoh, obdurate and furious, led on his troops into the new-formed channel; and already by anticipation seized in the grasp of his mighty malice, the prey which he intended to tear and devour. "And it came to pass, that in the morning-watch the Lord looked upon the host of the Egyptians through the pillar of fire and of the cloud, and troubled the host of the Egyptians, and took off their chariot-wheels, that they drave heavily: so that the Egyptians said, Let us flee from the face of Israel: for the Lord fighteth for them against the Egyptians. And the Lord said unto Moses, Stretch out thine hand over the sea, that the waters may come again upon the Egyptians, upon their Chariots, and upon their horsemen. And Moses stretched forth his hand over the sea, and the sea returned to his strength when the morning appeared; and the Egyptians fled against it; and the Lord overthrew the Egyptians in the midst of the sea. And the waters returned, and covered the chariots, and horsemen, and all the host of Pharaoh that came into the sea after them; there remained not so much as one of them."

What a scene did the light of morning exhibit to Israel! Pharaoh's chariots, his chosen captains, and all his host, had perished; "the depths had covered them, they sank into the bottom as a stone." But, as if the waters refused to harbour even the bodies of these enemies of the people of God, they were no sooner drowned than thrown, by the indignant billows, upon the sea-shore. See their ranks broken, their persons disfigured, their glory for ever extinguished! Their unburied and unpitied remains proclaim how fearful a thing it is to fall into the hands of God, and how dangerous it is to venture upon "touching" his people, which is, in effect, "touching the apple of his eye."

Anxious to celebrate so miraculous a victory, a victory achieved without a battle, and by the special interposal of an omnipotent arm, Moses composed that celebrated song of thanksgiving which is recorded in the fifteenth chapter of the book of Exodus. It is remarkable, not only on account of its intrinsic excellency, but as being composed six hundred and forty-seven years before the birth of Homer, the best of heathen poets, and, therefore, the most ancient piece of poetical composition in the world. It is characterized by the beauty and boldness of its imagery, the strength of its language, and the piety of its sentiments. If brought into comparison with the finest specimens of human genius that have since delighted mankind, its superiority must instantly be established.

According to the practice of the age, Miriam, with whom we are particularly concerned at present, appeared at the head of the women to congratulate Israel upon this splendid event, in responsive strains and dances. She was anxious only to aid the universal joy, and express in every possible manner her accordance of sentiment with that of her two illustrious brothers, Moses and Aaron, and the thousands of Israel. Happy was it for Miriam, that, instead of leading the unhallowed and prostituted festivities of heathen gods, she was "educated in the Jews' religion;" and, from infancy to maturer years, had been taught to sing the praises of the great I AM! Nor did she merely mingle her undistinguishable notes of joy with her country-women and her nation; but, from the ardour of her zeal, and the general superiority of her character, she took the lead in these devotional raptures. Her early advantages, and her pious connexions, had contributed essentially to the formation of her future character. They not only contributed to impress a holy bias upon her mind, but to prepare and mould her into that characteristic pre-eminence, by which she occupied so conspicuous a station among the Israelites, and was ranked with their two illustrious leaders. [18] What might not be anticipated from the singular concurrence of such means in her favour? She was the sister of a man who refused the honours of a court, and perhaps of a crown, to incur a voluntary degradation with the afflicted people of God; and with him she enjoyed a familiar and incessant intercourse. She had, besides, received her earliest lessons in the school of adversity, and was become an eminent proficient in sacred knowledge.

Let us duly appreciate, but be cautious of overrating, the advantage of religious education. It did not necessarily follow, from the means which Providence so amply and so graciously dispensed to Miriam, that she should become a truly religious person, much less that she should acquire such distinction in Israel; but while we gratefully admit, that good instruction is calculated to effect the best results, and will commonly produce them, it does not infallibly secure the end; nor can it at any time prove available, independently of the blessing of God. With the use of that system of means which is established in the providential arrangements of Heaven, his concurring sanction may be expected; although, to show the impotency of mere means, and to fulfil the secret purposes of the divine government, they are sometimes totally inefficient. It was the privilege of Miriam to be born an Israelite, and to have pious relatives; and it is our advantage to live in an age, and to be born in a country, blessed with the pure light of the Christian revelation. But religion is personal in its nature; and unless our advantages be improved, it is in vain that we have possessed them. Providence may give us Abraham for our father, and impenitence may incur perdition for our portion! It was to the most distinguished, and to the most boasting of the Jewish fraternity, that Jesus Christ afterward declared, "I know you, that ye have not the love of God in you."

The conduct of Miriam, on the triumphal occasion already mentioned, exhibits a striking contrast to that of Michal, the daughter of Saul, when at a subsequent period, the ark of God was brought from the house of Obed-edom into the city of David. Harps, psalteries, timbrels, cornets, cymbals, and all kinds of musical instruments, were put in requisition upon that interesting day; and David disarraying himself of the dress of royalty, and substituting the lighter linen vestment of the priest, danced before the ark in a devout ecstacy. But Michal, instead of uniting in the shouts of universal gladness, and extolling her husband's humility and zeal, addressed him in this taunting language, "How glorious was the king of Israel to-day, who uncovered himself to-day in the eyes of the handmaids of his servants, as one of the vain fellows shamelessly uncovereth himself!" From David's vindication of his behaviour, and from the punishment inflicted on this inconsiderate woman, we perceive how little capable irreligious characters are of estimating the nature and value of those extraordinary acts of piety, for which eminent saints have been always distinguished; and how displeasing to God is their proneness to vilify those whom they ought rather to admire. In the present instance, however, Miriam inspires the song, and leads the dance, vying with the other sex in expressions of praise, and recognizing with equal joy an interposing Providence. While Moses exclaims, "I will sing unto the Lord;" Miriam, with no tardy zeal, utters the responsive and animating strain, "Sing ye to the Lord, for he hath triumphed gloriously, the horse and his rider hath he thrown into the sea."

Union in religious exercises is conducive to holy pleasure, and no sight can he more gratifying than that of brethren and sisters engaging with heart and voice in the praises of God. Within the small circle of a single family, what a considerable portion of happiness--such as the world cannot possibly supply--is dispensed, when every heart is in tune to devotion, and no discordant sympathies blend with the universal feeling of pious delight. It resembles a young plantation, which the gentle gales of the south bend in the same direction--all under the same divine influence, all tending to the same point. But never had witnessing spirits before beheld such a scene on earth, as that of a *whole nation* assembled to celebrate the praises of Jehovah--never till the day of deliverance from the Red Sea, had they before listened to such acclamations as those of all the tribes and tongues of the thousands of Israel united in one general, instantaneous, and harmonious song. Now a world, which having been characterized by its apostacy, was marked by signs of displeasure--a world from which only a few notes of holy praise, a few strains of sincere devotion, had ascended to heaven from individual saints during the long course of more than *two thousand five hundred years*--seemed beginning to redeem its character; and rise to the dignity of serving God!

If blessed spirits were not permitted to break silence, and mingle their congratulations with man, as they did when incarnate mercy descended to Bethlehem, who can doubt the reality of their sympathy and satisfaction, when the songs of Moses and Miriam were thus emulating "the song of the Lamb?" Faith travels onward to a future and still happier day, when *every* redeemed individual, from amongst men, shall be permitted to utter his voice in the great chorus of eternity, in which the millions of the human race, who have "washed their robes and made them white in the blood of the Lamb," shall unite with the unfallen universe in the praises of Heaven. By the visions of the apocalypse, we are admitted to a view of the employments of that celestial state, and the very prospect of it is highly calculated to kindle a warm devotion. How truly trifling do all the pursuits of time appear to the exercises and enjoyments of happy beings around the throne, who, elevated above this mortal sphere, behold the unveiled glories of God and the Lamb, and drink immortal bliss from "the fountain of living waters." The many angels round about the throne, and the living creatures and elders, whose number is ten thousand times ten thousand, and thousands of thousands, are represented as *uniting* in the same immortal song, adoring the same Lord, and celebrating the same redemption. It is thus--exhilarating anticipation!--the devotions of time will expand into the songs of eternity; thus the services of earth issue in the raptures of heaven!

The course of the history of Israel at length introduces us to a very different, but perhaps a no less instructive scene. Miriam must not only be contemplated in a new, but unpleasing light. Hitherto she had been the coadjutor of her brother Moses, but now becomes his opponent, pursuing a line of conduct, in consequence of indulging a guilty passion, which usually produces the most deplorable effects, and which we cannot but lament should have been so conspicuous in this illustrious woman. The circumstance alluded to is recorded, with the characteristic fidelity of the inspired historians, in the twelfth chapter of the book of Numbers.

"Wrath is cruel, and anger is outrageous; but who is able to stand before *Envy?*" To this latter principle must be attributed the plot in which both Aaron and Miriam engaged to diminish the reputation of Moses. This was not indeed the ostensible reason, but it was their real design; and occasioned the severe, but just chastisement which was immediately inflicted. Seldom do any of the baser passions act without combining and blending themselves with hypocritical pretences, in order to conceal from view their own hateful deformity. This will be found particularly the case, when they prevail in persons who have acquired respectability and influence, and who are not given over to total blindness and hardness of heart. Artifice may sometimes conduce to success, but it usually betrays character.

Aaron and Miriam spake *against* Moses, but not *to* him. If they had observed any thing objectionable in his administration of public affairs, it would have been candid, fair, and kind, to have taken a private opportunity for expostulation or inquiry. Not only was he extremely accessible, but they were his relatives, and in habits of daily intimacy and communication. They knew him well, and saw him often. Such a conduct would have done them honour, and although their surmises had proved incorrect, Moses would have applauded their ingenuousness. But, alas! these dear relatives, and otherwise good and great characters, had become envious of their brother; and acting conformably to the invariable meanness of such a spirit, they secretly circulated reports in the camp tending to disparage his excellence, for the purpose of advancing their own pretensions to popular estimation. Their arrogance is sufficiently apparent from their words, "Hath the Lord indeed spoken ONLY by Moses? Hath he not spoken ALSO by us!"

Can this be *Aaron?* Can that be *Miriam?* The one the *brother*--the other the *sister* of Moses? Persons too, venerable for their years, and for their office, and only next in honour to the great legislator and leader of Israel? It may have comported with the ambition of a Pagan to exclaim, "I had rather be the first man in a village, than the second in a kingdom;" but is such language befitting the lips of saints and prophets of the true God? Was not *Aaron* the person that sought the intercession of his brother when he had committed idolatry? Was he not consecrated a high priest unto God? Was not *Miriam* his elder sister, who acted so conspicuous a part in his early preservation, watching his bulrush-cradle when exposed to the waves and the monsters of the Nile? Was it not *Miriam* that accompanied him in his prosperities, that hailed his increasing glory, that aided his triumphant songs when the Egyptian army was submerged in the Red Sea? and can *Miriam* be envious? Strange infatuation!

But, perhaps, we are really censuring ourselves. Listen to the unbiassed voice of conscience. Does it not thunder in your ears, "Thou art the man?" Art thou insensible to its powerful and just remonstrances, "Wherein thou judgest another, thou condemnest thyself; for thou that judgest doeth the same things?" O beware of this mean, creeping, reptile spirit! Persons in eminent stations may, in a certain degree, expect to suffer from the wiles of envy: But to suffer from those of their own household, and from persons on whose friendship they have had the greatest reason to rely, must be peculiarly afflictive. If it be possible to add one drop to the bitterness of such a portion, it is by being envied, and consequently depreciated, by those who are *associated in the same sacred office*. A remark upon this subject cannot be misplaced, the history seems rather to claim it. A mortal creature cannot be invested with a more important commission than that of the ministry of the word. So highly did the apostle of the Gentiles appreciate his work, that, gifted as he was in every requisite to discharge it with honour and success, he exclaimed, "Unto me, who am less than the least of all saints, is this *grace* given, that I should preach amongst the Gentiles the unsearchable riches of Christ." But if each heavenly ambassador be really convinced that he and his brethren are intrusted with an office at once so dignified in its nature, so useful in its design, so extensive in its duties, that no one can adequately fulfil for himself what would be sufficient to expend the energies of an angel; and that the combined exertions of all the preachers that ever have, or ever will, minister in holy things, cannot *wholly* occupy the sphere of possible usefulness, were every power of the mind, and every moment of time, made tributary to the service--if this were duly considered, surely instead of envying, depreciating, and thwarting each other, perfect love must prevail, and mutual assistance be incessantly rendered. The world is sufficiently disposed to reproach the servants of the sanctuary; they should not undervalue each other. Nothing can exceed, and no words can express, the littleness of attempting to construct our own fame upon the ruins of others; and when this temper exists, as it sometimes unquestionably does, amongst those who teach humility, it is singularly detestable. Ministers of the divine word should be guardians of each other's reputation, aware that the honour, and in some degree the success of it depends upon the *character* of its publishers and representatives. Miriam and Aaron should have been the last, while, such is human nature, they were the first, to envy Moses!

Mark the origin of those depreciating reports which they contrived to put in circulation. They had taken some offence respecting Zipporah, his wife, who is called the Ethiopian woman. The precise occasion of this offence cannot, and need not, be ascertained. Some have supposed it was on account of his having married her; but as this had taken place forty years before, and, being perfectly legal, could have furnished no just ground of crimination, the probability is, that some recent occurrence, grounded perhaps on personal and long cherished antipathy, produced a difference. Some private contention might have existed; that ungovernable member, the tongue, had inflamed resentments; and a revengeful spirit fastened the blame upon Moses, whose only offence was, probably, some meek and pacifying word.

But what connexion subsisted between the marriage of Moses with an Ethiopian woman, and the pretentious of Aaron and Miriam to an equality with their illustrious brother? Truly, none at all. Their conduct is a striking display, not only of the virulence of envy, but of the progress and resentful nature of anger. It always wanders from its subject, and ranges around for new materials upon which to operate. It possesses the perverse capacity of converting every thing into an element of mischief, of inventing circumstances and envenoming objections. It seeks to enlist others into its services, and to bring every thing into a confederacy against the peace of its object. It is limited by no bounds, and restrained by no considerations; it will often, like the exasperated judge of Israel, pull down ruin upon his own head, for the sake of destroying others. The present contention began about Zipporah, but it ended in Moses himself. It was, perhaps, at first, a common-place strife; but at length it assumed the shape of a settled hostility. It was but a spark, and if angry passions had not blown it, soon it might have gone out; imprudence and revenge raised and extended it into a vast conflagration.

Family quarrels are, of all other dissentions, the most to be deprecated. We should be careful to prevent them, and if they occur, take effectual and speedy measures for their extinction. Let us not be tenacious of our own opinions, or determined upon practising our own plans. It becomes the Christian, both for his own sake and for the interest of religion, to make every possible sacrifice to peace. Pour the oil of gentleness upon the stormy billows of strife: ever remembering that "a brother offended is harder to be won than a strong city, and their contentions are like the bars of a castle."

One expression in this narrative merits particular notice. Let the envious detractor tremble at the words, "the Lord heard it." It requires not the tone of thunder to penetrate the ear of God: his omniscience perceives the secret whisperings of slander, and even the inaudible and unexpressed surmises of a perverted mind. Moses may have been ignorant of the industrious malignity of his brother and Miriam, or disregardful of any intimations on the subject; for a person of integrity is unwilling to believe, without very compulsory evidence, the dishonesty of others; or, if it cannot be discredited, he will patiently pursue that course which will eventually place injured innocence in the point of complete vindication. In this he resembled the great Exemplar of every virtue of whom he was an eminent antitype, and of whom it is recorded, that "when he was reviled, he reviled not again, but committed himself to him that judgeth righteously."

But whether *Moses* did or did not hear, or, hearing, disregarded the detractions of his nearest relatives, *God* observed them, and instantly came down to express his displeasure. The two delinquents were summoned to the door of the tabernacle of the congregation, with their much-injured brother: the glory of the Shekinah appeared, and the solemn voice of the divine majesty issued from the cloud of his presence. The superiority of Moses was proclaimed, and an unanswerable question proposed to them, "Wherefore then were ye not afraid to speak against my servant Moses?" As an indication of anger, the symbolic cloud instantly removed from the tabernacle; and Miriam, the most forward, and perhaps the first in this transgression, became "leprous, white as snow."

Aaron was shocked at the sight, and had immediate recourse to the man he had before so defamed, humbly requesting him to pass over the sin they had perpetrated, and entreating his powerful intercession with God on behalf of their afflicted sister. Moses, obeying at once the impulse of humanity, piety, and fraternal attachment, pleaded for her restoration. He was graciously heard. Miriam was excluded from the camp only seven days, during which the journeyings of Israel were suspended, to express the displeasure of God at their concurrence in her transgression, and to show the kind intermixture of mercy with judgment in the divine proceedings. After this, the people removed from Hazeroth, and pitched in the wilderness of Paran.

[Sidenote: Years before Christ, about 1451.]

With this instructive story the history of Miriam closes, excepting the brief notice of her death at The encampment at Kadesh, where she was buried. Josephus relates, that after interring her with great solemnity, the people mourned for her a month. This occurred in the fortieth year after the departure from Egypt, Eusebius says, that in his time her sepulchre was still to be seen at Kadesh.

Whether the imputation be true or false, that women are particularly addicted to the vice of slander, it cannot be deemed unsuitable to suggest a caution upon this subject. Character is a sacred thing, and it is unworthy of you to trifle with it. To sit in judgment upon others, and to pronounce a hasty verdict upon actions which may be carelessly misrepresented, or words, if not intentionally, yet heedlessly misquoted, without affording an opportunity to the condemned individual to speak for himself, is unjust in the extreme. But how many excellent persons are made the butt of ridicule, or tossed about as the playthings of a gossipping spirit, which, incapable of a direct charge, gratifies its malignity by infusing calumnies into the too listening ear of prejudice. An idle report is, by this means, magnified and circulated to an incalculable extent; or the infirmities of excellent characters animadverted upon, for no other purpose than to fill up the waste moments of a ceremonious visit. Women should assume their proper rank, by aspiring to the dignity of rational intercourse; and not degrade themselves, and disquiet society, by engaging in petty warfare against the reputation of others.

Let what is termed *religious conversation* turn rather upon *things* than *persons*; otherwise men in public station, perhaps of equal though dissimilar excellence, will be in danger of undue praise or excessive depreciation. The favourite preacher will be unmercifully extolled, and the unpopular one as cruelly degraded. A clashing of opinion will be likely to produce rivalries, and invigorate partialities; till, probably, the effect of their respective labours is lost upon these fair but injudicious critics. Let young women, especially, take the hint, and "set a watch upon the door of their lips." Beware of indiscriminate censure, or extravagant applause. Regard the ministers of the word as the servants of God. Receive instruction from their lips with all humility, pray for their increasing wisdom, and tenderly cherish their good name. If a Moses, with all his excellencies, seem to you to assume, or in any respect to commit an error, do not be the first to publish it abroad in the camp, or to aggravate, by misrepresentation, a failing which is blended with such acknowledged worth. Remember, it is as likely that *you* should be mistaken in your judgment, as that *he* should be faulty in spirit or conduct; and that if your detractions be not visited with an outward token of displeasure, resembling the loathsome deformity of Miriam, which required a veil, they render you most unlovely in the sight of God and man. "The tongue is a fire, a world of iniquity: so is the tongue amongst our members, that it defileth the whole body, and setteth on fire the course of nature, and it is set on fire of hell. For every kind of beast, and of birds, and of serpents, and things in the sea, is tamed, and hath been tamed of mankind: but the tongue can no man tame; it is an unruly evil, full of deadly poison."

The situation of Miriam during her exclusion from the camp suggest an observation on the debasing nature of sin. When engaged in the exercises of religion, and taking the lead in the celebration of the overthrow of the Egyptian army by the interposing providence of God, she appears the glory of her sex and the ornament of her country; but from the moment she indulges a guilty passion, her honour is tarnished, her dignity degraded, and her pre-eminence lost; the moral defilement she has contracted is marked by an external deformity, and issues in a degrading separation. Miriam is deeply conscious of her guilt, and confounded at its bitter consequences: she feels that she is a sufferer because she was a sinner; and would no doubt have made any sacrifice could it have been possible to regain the forfeited paradise of peace and innocency. But we have here a specimen of the inevitable consequence of sin. It does not indeed generally incur immediate and temporal punishment; but it degrades the perpetrator of it in the eyes of God, in the opinion of others, (especially the wise and good,) and in his own sight: it lowers him in the scale of being, at once diminishing his reputation and contracting his means of usefulness. If the face of Miriam recovered its beauty, and the eyes of Israel could discern no external blemishes, it is questionable whether a scar would not ever after be discernible upon her character: and even should her indulgent friends have forgotten, and God have graciously forgiven her past iniquities, Miriam, as a true penitent, would scarcely ever forgive herself: the very consciousness of pardoning mercy would often renew the sensations of penitence; and moments of holy joy would ever after be bedewed with tears of humiliation.

From this example it is further obvious, that the hope of escaping the divine displeasure on account of sin, under the notion of being the professed people of God, is altogether delusive; sin is detestable in the eyes of perfect purity *wherever* it exists, and can neither escape detection nor elude chastisement. Its perpetration by his own people is rather a reason for more signal and exemplary chastisement, than for any kind of exemption from it; because the motive to obedience arising from gratitude and other sources is proportionably stronger; and because a contrary proceeding would tend to disparage the divine government, by affording a plausible pretence to the doctrine of salvation *in* sin, and not *from* it. The eminence of Miriam rendered her disgrace the more requisite as a punishment, and the more salutary as an example: the leprosy in her face was a practical lesson, which every Israelite could not fail of understanding, and probably would not soon or easily forget.

It is, besides, not only the necessary tendency of sin to procure its own punishment, but such is the appointment of God: it constitutes an essential part of the great system of his moral government to unite them together; and no mortal power can disconnect them. Sooner or later every transgressor must be humbled; he *must* fall--by judgment, or by penitence--before the sword of excision, or into the arms of mercy. Happy for us if external visitations produce internal prostration of spirit; if, instead of stiffening ourselves into resistance, we bend to the inflictions of parental chastisement; and if present and temporary sufferings excite a feeling which will supersede the necessity of future and more awful visitations.

If, again, Miriam were so severely visited for speaking against *Moses*, how fatal will prove the consequences of resisting *Christ!* The secret whisperings of envy and ambition against the *servant* of God, occasioned a public and awful punishment: what tremendous wrath may not they expect who reproach or disregard his beloved *Son!* "If they escaped not, who refused him that spake on earth, much more shall not we escape if we turn away from him that speaketh from heaven."

This remarkable manifestation to Miriam, Aaron, and Moses, may remind us of that period which is hastening on the rapid wings of time, when the descending Judge of the universe will "come in the clouds of heaven with power and great glory," "the glory of the Father and all the holy angels," to summon every class, and all the generations of mankind, to his tribunal, and pronounce their final, irreversible, everlasting doom: then, like Moses, his servants will be vindicated from every charge, honoured by witnessing celestials, admitted through the gates into the city of the New Jerusalem, be emparadised forever in the embraces of their God. Then, like Miriam and Aaron, a guilty race, which has plotted against the righteous, and opposed by their impenitence, if not their actual persecutions, the prosperity of his cause and people, will be driven, not into temporary exile and disgrace, but into ever-during darkness. "These shall go away into everlasting punishment, but the righteous into life eternal." The pride of Miriam was intelligibly marked upon her smitten countenance; and the sin of transgressors will be written by the finger of God in appropriate and conspicuous characters upon their immortal destinies. Thus will the perfections of the Deity for ever blaze in the flames of perdition, and irradiate the temple of glory!

Finally, imitate the conduct of Moses, who, on this occasion, so nobly displayed a conduct which the Redeemer of the world thus inculcated as an essential part of his religion: "Pray for them that despitefully use you and persecute you." His intercession for Miriam, who had so cruelly injured him, was prompt and ardent; instead of resenting her calumnies, or triumphing in her merited affliction, he prayed for her recovery! Here we see the very spirit of the Gospel under the law! a Christian in the habit of a Jew! Superior to the age in which he lived, he seemed in character and temper to have anticipated a far distant period of evangelical illumination; to have caught, so to speak, by ascending the summits of faith and hope, some of the yet unrisen splendour of the Sun of Righteousness; to have been in a sense the *disciple*, as he was the most illustrious *antitype* of Christ, even centuries previous to his incarnation! The cross is indeed the centre of union and the point of attraction to all ages and nations. There the antediluvian and patriarchal saints associate with those of later times, imbibing one spirit, coalescing upon one principle, meeting in one sacred spot, conjoined in one fraternal band! The wise and the good of a former dispensation looked forward with anticipating pleasure to the great event, which we are permitted to contemplate with retrospective joy. Hail, happy hour! when we shall meet with all the redeemed in one glorious assembly; not as at present, *by faith*, on mount Calvary, but *in reality*, on mount Zion-- in a world where the imperfections of Christians shall be removed, and their excellencies completed--where Miriam shall not envy Moses, nor Moses be exhibited in contrast with Miriam!

Naomi, Orpah, and Ruth Chapter VII

Section I

Domestic life furnishes the most attractive and the most instructive species of history. If it do not present an equal diversity of incident with the narratives of rising or falling empires, in whose mighty concerns every passion of human nature is interested, it possesses the superior advantage of "coming home to men's business and bosoms."

The scene of *general history* is frequently placed in a region which, to the great proportion of mankind, is inaccessible; and however we may admire its principal actors, they seldom furnish examples capable of being exhibited for imitation. The sphere in which they moved is so totally different, so far remote from that in which our duty usually lies, that the knowledge of their achievements can conduce but little, to the great purposes of practical improvement. The story of *private life* possesses a very different character; we are at once introduced to our *own* sphere; and although it may relate to a class in society either very much inferior or superior in point of station to ourselves, it necessarily brings into review relations which we all sustain, situations we have all to occupy, and duties we have all to discharge. Whether, therefore, a princess or a peasant be the principal actor, the central point round which every circumstance revolves, and from which it derives interest and distinction, it claims and will repay our serious attention.

Independently of these general considerations, the history of Ruth, in connection with that of Naomi and Orpah, has been always regarded as singularly interesting: it is a most pathetic tale, illustrative of the operation of the tenderest of the domestic affections, in unison with genuine religion: it exhibits the most artless simplicity of manners, the most virtuous sensibilities, and the most affecting interpositions of Providence. It is at once romantic and true, sublime and simple, marvellous and natural: it constitutes, moreover, a connecting link in the great chain of providence, and an important incident in the history of redemption.

The sacred book, which derives its name from RUTH, was in all probability written by Samuel: this is the concurrent opinion of Jews and Christians. It may be considered as supplementary to the book of Judges, an introductory to the history of David, whose descent from Judah through Pharez is distinctly traced in the genealogy of Boaz.

According to Jewish tradition, Ruth was of the royal race of Moab, a nation descended from Lot, and settled on the borders of the salt sea in the confines of Judah. She married Mahlon, the son of Elimelech, who lived in Moab in consequence of a famine which prevailed in Judea. After his death, relying on the promises made to the tribe of Judah, to which her husband belonged, she became a proselyte; and thus the Holy Spirit, by recording the adoption of a Gentile woman into that family from which the Messiah was to descend, might intend to intimate the comprehensive design of the Christian dispensation. "It must be remarked also, that in the estimation of the Jews it was disgraceful to David to have derived his birth from a Moabitess; and Shimei, in his revilings against him, is supposed by the Jews to have tauntingly reflected on his descent from Ruth. This book, therefore, contains an intrinsic proof of its own verity, inasmuch as it records a circumstance so little flattering to the sovereign of Israel [19]; and it is scarcely necessary to appeal to its admission into the canon of Scripture for a testimony of its authentic character; or to mention that the evangelists, in describing our Saviour's descent, follow its genealogical accounts." [20]

[Sidenote: Years before Christ, about 1818] This book commences with a statement of the calamitous situation of Israel in consequence of a famine, one of those messengers of divine displeasure sometimes commissioned to scourge a guilty land, and chastise them into obedience. Elimelech, a resident in Bethlehem-Judah, was compelled, probably with many others, to quit his beloved home, and seek a temporary subsistence in the country of Moab, which, although favoured at this time with the blessings of temporal prosperity and abundance, was destitute of those religious means, without which, in the view of a good man, Eden would lose its charms, and life its value. He took with him his wife Naomi and his two sons Mahlon and Chilion; and, under the guidance of that Providence which once tamed the lions and restrained the fires of Chaldea, found an asylum in the bosom of Israel's enemies.

In this exile, a family so ancient and reputable sunk into such degradation excites our compassion; still more so, when in tracing their adventurous history, we find them assaulted by new forms of sorrow and calamity. Elimelech dies, and Naomi is left with her two sons. The young men afterward marry, the one Orpah, the other Ruth, both natives of Moab. It seems as though the disconsolate widow were beginning to dry up her tears, and to rebuild her fallen house by those matrimonial alliances which tended to naturalize them in the country; but whether the use of these idolatrous materials was displeasing to God, or whether it was deemed requisite to detach the mind of Naomi, by repeated afflictions, from a soil in which her affections were becoming too deeply rooted, her two sons also died in a few years, and the three females were left to grapple with adversity alone. The original state and character of the young women is uncertain, but they became proselytes to the Jewish religion. They might have become so previously to their union with their now departed husbands, whom, if the sacred narrative had been more detailed and minute, we might possibly have had occasion to applaud for their pious discrimination, rather than to censure or suspect for impropriety of conduct; at least, under all the circumstances, we are by no means justified in severe animadversions upon their choice. But, whatever might have been their intentions, the Supreme Disposer was working with a wise but mysterious secrecy, to promote his designs which were linked with a succession of events extending to far distant generations. Poor Naomi! how desolate thy condition! how deep thy depression! Wave after wave rolls over thy defenceless head! And yet, where is the human being to whom no comforts are left? Thy daughters remain, and even if they had been removed, thy pious spirit would not have sorrowed over their graves, as one that has no hope! Thy religion has supplied thee with sources of consolation unknown to the world, and indestructible by calamity, time, or death--"The eternal God is thy refuge," "and underneath are the everlasting arms."

The rapid changes in this family cannot fail to remind us of the instability of earthly possessions and enjoyments; nor ought we to forget the wisdom and the goodness of that divine superintendence, which holds all these changes in subserviency to his will. How impressive is the language of inspiration, "we all do fade as a leaf;"--and how illustrative of the present tragical history! When the sun of summer beams upon the growing landscape, and, ascending some eminence, you survey the valleys covered over with corn, the hills adorned with verdure, the trees bending their abundant foliage to the gale, the flowers in "yellow meads of asphodel and amaranthine bowers," perfuming the air with their odours, you seem for a moment to inhabit regions of enchantment and perpetual beauty. A month or two intervenes--you reascend your former elevation, once more to feast the senses--to admire and adore the Dispenser of these blessings--but O how faded! The bright beams of the sun are shrouded in a wintry cloud--the corn has disappeared--the flocks retire--the trees are bereft of their foliage--the flowers lie scattered on the ground. Such, such is human life; thus we and our families fade! to-day in vigour--to-morrow in dust! Where are generations past? where are our ancestors? where our immediate predecessors? where our early associates, and many of the individuals that have enlivened our social hours in maturer life? Like the leaves which cluster on the ground in autumn, and almost obstruct the path of the traveller, they seem to have dropped in quick succession, and to lie in faded heaps on the road that leads into eternity. And, alas! with an indifference too nearly resembling that which is apparent in the unheeding passenger, who tramples autumnal foliage beneath his feet, we tread on the graves of departed ages, and neglect to imitate the example of the pious dead.

Pause and reflect, "we *all* do fade." Whatever our circumstances or connections, the inevitable dominion of death extends over all. The leaves may occupy a higher or a lower station on the tree, they may be suspended on the loftiest or the lowliest branches--but they *all* drop off; and we may be rich or poor, learned or illiterate, young or old, the house of the grave is "appointed for *all* living." Providence in mercy permits the union of families long to remain unbroken; and, at length, in *mercy* too--whatever the suggestions of despondency--dissolves it. The parent expires, and the children follow; till, perhaps, the *name* only survives, like a tree bared to the storm of winter thrown down by the blast, and at length rotting into dust.

Mournfully fascinating, however, and instructing as these considerations appear, they must not divert us longer from the narrative. Naomi, at the distance of ten years, cherished a constant anxiety respecting what passed in Israel; and, weaned by repeated trials, if not still more so by Moabitish idolatry, from her present situation, she heard with pleasure, "that the Lord had visited his people, in giving them bread:" upon which she determined to return, and take her two daughters-in-law with her into Judea. This secondary kindred often proves a source of the most unhappy jealousies and animosities in domestic life, but the harmony in which these women lived, and with which they concerted measures for their removal, indicated at least the goodness of all their dispositions. They were, besides, in equal distress. Affliction, in almost every form, is beneficial in its tendency; and nothing is more calculated to strengthen mutual attachment than common calamity.

How often is distress, similar to this, aggravated by unkindness! Moroseness on the one part, and undutifulness on the other, excite the mother-in-law against the daughter-in-law, and the daughter-in-law against the mother-in-law; whereas reason, religion, and even self-love, require a different conduct. The poverty of Naomi was no objection to Orpah and Ruth to accompany her in her departure from Moab; but at once, abandoning every minor or selfish consideration, they prepared to attend her unprotected way. They would not suffer her to drink alone of the bitter cup, but resolved to encourage her by sharing it.

A bitter cup indeed it was. Who can imagine, without a painful sympathy, the situation of three friendless women, each a widow, and quitting a country where they left behind so many sad recollections! There they had lost the dearest of earthly connections, who, had they been preserved to this hour, would have soothed their sorrows, sustained their spirits, and accompanied their journey! The voice of parental and conjugal tenderness was silent in the grave! Their natural timidity had no shelter-- their tears were wiped away by no kind hand--their steps were supported by no sustaining arm--the world was a barren wilderness before them-- they seemed to be alone, as after a ship-wreck--and they had no immediate refuge but in themselves, and--for there was still another hope, an observant friend, a helper to the needy in his distress--in GOD!

Having proceeded a short distance, Naomi, overwhelmed with a sense of the disinterested kindness of her daughters-in-law, even more than with her own affliction, begged them to leave her, and return to their respective homes. She adverts to their past amiable and affectionate conduct; and severe as parting would prove to her maternal heart, she wished them still to be happy in the Sand of their nativity. Commending them to the benediction of the God of Israel, and expressing her desire for their happiness in the formation of future connections, "she kissed them" in token of a long and last farewell.

What fondness and what agony blended in that embrace! What a separation! It was no moment for words; the lovely daughters could only weep! A thousand past endearments recurred to their memory, a thousand uncertainties springing from the bosom of futurity, presented themselves to their minds. They had cherished a mutual esteem--they were blended into one in feeling, in interest, in all that can render life desirable. Their dark path had hitherto been enlightened by the beam of affection;--and was the sun to set upon their day for ever?

Alas! what a land of mourning is this! what heart-rending separations are we called to experience on earth; and what an hour of parting from the tenderest of connexions will soon arrive, when, death interposing his authority to break the ties of nature and of friendship, we must bid adieu to those who would indeed gladly accompany us, but *must* survive to walk alone in the wilderness.

We are, however, attributing too much to this formidable power. He may break the ties of nature--but he cannot dissolve the union of *Christian* friendship. The pious shall meet again in a region uninfested by malignity, and where the long annals of everlasting ages shall record no day of separation, and no instance of death.

It was kind, it was disinterested, it was maternal, in Naomi to propose this parting; but they were not to be persuaded. As soon as tears permitted utterance, they exclaimed, "Surely we will return with *thee* unto *thy* people."--"We have taken our resolution, and cannot depart from it. To go *with* thee is indeed a trial--but to go *from* thee is incalculably worse. Thou shall not be forsaken. We will be inseparable." Naomi remonstrated, and kindly repeated her commands. She called them *daughters*, an appellation they had well merited by their ardent and unabated attachment, earnestly entreating them to "turn again; and" intimating that they could not reasonably entertain a hope of her having sons whom they might marry, and therefore they could not accompany her without detriment to themselves. She was afflicted at the idea of their being widows in the days of their youth; and especially that, for her sake, they should continue in so solitary a condition, voluntarily resigning to her comfort the joys of connubial love.

Again they wept--but from this moment, Orpah and Ruth take a different course. The former fails in her resolution, embraces her mother-in-law, and returns; the latter "cleaves to her," and remains the solitary example of unconquerable affection, the heroine of the future narrative.

In the character of Orpah, we perceive an exemplification of that imperfect obedience which characterizes those who have been induced to pay some degree of attention to the gospel of Christ, but who have been influenced by certain subordinate motives to retrace their steps. She contemplated future poverty with alarm, and cannot be exculpated from a charge of secretly preferring the service of Chemosh, the Moabitish god, to the service of Jehovah. Her affection for Naomi had, perhaps, induced her hitherto to dissemble; and though she persevered to a considerable extent, when the final resolution was to be taken, she paused--hesitated --trembled--and drew back. She could not part with *all* for this service. In the days of Christ, many treated him with respect, listened to his words, admired, and like the young ruler, even wished to become his follower, but excited the best hopes only to disappoint them. Happy, thrice happy, they who take up the cross, and follow him through much tribulation; nobly resisting the allurements of the world, the demands of earthly friendship, and even the interdictions of human authority, for the sake of Christ and his gospel! The martyr's *crown* awaits them, for they display the martyr's *spirit*.

At a superficial glance, the address of Naomi to Ruth, upon this occasion, seems altogether extraordinary; "Behold, thy sister-in-law is gone back unto her people, and unto her gods; return thou after thy sister-in-law." Did she then really wish to urge this young widow to imitate the conduct of her sister, not only in returning to her relations, but to the service of the gods of Moab? Whatever opinion she entertained of her daughter-in-law's piety, could she really be desirous of placing her in circumstances of such temptation and danger? This supposition would be at least uncharitable, and contradicts probability. It was rather a trial of her sincerity in religion, and an evidence of her determination to use no compulsory measures, not even maternal influence, to coerce her conscience. Her language was, besides, premonitory and warning, similar to the permission given to Balaam, who though apparently admonished to go and curse Israel, was really interdicted.

Ruth received the appeal in a manner worthy of her character, and the most satisfactory to Naomi. "Entreat me not to leave thee, or to return from following after thee; for whither thou goest I will go, and where thou lodgest, I will lodge; thy people shall be my people, and thy God my God. Where thou diest will I die, and there will I be buried: the Lord do so to me and more also, if aught but death part thee and me." If the pious origin of this attachment were not sufficiently apparent, we should be tempted to call it romantic; but founded as it was in religion, we must contemplate it as a rare specimen of a perfection in friendship, scarcely ever attained in the cold and chilling atmosphere of this world. Nothing could have so ripened and matured it, but the beamings of heavenly love, which rendered even an unfriendly soil productive of so choice a fruit.

Notwithstanding the indigent circumstances of Naomi, her daughter-in-law persisted in accompanying her, and thus voluntarily chose affliction with the people of God in preference to hereditary affluence and distinction. With deliberate resolution, and persevering consistency, she adhered to her purpose, calculating upon all the inconveniences that might result, but not fearing them. She turned her back upon the glory of the world, neither dreading its frowns nor soliciting its patronage. She knew that she could live happily without human applause, but not without divine approbation. Her early prejudices were subdued by principle, and she felt no hesitation in discarding the gods of Moab to procure the love of the God of Israel. In fact she *did* choose the path of true honour and renown. The servant of God is the greatest character in the universe, and will eventually be exalted to a situation which will fully and for ever disclose the perfect nothingness of terrestrial glory, and the shadowy nature of all that mortals have been deluded to imagine substantial.

This part of the history may serve to suggest the beneficial inquiry, whether we habitually cherish an equal zeal for our religion, with that which this young Moabitess manifested? It would be easy to descant upon the superiority of our advantages, and to urge our increased responsibility; but do we equal her in the firmness of our faith, and the steadfastness of our profession? It may not be a question, whether we are likely to be called to similar or equal trials; but the most important consideration is, whether through the grace of God we stand prepared for *whatever* trials await us in the path of duty; and whether, with fewer difficulties and greater advantages, we at least display an equal decision of character? We have Sabbaths--do we keep them? We have Bibles--do we read them? We have religious and social opportunities--do we improve them? We have pious friends--do we, like Ruth, cleave to them? Do we come out from the world, and are we separate, saying to the church of Christ, and adhering to our purpose, "We will go with you, for we have heard that God is with you?" Association is a test of character. The companion exhibits the man.

Candour and sincerity may be recommended from this example, as the best policy. We should not be ashamed of our religion: an open avowal, like that of Ruth, which prevented any farther importunity to return to the idolatries of Moab, is calculated to prevent a thousand perplexities into which the wavering, the timid, and the dissembling, inevitably fall. Persons of this description fail in every respect. They dissatisfy both parties, sacrifice their own peace of mind, and incur all the pains, without securing any of the pleasures of genuine piety. Hesitating between a sense of duty and an inclination to sin, trembling amidst conflicting attractions and opposing interests, they never attain to dignity of character or repose of spirit. They lie at the mercy of every foe, of every passion, of every change. Without the pilotage of principle, they know not what course to take, and are every moment in danger of a fatal wreck. "He that wavereth is like a wave of the sea, driven with the wind and tossed! ... A double-minded man is unstable in all his ways."

It is unquestionably a duty devolving on all who believe in Christ, to "confess him;" and to this candid avowal he has himself attached, not only the purest felicities on earth, but the honour of a public acknowledgment of their persons and services before assembled ages in the day of judgment, together with a final admission into the paradise of his presence. It is indeed criminal to profess attachment to him when we do not feel it, and it is also highly improper to cherish such an attachment without daring to avow it. If the former must be characterized as hypocrisy, the latter cannot be exculpated from the charge of sinful timidity; if the one be presumptuous boldness, the other is unholy fear.

To avow our principles, on all suitable occasions, with unshrinking firmness, is essential to integrity, and distinctly claimed by religion. The worldly motives which influenced some of the chief rulers in the days of our Lord, if not to disavow, at least to withhold their public concurrence with his doctrines, are mentioned in the gospel to their everlasting dishonour. They are not exhibited as specimens of violent hostility, but of that spirit of neutrality which resulted from political feelings, and which, being no less deemed a real enmity, will receive its appropriate condemnation. "Nevertheless, among the chief rulers also many believed on him; but because of the Pharisees they did not confess him, lest they should be put out of the synagogue. For they loved the praise of men more than the praise of God."

This kind of preference seems to be the result of strange infatuation, the origin of which demands a serious inquiry. In part, it may be accounted for from the impression which sensible and near objects produce on the mind, in comparison with those which are less obvious and more distant. Visible things attract attention, while those which are invisible, being placed beyond the sphere of sense, remain unnoticed. An object which is really greater, appears less when it is more remote. Eternity seems, in human estimation, extremely distant; its crown of glory afar off; all the possessions of the New Jerusalem disappear from view, when covered with the mists of futurity. We are easily affected by loud applauses, gay scenes, and temporal good. The secret whispers of an approving conscience are less audible, the smiles of God less perceptible to a depraved and earthly mind. In addition to which, temporal inconveniences or dangers are frequently connected with a conduct which secures the approbation of God; a criminal apprehension of which produces indifference and distaste for religion. When the choice lies between shame, poverty, affliction, the sacrifice of worldly interest, and even death itself in the one balance--and temporal distinction, affluence, ease, advancement, in the other--many will hesitate, with Agrippa, few determine, with Moses. In the present history one was taken, the other left. The experiment has been since sufficiently tried upon a large scale, and proofs are perpetually accumulating, that the temper and conduct of Orpah were coincident with those of the great majority in the world.

The narrative of the journey to the place of Naomi's early residence, is comprised in one short sentence; "So they two went until they came to Bethlehem." We are left in ignorance of those circumstances which curiosity would wish to explore in so remarkable a removal. Who can doubt, that in a distance of at least one hundred and twenty miles over mountains and rivers, these female travellers, unprotected, friendless, on foot, and seeking day by day a precarious assistance from the wild luxuriancy of nature, or the occasional hospitality of the stranger, must have encountered repeated perils, and often deemed themselves irretrievably lost. But there was an eye that watched them, of whose observance they were not ignorant; an arm that protected them, on whose powerful support they leaned by faith, and leaned not in vain. *He* can never be destitute who has *God* for his father; *he* can never be lost, in whatever region he wanders, who has *God* for his guide! In the adventurous journey of life take his proffered aid, ye children of adversity! repose in his goodness, having committed your way to him, ye widowed mourners! while God is on his throne, ye cannot inhabit a fatherless world, ye cannot be destitute of efficient aid! "A Father of the fatherless, and a Judge of the widows, is God in his holy habitation."

In a small town, like Bethlehem, the arrival of these strangers would naturally awaken inquiry. After an absence of ten years, the inhabitants probably never expected to see Naomi again. Such is the vicissitude of human affairs, that within a few years many strange mutations occur, even in places of no great extent. Of her former friends or acquaintances, some were, no doubt, consigned to the grave; and her own appearance and circumstances were so altered since her departure, that the voice of friendship, the congratulation of love, seems to have subsided into the idle language of wonderment, "Is this Naomi?"

It is--but the mention of her name is a caustic to the wounds of her heart. The endearments attached to that beloved and significant appellation are fled with departed time, and Bethlehem no longer beholds her in a situation to command respect, to excite envy, or to purchase attention. Her husband, her children, are no more!--one, one only comfort remains--one friend, one solace in adversity--one ray of light in the dark hour! Amidst universal desertion, RUTH has not forsaken her; but is become her joy in sorrow, her companion in solitude, her prop in decrepit age! Can we wonder that she wishes to discard a name which awakened such recollections, and only recalled the *dream* of happiness? "Call me not *Naomi*,--call me *Mara*; for the Almighty hath dealt very bitterly with me. I went out full, and the Lord hath brought me home again empty; why then call ye me *Naomi*, seeing the Lord hath testified against me, and the Almighty hath afflicted me?"

There is something in these words which charity requires us to excuse. If, under the peculiar circumstances in which she was at present placed, the name of NAOMI, which signifies *pleasant*, distracted her, and she wished rather to adopt that of Mara, importing *bitterness*, her impatience must not be interpreted in the worst sense. After long absence, it is natural to anticipate a return home, and a rush of joy pervades even unfeeling minds, when the spire of their native *village*, the smoke of their native *hamlet*, especially the roof of their native *cottage*, first strikes upon the sight. Friends, family, neighbours, early scenes and pleasures, recur with a force which gives the air of enchantment to the long-lost scene. But every feeling of this nature was, in the case of Naomi, checked by different associations; the darkness of the sepulchre converted this day into midnight, and this lovely spot into a desolate wilderness!

There is, moreover, something in Naomi's remonstrance, which sympathy would lead as to pity, and experience, in some degree, to blame. She commits an evident mistake in attributing the dispensations she had suffered, to a *testimony against her* on the part of the supreme Disposer. Viewing past events through the discolouring medium of present affliction, and incapable of perceiving their secret and concurrent design, she forms a conclusion, which is rather the effect of temporary depression of mind, than of a settled conviction of judgment. We cannot doubt, indeed that the impression was evanescent; but it seems allied to that of the impatient patriarch, who exclaimed, "All these things are against me." *That* eminent servant of God enjoyed the privilege of living to a period in which the divine purposes were fully developed, and of seeing that what he deemed hostile circumstances, were really conducive to the most wise and felicitous results. Had Jacob departed during the interval, and while the mysterious plan was yet unaccomplished, his grey hairs would have gone down with sorrow to the grave, and the cloud of mystery would have been suspended over his dying hour. Such is the usual lot of the righteous. Life, in general, does not afford a space sufficiently ample, a period sufficiently protracted, for the complete execution of the great purposes of Infinite Goodness with regard to our real interests; and we murmur, because we cannot penetrate his arrangements. Patience, however, should be supported by the consideration that either in this, or in a future state of existence, the day of satisfactory explanation will arrive.

But there is a sentiment pervading the whole of this appeal, which, notwithstanding its partial defects, piety must warmly approve. Every thing is imputed to "the Lord." Naomi sees his hand in whatever occurrence she has witnessed. To him she imputes the fulness of her prosperity, and the emptiness of her adversity. In *every* change, in *every* place, she beholds and bows, to the ALMIGHTY. When this is happily the prevailing sentiment, the storm of angry passions will soon subside, the murmurings of discontent cease, and the clear shining of comfort break forth from behind the cloud.

"The Lord God omnipotent reigneth." This is enough! Angels and blessed spirits shall not monopolize the strain of gratitude and acknowledgment. Mortal voices shall join immortal harps, saying, "HALLELUJAH!"

Section II

Tales of fictitious wo, and of splendid distress, may alone be capable of fascinating those who recline on the lap of luxury, and who seek amusement, without soliciting instruction; but, among persons who possess any taste for genuine simplicity, any delight in the sacred employment of tracing the operations of infinite wisdom in the works of Providence, any desire for their own mental and spiritual improvement, and who have not yet learned of dissipated folly to despise

"The short and simple annals of the poor;"

the remaining circumstances of the narrative introduced into the preceding chapter, cannot fail of exciting interest.

That God, who promised Noah, that "while the earth remaineth, seed-time and harvest, and cold and heat, and summer and winter, and day and night, shall not cease;" and who "visits the earth and waters it, greatly enriching it with the river of God which is full of water, and prepares them corn when he has so provided for it;" having at this period dispensed fertility to the fields of Bethlehem, the humble travellers from Moab chose, or rather, were appointed by a superior influence to return in the season of barley-harvest. This was probably at the commencement of the month of May. [21]

But whither shall the wretched fugitives turn for assistance and support? It was indeed a time of plenty, but they were in extreme poverty. Golden harvests waved around them, but having no fields to reap, they were sorrowful amidst universal gladness, and depended upon precarious means of subsistence.

Ruth proposed to her mother-in-law to allow her to go and glean in any field where she could obtain the permission of the proprietor; to which Naomi readily consented. *As* a Moabite, she was probably ignorant, that what she regarded as a *favour*, was bestowed upon the needy as a *right* by the God of Israel. "When thou cuttest down thine harvest in thy field, and hast forgot a sheaf in the field, thou shall not go again to fetch it: it shall be for the stranger, for the fatherless, and for the widow; that the Lord thy God may bless thee in all the work of thine hands." This law is more than once repeated, and Ruth had a peculiar claim upon the liberality of its provisions, as uniting all the three species of wretchedness in her individual case. She was indeed a *stranger*, an *orphan*, and a *widow*.

The proposal of Ruth upon this occasion is, in many respects, illustrative of her estimable character. It furnishes a specimen of that *respectful treatment* which is due from the younger relative, to those whom venerable age and long experience have rendered their superiors. She would do nothing without Naomi; but consults her wishes, and seeks her concurrence in attempting to procure subsistence by means which she deemed the best adapted to their present poverty. A churlish temper would have submitted with extreme reluctance, and many taunting reproaches to what might easily have been represented as the drudgery and degradation of the gleaner's field; but this excellent daughter-in-law displayed a spirit most worthy of imitation.

Her *reflecting kindness* may be recommended to the notice of the inconsiderate and unfeeling. Offering herself to the laborious but necessary service, she is far from hinting any wish that Naomi should either accompany her to the field, or take measures to spare her, by seeking the aid of her richer relations, or the casual contributions of others. She wished to extend her support to the wearied and decaying nature of her beloved relative, and to use every possible exertion to alleviate her anxieties, to minister to her comfort, and to assist her infirmity. "Let *me* now go to the field." Amiable, generous, kindhearted woman! Thou wert anxious to procure for thy poor, afflicted, aged mother, all the repose which her advanced life seemed to require, to wipe away the tear from her dimmed eye and farrowed cheek, and as far as possible, to dissipate the clouds that hovered about the setting beam of her earthly existence!

If there be one scene of domestic life pre-eminently attractive, it is that of a lovely daughter manifesting a promptitude and zeal to alleviate the sorrows, and to aid the weekness of a parent, by those nameless and numberless assiduities which bespeak a genuine affection. Her own works praise her, and the mere flatterer's tongue is awed into respectful silence. How deplorable is it to witness the impatience of some young persons who think every little exertion an insufferable effort, a trouble, and a fatigue; and who forget the maternal fondness which cherished their infancy, the wakefulness that guarded their sickness, the love that never slept.

As Ruth was characterized by a virtuous sensibility, the proposal she made distinguished her also as *active and industrious*. Although her mother-in-law was advanced in years, she being in the vigour of her days, determined to devote her health and strength to procure subsistence. She did not waste her time in complaining, or sit down in a state of inactive despondency; but was alive to the duties of her lowly station. The poorest individual, who cheerfully fulfils his obligations, and exerts himself by an honest industry to maintain himself and his family, is inexpressibly more respectable in a wise man's estimation, than pampered luxury lolling on the couch of indulgence, and dreaming away existence in slothfulness and pomp. Real worth unquestionably consists in the proper occupation of that sphere, whatever it may be, which Providence has assigned us: and that person who is "not slothful in business," but "fervent in spirit, serving the Lord," secures the esteem of the good, and what is infinitely more important, the approbation of God. Idleness is no less a perversion of the designs of nature, than detrimental to our personal happiness. It not only renders its unhappy devotees useless to society, but burthensome to themselves.

All beings, through every gradation of existence, from the toiling emmet to the flaming angel, are formed for activity and exertion. Nor ought we, who are privileged to live under the Christian dispensation, to forget, that Jesus Christ himself, by his humble appearance and lowly occupation, as the Son of a carpenter, has elevated honest industry to a just and honourable distinction.

Accidentally, so far as related to herself, Ruth went and gleaned in the field of Boaz; but she was guided by an invisible hand. This proprietor was a man of great opulence, and a relative of Naomi. Coming from Bethlehem to his reapers, and having exchanged their mutual salutations according to the pious custom of the times, [22] he inquired of the superintendent, or steward, the name of the young woman he observed gleaning amongst the sheaves. Ruth, it appears, attracted his particular notice. Even a superficial reader might be struck with the astonishing providential coincidences in this story; and nothing but the most perverse infidelity can refuse to admit, that the God who had conducted this interesting widow from Moab to Bethlehem, and from Bethlehem into the field of the reapers, guided the steps and awakened the solicitude of Boaz on this occasion.

"And the servant that was set over the reapers answered and said, It is the Moabitish damsel that came back with Naomi out of the country of Moab. And she said, I pray you let me glean and gather after the reapers among the sheaves; so she came, and hath continued even from the morning until now, that she tarried a little in the house." The rich are frequently reluctant to acknowledge their poor connections, and in the great majority of instances, a discovery like this would rather have averted than conciliated the regards of an affluent proprietor from the humble individual he found to be the daughter-in-law of his indigent relative. Superior, however, to unwarrantable prejudices and ridiculous vanity, Boaz listened to the tale and immediately addressed her in affectionate terms. It is by no means improbable, that a blush of shame crimsoned his cheek, from the recollection of his past negligence in suffering Naomi to pine away in solitary sadness and penury, when it was in his power to have afforded her relief. Reasons *might* have existed to justify this delay, though they must have been very imperious to furnish even a plausible pretence for such indifference; but the best construction we can put upon his conduct is to suppose, that, like many worthy and benevolent men, he was dilatory in the execution of measures which he might have planned to discover and relieve the necessities of his kindred. The law of love was in his heart; he hastened to make reparation, and kindly enjoined her to glean in no other field, to keep fast by his own female servants, and to drink whenever she chose out of the vessels which were replenished from time to time for his reapers. He further issued orders to the young men employed in his service, to show every kindness, and to observe the utmost decorum towards her, upon pain of his displeasure.

It is observable, that Boaz addressed her by the tender epithet of *daughter*, adopting the language while he displayed the affection of a parental protector. Ruth had forsaken every Moabitish friend and relative, to share the fortunes of Naomi. Her birth-place, her home, her connections, all were relinquished for the privileges of her new relationship and adopted country, although to her eye nothing was presented but poverty and want. But her loss was gain; in Naomi she found a mother--in Boaz a father--in Bethlehem a home--in Judaism the religion of heaven, and the way to God. And shall they be eventually losers, who forsake all things for Christ and his gospel? Listen, ye youthful readers of either sex, and be wise--"Every one that hath forsaken houses, or brethren, or sisters, or father, or mother, or wife, or children, or lands, for my name's sake, shall receive a hundred-fold, and shall inherit everlasting life."

The reply of Ruth is singularly expressive of her characteristic modesty, humility, and goodness, The wealthy proprietor of the field had unexpectedly discovered in one word the history of this stranger: but she was wholly ignorant of the string that had been touched, and with artlessness replies, "Why have I found grace in thine eyes, that thou shouldest take knowledge of me, seeing I am a stranger?" This is equally the language of astonishment and gratitude. Little did she imagine the mighty consequences of this casual interview, or the real origin of this extraordinary kindness. Her susceptible and affectionate heart would have acknowledged the *smallest* favour, while some, and unhappily too often, the most dependent and the most indulged of the children of indigence seem scarcely thankful for the *greatest* obligations. It ought not to prevent our charity, but it may well excite our surprise, to find that needy persons are sometimes disposed to claim as a right what is bestowed as a boon.

Boaz intimated that the principal circumstances of her past life had come to his knowledge, and conveyed the most delicate commendation into her modest ear. He said, that he was aware of her whole behaviour to Naomi, with the sacrifice she had made of her native land and connections, and pronounced upon her an affectionate, solemn, and pious benediction: "The Lord recompense thy work, and a full reward be given thee of the Lord God of Israel, under whose wings thou art come to trust." To the same refuge from painful convictions and impending judgments may every reader instantly repair, embracing, by a devout faith, that glorious Light of the world, and Saviour of men, who was prefigured, in all the splendours of his love, by that miraculous brightness which shone between the wings of the cherubim in the ancient temple, and pointed the Jewish worshipper to "God manifest in the flesh."

Virtually disclaiming the praise which the opulent stranger had conferred, and far from imagining that she deserved, or had reason to expect any reward of God for conduct which she considered as no other than what a proper sense of duty demanded, Ruth thought herself honoured in the notice which she had received, respectfully acknowledged the condescension, and solicited its continuance. "Let me find favour in thy sight, my lord; for that thou hast comforted me, and for that thou hast spoken friendly unto thine handmaid, though I be not like unto one of thine handmaidens." Boaz repeats every kind assurance, invites her to share the rural repast, to "eat of the bread, and dip her morsel in the vinegar;" and with his own hand plentifully supplies her with "parched corn."

The sentiments of this excellent woman for the comparatively trifling kindness of her kinsman, may serve to reprove our cold returns, our disproportionate gratitude to the Supreme Benefactor, who daily loads us with temporal benefits, and constantly replenishes the cup of spiritual blessing; he, indeed, "comforts us;" in his word he "speaks friendly to us;" and we have, individually, abundant reason to confess, "I am not worthy of the least of all the mercies and of all the truth which the Lord has showed unto his servant."

The rural repast being ended, and Ruth having withdrawn into the field to pursue the humble labour of gleaning, which necessity and affection for an aged parent alike concurred to prompt, Boaz enjoined his reapers not only to allow her to glean, and to glean among the sheaves, but to "let fall some of the handfuls on purpose for her, and leave them that she may glean them, and rebuke her not." Her real thankfulness and amiable diffidence procured her these additional favours, and seem to have inspired the noble benefactor with a feeling which was afterward matured into love and consolidated in marriage. Let the poor beware of that cold indifference in the reception of benefits which freezes up the stream of benevolence, and chills the heart of the most liberal friend; let them equally avoid that forwardness which seems to demand, rather than to solicit kindness. Boaz, on this occasion, enjoyed a Double feast; with condescending familiarity he partook the frugal meal with his labourers, encouraging them by his presence and piety; with pleasure he fed the hungry stranger, cheerfully dispensing a portion of what he thankfully received from the Lord of all, whose bounty had enriched his possessions, and thus enjoying the luxury of doing good: this was indeed to his benevolent spirit, a feast which all the wealth of a Croesus could not otherwise have procured.

Boaz may be exhibited as a specimen of that prudential charity which should always regulate our distributions. He might have supplied Ruth at once from his ample repository of grain, or from the sheaves of the golden harvest; but he chose, on the contrary, to encourage her industry, though he kindly mitigated her toil. Indiscriminate gifts may rather favour idleness than relieve necessity; and it is as much a duty to see to the mode of distributing help to the needy, as to render them the requisite aid: besides which, the poor are more likely to value and to use properly what has been industriously acquired, than what is lavishly, however, as to its principle, benevolently communicated. Alleviate the toil of the necessitous, but do not prevent their useful employment of time and means. Industry is the law of the universe; and the Supreme Disposer of human affairs has appointed that "in the sweat of his face man should eat bread till he return unto the ground."

To Ruth this was one of the happiest evenings of a life which had been chequered with vicissitude, and of late particularly beclouded with, sorrow. How different were the feelings with which she returned to the cottage of her mother-in-law from those which afflicted her bosom when she quitted it in the early part of this memorable day.

Distressed and friendless she had gone forth; "not knowing whither she went," anxious only to procure some scanty subsistence for the day to satisfy the cravings of appetite, and to sustain the weakness of her dear and aged relative; but she returned laden with the spoils of the harvest field, an ephah of barley; she had been noticed by a very liberal proprietor of the soil, and invited to continue gleaning in his field. With what heartfelt satisfaction did she present the fruits of her first-day's exertion at the feet of Naomi, and sit down to share that kind of comfort to which Solomon has so strikingly alluded--"Better is a dinner of herbs where love is, than a stalled ox, and hatred therewith."

What family in Bethlehem was so truly blessed as these two poor women? Where, in the whole city, was concentrated so many sweet enjoyments, so many pure unsophisticated pleasures as met beneath this dwelling? Who would not rather turn into that lowly door, and listen to the inspired record of the conversation which took place between, its pious inmates, than hear the music which shakes the lordly roof, or witness the unmeaning gayety that riots in its apartments?--The good matron inquired where she had been gleaning; and seeing the ample supply she had procured, eagerly demanded where she had wrought: but unable, in the exultation and overflowings of her gratitude to wait for an answer, she pours forth her benedictions upon the unknown benefactor: "Blessed be he that did take knowledge of thee!" Her daughter informed her it was BOAZ; a name welcome to her ear, and calculated to kindle a hope in a bosom long filled with distracting griefs: she was reminded of former favours: she remembered his constant friendship to her family, and uttered an instantaneous supplication to Heaven for blessings upon his head. Unable herself to requite his kindness, she well knew who could recompense it, and therefore prayed, "Blessed be he of the Lord, who hath not left off his kindness to the living and to the dead!"

Such is the commerce between the benevolent rich and the pious poor; the former bestows subsistence, the latter blessings. How miserable, how *deservedly* miserable is an incommunicative selfishness! Happy the man who can say with Job, "When the ear heard me then it blessed me; and when the eye saw me it gave witness to me: because I delivered the poor that cried, and the fatherless, and him that had none to help him. The blessing of him that was ready to perish came upon me, and I caused the widow's heart to sing for joy. I was a father to the poor."

With what astonishment must Ruth have heard, "The man is near of kin unto us, one of our next kinsmen!" but she did not arrogantly assume her right to what she had received, or, presuming upon the dignity of her relationship, propose to make immediate application for that support which he was so well able to afford: this would have been the first thought of an ordinary or a selfish mind. On the contrary, she expatiates, with a satisfaction which heartfelt gratitude and pre-eminent goodness alone could have inspired, upon the marked attention of Boaz--"He said unto me also, Thou shall keep fast by my young men until they have ended all my harvest." Naomi advised her to accept this bounty, lest, by gleaning in any other field she might seem to undervalue the permission, or to cherish an offensive dependency of spirit. With her characteristic meekness, Ruth assented, continuing to pursue her mean occupation during the weeks of harvest, and returning every evening to share with Naomi her humble cot and her scanty fare.

During all this time, the mind of the affectionate mother-in-law was meditating a plan to promote the future happiness of her daughter. Past the period of marriage herself, she knew that Ruth might yet adorn, as well as obtain an accession of comfort from such a connection. If the young woman were satisfied with her obscurity, and content to provide a precarious subsistence for herself and her venerable relative by the labour of her hands, Naomi was superior to that selfishness which would rather have aimed to retain her in perpetual subserviency to her convenience, than seek to augment her joys, advance her interests, and raise her to her proper sphere of usefulness. Having made every possible sacrifice to her and her religion, she deemed it the part of maternal kindness to avail herself of the existing laws respecting matrimony, to connect her with the noble minded Boaz.

This solicitude she took the first opportunity of expressing, and directed her to measures, which, if they appear extraordinary to us, might not have been unseemly or unusual at that period and in that country. A few years are sufficient to operate a complete revolution in existing customs; it cannot therefore be surprising, that the manners of another quarter of the globe, at the distance of more than thirty centuries, should essentially differ from our own. To judge of their propriety by our standard is manifestly absurd; and to make great allowances for the state of society is, in cases of extreme variation, obviously necessary. After all, the conduct of Naomi may not be capable of entire vindication; though we are certain it proceeded from a sentiment of pure affection, and was connected with important results in the order of Providence: it is, moreover, recorded without the slightest hint of disapprobation.

Ruth was directed by her mother-in-law to repair with the utmost secrecy to the threshing-floor; and, when Boaz, conformably to the simple manners of the age, retired to rest among the heaps of corn, to place herself at his feet. When be spoke, she was to answer frankly, and await the intimation of his will. She did so: Boaz made the inquiry, and promised all that a sense of her virtues and a knowledge of her rights dictated. The law authorized the present application on her part at the instigation of Naomi, in order that the possessions of the family might not be alienated. Kinsmen were required to intermarry, and in case of refusal the near relative was treated with the utmost public indignity. Boaz perfectly understood this legal claim; and, notwithstanding his evident partiality to Ruth, ingenuously informed her, "There is a kinsman nearer than I." If he performed the kinsman's part, law and piety required acquiescence; if not, he solemnly avowed his own resolution to do so. Ruth departed before it was light, and carried the intelligence home. Boaz availed himself of the earliest opportunity in the morning to bring the affair to a decision; he went up to the gate, stopped the relative to whom he had alluded as he was passing by, and appealed to ten of the elders of the city. He at first agreed to the redemption of some family inheritance which belonged to Naomi; but, upon intimation that if he purchased the land he must marry Ruth, he declined it, giving full permission to his relative to enter into this contract. The mutual regard subsisting between Boaz and Ruth rendered this a most welcome circumstance, and the former immediately called upon the elders and all the people who were assembled on the occasion, to hear witness to this, as a fair, public, and honourable transaction. "So Boaz took Ruth, and she was his wife."

In some cases, where the matrimonial connection has been founded upon a dereliction of principle, and formed in defiance of the suggestions of common prudence, of parental kindness, and even of the interdictions of Heaven itself, we feel compelled to express our grief, rather than offer our congratulations; but where, as in the present instance, the voice of nature harmonized with that of reason, conscience, and God, who can hesitate to approve the union, and to anticipate that delightful result which has been so well expressed in poetic numbers?

> "Hail, wedded love! by gracious Heaven design'd,
> At once the source and glory of mankind!
> 'Tis this can toil, and grief, and pain assuage,
> Secure our youth, and dignify our age;
> 'Tis this fair fame and guiltless pleasure brings,
> And shakes rich plenty from its brooding wings;
> Gilds duty's roughest path with friendship's ray,
> And strews with roses sweet the narrow way."

If, in all the circumstances that lead to this union, the interpositions of Providence be not always, perhaps not frequently, so marked, incontrovertible, and striking, as in the history under consideration, let it never be forgotten, that such a wise and good superintendence really exists, and may, in every instance, be traced in some degree by the devout observer. If our ways be committed to the Lord, he will direct our paths. Amidst the ardour of youth, we are not always capable of discerning what is really obvious, or of fully believing what is infallibly true: but years teach wisdom; the developements of futurity often throw light upon the mysteries of the past; in the coolness and quiet of the eventide of life, and even before that period, how commonly do good men acknowledge the kindness of those once distressing dispensations that thwarted their juvenile susceptibility. In the adverse, as well as the prosperous events of the life of Ruth, she could perceive that "all things worked together for her good;" and no reflecting Christian will hesitate to appropriate the same sentiment to himself. A plan was laid in the divine mind, in the execution of which she often acted unconsciously: the birth, the education, the original circumstances and residence, the removal, the final elevation of Ruth, were all essential parts of the scheme, links in the chain of mercy; and the same may be affirmed respecting the life of every pious individual.

One circumstance demands particular notice. Neither in Boaz nor in Ruth can we discern the least symptom of *precipitation*; they suffered Providence to work its own way, to accomplish, without any obstruction from their unholy haste and heedlessness, its own purposes; in neither of them is discernible the least trace of a wish to seek their own gratification irrespectively of the will of Omniscience; they were in a sense passive, resigning themselves wholly to the disposal of God; they did not force a passage through intervening impediments with an indecent and impious resolution of spirit, as if they could not, or would not be happy excepting in their own way, but "waited patiently for the Lord."

Young persons sometimes attempt to outstrip Providence, and dare to chide its lingerings, or to murmur at its decisions; they set up for separate empire, and imagine they can create their own paradise; a conduct which ultimately proves as fatal to their comfort as it is now to their respectability. It is an advantage for young people of both sexes, which cannot be too highly appreciated, to have judicious, and especially parental advisers. Let them not impute their kind suggestions to the frigidity of age when they do not keep pace with their own warm feelings, but consider that they are likely to know more of the world, and to deserve their attention after amassing a stock of experience. Why should their good advice, or even their urgent importunity, be deemed officious or be treated with contempt? If mistaken, they are not, or ought not to be, peremptory. If not obliged to *follow* their opinion, young persons are certainly required, by every motive of duty, and even of self-interest, to *hear* it. Were it admitted that Ruth erred in some degree from her excessive obsequiousness to Naomi, yet her general spirit and temper merit the strongest encomium, the deepest study, and the closet imitation.

Tragical as was the commencement of this history, its termination presents a very different aspect. We beheld the family of Elimelech sinking fast in human apprehension into oblivion, and his name beginning to cease in Israel; we now witness its restoration and prosperity: it has emerged from its obscurity into splendour, and shines with imperishable glory on the page of inspiration. The aged tree, which time had well nigh lopped of every branch, sprouts out afresh, and shoots forth with new vigour and luxuriancy. We should learn never to despair of Providence, never to relinquish hope, never to imagine that "any thing is too hard for the Lord." Time, and change, and death, whatever revolutions they may occasion in general society or in individual families, not only cannot prevent, but, by their diversified operations, shall conduce to accomplish the purposes of Heaven. "Time and change," exclaimed Job, "are against *me*." True; but they cannot countervail *Omniscience*.

We naturally congratulate our favourites upon their prosperity; and the interest we must feel in the history of Ruth swells into the highest satisfaction upon reading the closing part of the narrative. We hear of the birth of Obed, who derives additional importance from the illustrious line of his descent. A few generations conduct immediately to the MESSIAH. All the neighbourhood celebrates the event, and we have equal reason to hail and proclaim it: "And the women said unto Naomi, Blessed be the Lord, which hath not left thee this day without a kinsman, that his name may be famous in Israel; and he shall be unto thee a restorer of thy life and a nourisher of thine old age: for thy daughter-in-law, which loveth thee, which is better to thee than seven sons, hath borne him. And Naomi took the child and laid it in her bosom, and became nurse unto it. And the women her neighbours gave it a name, saying, There is a son born to Naomi; and they called his name Obed: HE IS THE FATHER OF JESSE, THE FATHER OF DAVID."

Ordinary minds avoid, as much as possible, recurring to past periods of indigence and inferiority of station. Any reference to such circumstances is deemed offensive, by people of the world who have been elevated from low situations to opulence and rank, and whose arrogant nothingness proves they have descended in moral worth and real respectability exactly in proportion as they have risen in temporal distinction. But every thing we know of Ruth tends to convince us that, if a detailed account of her private life had been given, it would have been highly honourable to her sensibility and her piety. How often, and with what feelings, would she pace the field where, in the situation of a humble gleaner, she first met with Boaz. With what emotions would she trace and retrace her own eventful story! And especially, with what devout gratitude would she call to mind the days of her idolatry in Moab, and the happy era of her spiritual emancipation! In her own past character, in her infatuated sister's defection, what motives to praise would arise, and what tears of mingled pain and pleasure would she shed! And shall not we, who have "tasted that the Lord is gracious," cherish a sense of our obligations to redeeming mercy, and "remember all the way which the Lord our God hath led us these years in the wilderness, to humble us and to prove us, to know what was in our hearts, whether we would keep his commandments or no?" Sweet are the recollections of piety, and acceptable the offerings of a grateful mind! How inferior to these the trees of Lebanon in sacrifice, or all the spicy mountains of Arabia in a blaze! From what depths of sin, what delusions of mind, and what danger of soul, has "God in Christ" delivered us! "Once far off," we are now "brought nigh"--"sometimes darkness, now light in the Lord"--"you hath he quickened, who were dead in trespasses and sins."

But far more exalted pleasures of memory and retrospection await the Christian in a future world. Having ascended above this cloudy spot into the glory of the divine presence, it will be his pleasing and privileged employment to retrace the events of past existence, when nothing but a *remembrance* of the struggles and conflicts of this mortal state will remain, to enhance the raptures of eternal victory. What is crooked will then be made straight, what is perplexing will become plain, what is unknown will be revealed. Amidst the songs of heaven it will heighten our blessedness to recollect the sorrows of earth as *past*--clothed in the robe of salvation and triumph, it will be grateful to recall the time when we *wore the armour* and *strove in the field*--arrived in port, it will be inexpressibly delightful to recur to the storm as then for ever *gone by*!

Deborah Chapter VIII

Section I

After the death of Joshua, which occurred in the hundred and tenth year of his age, and in the two thousand five hundred and seventy-eighth of the world, the people of Israel were in a very fluctuating, unsettled condition, having no regularly appointed governor; and the book of Judges, supposed to have been written by Samuel, exhibits a striking picture of the disorders incident to such a state of civil disorganization. "Let every soul," then, "be subject unto the higher powers;" remembering that, as "rulers are not a terror to good works, but to the evil," while we are properly submissive to their authority, we should be grateful to God for their appointment.

Although the Israelites, who had been commanded to extirpate the nations of Canaan, pursued their conquests for some time, they gradually relapsed into a neglectful inactivity, permitting the inhabitants of the land to remain in tributary subjection. Whatever personal objections they might feel, and whatever apparent contrariety there might have been between their views of strict justice and the explicit directions of Heaven, they were bound to execute the divine will with a prompt unhesitating compliance. If general rules of conduct were not perfectly superseded by the paramount authority of an express direction from God, the great principle of positive institutions would he annulled, and the prejudices, passions, and misconceptions of a fallible creature, might, in certain cases, interfere with the acts of supreme legislation. Though, to strengthen the principle of obedience, and, as far as possible, to render "a reasonable service," it may often be proper to inquire "*why*--" such is our present incapacity, or so profound and vast the mysteries of divine administration, that in general our inquiries must be limited to the great question, "*what*--is enjoined?" His conduct does not require our vindication, while his commands claim our obedience.

Nor does a rebellious spirit merely incur censure; it inevitably exposes to punishment. The people upon whom Israel neglected to execute the purposes of Infinite Justice, became, according to prophetic intimations, "snares and traps to seduce them to idolatry," and "scourges in their sides, and thorns in their eyes." They were in subjection eight years to Cushan, king of Mesopotamia, till judges, of whom Othniel was the first, and Samuel the last, were raised up for their deliverance.

After the signal interference of Heaven on their behalf, in the successes of their first judge, which terminated in a peace of forty years, the "children of Israel did evil again in the sight of the Lord, and the Lord strengthened Eglon, the king of Moab; against Israel," by whom they were enslaved eighteen years. After which, Ehud, a Benjamite, became their deliverer, by assassinating the king of Moab, and another peaceful interval of eighty years elapsed: but such was the strange perversity of this extraordinary nation, that they abused their prosperity, and again apostatized from God. Nor will it be difficult or unprofitable to trace in ourselves some striking points of resemblance to them, and in the divine conduct that same character of love and forbearance which marks his dispensations to his church in all the successive ages of time, "They were disobedient, and rebelled against thee, and cast thy law behind their backs, and slew thy prophets which testified against them to turn them to thee; and they wrought great provocations. Therefore thou deliveredst them into the hand of their enemies, who vexed them: and in the time of their trouble, when they cried unto thee, thou hearedst them from heaven; and according to thy manifold mercies thou gavest them saviours who saved them out of the hand of their enemies. But after they had rest, they did evil again before thee; therefore leftest thou them in the hand of their enemies, so that they had the dominion over them; yet when they returned and cried unto thee, thou hearedst them from heaven, and many times didst thou deliver them according to thy mercies; and testifiedst against them, that thou mightest bring them again unto thy law: yet they dealt proudly, and hearkened not unto thy commandments, but sinned against thy judgments, (which, if a man do, he shall live in them,) and withdrew the shoulder, and hardened their neck, and would not hear: yet many years didst thou forbear them, and testifiedst against them by thy spirit in thy prophets: yet would they not give ear; therefore gavest thou them into the hand of the people of the lands. Nevertheless, for thy great mercies' sake, thou didst not utterly consume them, nor forsake them; for thou art a gracious and merciful God."

Jabin, king of Canaan, was raised up by Providence to disturb that long period of national tranquillity already adverted to, during which the religious character of Israel had so much degenerated: and it must be admitted to evince the unfailing regard of their divine Protector, rather to inflict corrective chastisement upon his people, than to suffer them to proceed with unchecked eagerness in a course fatally injurious to their real interests. In every individual concern shall we not gratefully confess, that "whom the Lord loveth--he chasteneth, and scourgeth every son whom he, receiveth?"

[Sidenote: Year before Christ, 1805 to 1235]

Jabin is said to have reigned in Hazor, a place situated, according to Josephus, in the tribe of Naphtali, on the lake Semechon. Joshua had reduced this place to ashes, and slew its former sovereign; but, probably, the present prince had availed himself of the criminal indolence of the Israelites to rebuild it. The captain of Jabin's army was Sisera, who was truly formidable; having, according to the inspired historian, nine hundred chariots of iron. This, for a petty prince of Canaan, was a most extraordinary force, by which Israel was kept under tyrannical domination for twenty years. Ardent cries were presented to Heaven in these critical circumstances; and he whose ears are ever open to the cries of the distressed, interposed by raising up an illustrious female to accomplish the plans of mercy. "And DEBORAH, a prophetess, the wife of Lapidoth, she judged Israel at that time." As no prophet is mentioned in Israel during their defection, this was a signal testimony of the divine favour upon their repentance; and while observing that out of the millions of Israel a woman was chosen to execute the great purposes of Heaven, we cannot but admire the inscrutable wisdom that appoints all persons to their stations, qualifies all agents for their particular instrumentality, and regulates all the movements of this lower world. Not a sparrow falls to the ground, nor an angel wings his flight, but in subserviency to the arrangements of an omniscient mind.

Deborah was a judge, as well as a prophetess; and a ruler over some, if not all their tribes. Some have supposed, that judges among the ancient Israelites resembled the Archons among the Athenians, and the Dictators among the Romans. The office was not hereditary, but conferred for life; and seems to have been considerably allied, although somewhat inferior, to royal authority.

We are struck with the simplicity of the age in which this prophetess and judge of Israel is represented as sitting under a palm-tree, to discharge her public and eminently important duties. It was between Rama and Bethel, in mount Ephraim. The subject is curious and interesting; we may, therefore, enter into some particulars.

The palm, or date-tree, is a native of Africa and the East, where it grows to the height of fifty or sixty, and occasionally a hundred feet. A cluster of branches issues from the top of it, eight or nine feet long, bending towards the earth, and extending all round in the form of an umbrella. The trunk is upright, and full of cavities, the vestiges of its decayed leaves, having a flat surface within, adapted to the human foot, and forming a kind of natural ladder, by which a person may easily ascend to the top. The lower part produces a number of stalks or suckers, which diffuse the tree considerably, and form a kind of bushy forest. This illustrates the scriptural term in the history of Deborah. "She dwelt under the *palm-tree;*" or, as it might be rendered, *in a forest of palms.* This tree was very common in Palestine. It abounded along the banks of Jordan, and particularly about Engeddi and Jericho; the latter place is designated, in Scripture, *the city of palms.*

"The extensive importance of the date-tree," says Dr. Clarke, "is one of the most curious objects to which a traveller can direct his attention. A considerable part of the inhabitants of Egypt, of Arabia, and Persia, subsist almost entirely upon its fruit. They boast also of its medicinal virtues. Their camels feed upon the date stone. From the leaves they make couches, baskets, bags, mats, and brushes; from the branches, cages for their poultry, and fences for their gardens; from the fibres of the boughs, thread, ropes, and rigging; from the sap is prepared a spirituous liquor: and the body of the tree furnishes fuel: it is even said, that from one variety of the palm-tree, the *Phoenix farinifera,* meal has been extracted, which is found among the fibres of the trunk, and has been used for food." [23]

In the East, it is very common for persons to live in tents, either entirely or during some of the most sultry seasons of the year. This was the patriarchal mode, and persons of considerable distinction are accustomed to pitch them for occasional residence. Mr. Harmer quotes Dr. Pococke as speaking of a pleasant place not far from Aleppo, where he met an Aga, who had a great entertainment there, accompanied with music under tents. Maillet mentions tents as things of course, in an account he gives of an Egyptian officer's taking the air with his lady in the neighbourhood of Cairo; and Chardin says, that Tahmasp, the Persian monarch, used to spend the winter at Casbin, and to retire in the summer three or four leagues into the country, where he lived in tents at the foot of Mount Alouvent, in a place abounding with cool springs and pleasant shades; and that his successors lived after the same manner until the time of Abas the Great, who removed his court to Ispahan. [24] It is sufficiently probable, therefore, that Deborah pitched her tent during a considerable period of the year, under some remarkable palm-tree which stood either alone, or in a forest of palms. There, for the purpose of convenient shelter in a sultry climate, and with primitive simplicity of mind and manners, she received the children of Israel who came to her for judgment, investigating their causes, and by her integrity and wisdom, promoting the happiness of her illustrious nation. The homage which mere external pomp compels is lighter than vanity, compared with that stirling solidity of character which no less ministers to the general good than to the individual's own reputation. He who rules over others, should aim to be enthroned in their affections; and they whom Providence calls to obey, should readily cherish, and, on all suitable occasions, express feelings of respect for their appointed rulers.

As the supreme magistrate of Israel, Deborah sent to Barak, of whom we know only that he was the son of Abinoam, and resided in Kedesh-Naphtali, requiring him to take ten thousand men of the tribes of Naphtali and Zebukin into the neighbourhood of mount Tabor; and, as a prophetess under supernatural influence of immediate inspiration, she assured him of the most perfect success against the hostile prepartions of Sisera. He was not only warranted to anticipate a decisive victory, but also the destruction of this celebrated general, of whom it was expressly affirmed that he should be "delivered into his hand."

It is not necessary to inquire by what particular means this divine intimation of success was communicated to the prophetess of Israel, whither by an audible voice, a nocturnal vision, an angelic messenger, or a secret impression; suffice it to know, that the great Disposer of human destiny has often adopted some and all of these methods to disclose the scenes of futurity to the mind, in proof that he is not only the ruler of nations, but the guardian of his church. Though he permit the rod to smite his people, it shall he broken in pieces whenever it has accomplished its work. On the present occasion, it was revealed to Deborah, that in the ensuing conflict Israel should certainly be victorious; and this disclosure of the event might be kindly intended to revive the desponding feelings of the pious part of the community under circumstances of painful depression. We are not authorized to anticipate, in our individual or national calamities, such a miraculous discovery, nor ought we to repine at the concealment of future events; but of this we may rest assured, if indeed the people of God, and the "called according to his purpose," the hostility of our worst enemies cannot eventually injure us--the "Captain of our salvation" will conduct, us to triumph--and the standard of victory shall be planted upon the graves of our foes.

Barak, it seems, started some objection to the message of Deborah, alleging, "If thou wilt go with me, then I will go; but if thou wilt not go with me, then I will not go." This extraordinary reply may, perhaps, be explained, by supposing it to be the language of that modesty which has so often characterized the greatest of men; and which, it must be admitted, is no less admirable than their most splendid achievements. Thus when the angel of the Lord appeared to Moses, announcing a divine commission to go to Pharaoh, and bring the children of Israel out of Egyptian servitude, he replied, "Who am I, that I should go unto Pharaoh?" and, during a long-continued conference, he stated a variety of difficulties, and manifested a degree of reluctance that excites astonishment. We are ready to charge him with an infatuation bordering upon insolence and presumption; nor, upon a first perusal, should we wonder to find him smitten to the earth for his strange hesitation and timidity; but a closer inspection of the narrative will convince us, that his reluctance, and apparent refusal, ought not to be attributed to any unwillingness to engage in the service of God, with a view of promoting his glory in the earth, but to a consciousness of his personal unworthiness. His objection was less to the *work*, than to *himself*; he did not so much tremble because *that* was arduous, as because *he* was, in his own apprehension, *unfit*. This was a feeling, however, which, under the circumstances of his call, we cannot vindicate; for, to say the least, it was excessive. Whatever estimate Moses in the one case, or Barak in the other, might have formed of themselves, the divine will ought to have been considered the only rule of action. We must never shrink from the course to which Providence calls us--allowing God, who cannot err, to choose his own instruments; and feeling that he who *commands* can *enable* us to perform the most arduous duties.

Animated by a zeal which nothing could repress, Deborah instantly complied with the condition upon which Barak proposed to engage in the war. In language expressive of an unconquerable heroism, a masculine energy of character and a devoted patriotism of spirit, she sent him word, "I will surely go with thee;" but accompanied this message with an intimation, that the honour of this exploit would in part at least attach to a woman, whom Providence had selected to execute the purposes of heaven upon Sisera. The little army being collected, the general and the prophetess hastened to the field of battle, anxious to revenge the wrongs of their insulted country, and to emancipate her enslaved provinces. A patriotism inspired *her* breast, and probably by this time animated *his*, which was kindled by a fire from heaven, which roused into vigorous action all the respective talents, and energies of their nature; and which, urging them forward to righteous war, a war against impiety and oppression, undertaken in the fear, and to promote the glory, of God, excited them to march to an anticipated victory.

Under these circumstances, it is as much to the honour of Barak, that he wished for the presence of the prophetess. Heroes are seldom anxious for the observant eye of piety to watch their movements, and to penetrate their camps. Alas! those whom we admire as the defenders of our country, we weep over as the corrupters of our morals; and too often the page which celebrates their prowess, is stained with the record of their rapacity. But, however unwelcome an attendant, let them remember that an omniscient eye witnesses both their private transactions, and their public career.

It is no less honourable to the character of this illustrious heroine and female head of Israel, that so far from cherishing any petty jealousies of Barak, and aiming at a monopoly of the reputation likely to result from the present undertaking, she assigned to him the post of honour, and contented herself with becoming his adviser. The superiority of her mind induced her to seek an inferiority of station; anxious only to ensure success, not to gain applause; to be approved of God, not to be altered of man. Happy would it be for us all in our respective stations, whether elevated by opulence or depressed by poverty, were we constantly influenced by a similar principle. Then should we be stimulated to the noblest duties, and fulfil the solemn injunction of our God and Saviour, "Occupy till I come."

Sisera, the captain of the Canaanitish army, having been informed of the movements of Israel, gathered together all his nine hundred chariots of iron, and encamped between Harosheth and the river Kishon. This hostile force, stretching along the circumjacent valley of mount Tabor, must have presented a formidable appearance; and it would not have been surprising, if even veteran troops, whose scared bosoms proclaimed their unretreating hardihood in battle, had been appalled to meet so mighty a preparation with only ten thousand men. But the spirit of a weak woman, when sustained by the living God, shall brave every danger. Faith shall triumph over fear, and the sword shall follow and fulfil prophetic inspirations. "Up," said Deborah to Barak, "for this is the day in which the Lord hath delivered Sisera into thine hand; is not the Lord gone out before thee?" If from this spirited appeal, it might be unjust to the military character of Barak, to cherish a suspicion that he manifested some degree of reluctance to attack the army of Sisera, overawed by his numerical superiority, we cannot help perceiving the wisdom and promptitude which actuated the conduct of Deborah. She had an eye to discern, and a courage to seize, an important crisis. But what most claims our admiration is, an incessant reference to Providence, which marks all her words and actions. Nothing of that boastful language, which indicates an arrogant mind escaped her lips. She evinced no self-adulation, and no undue dependence upon human resources. How many in similar circumstances, would have vushed forward to disproportionate battle with a blind impetuosity, trusting to *chance*, for the result: or, inspired alone by personal hatred against the foe, and a thirst for renown, would have hastened to conquer or to die! From our earliest days we have been taught to admire the heroes of classical story, and have followed with acclamations the conquerors of later ages, who seem to have rivalled the fame of a Themistocles or a Leonidas, and to have reacted the tragical sublimities of Salamis and Thermopylæ; but, in the present history, we see piety clad in the armour of heroism--the achievements of military valour ascribed solely to the higher cause of a divine superintendence--"The LORD hath delivered Sisera into thine hand; is not the LORD gone out before thee?"

Without detracting however from the military genius of Barak, or ascribing an undue pre-eminence to Deborah, it may be readily believed, that so disproportionate a force as that of the Israelites at first acted, and very properly acted, on the defensive, till a favourable conjunction of circumstances occurred; and, perhaps, some miraculous sign, or some divine inspiration on the mind of the prophetess, suggested the moment of attack. [25] It is in fact impossible to determine with any precision where human skill ceased to operate, and where divine interposition commenced; and so imperfect is our present acquaintance with the laws by which spirit and matter are connected, that our speculations will certainly be fruitless, and may therefore be pronounced unwise. Let us be grateful, that *the fact* of divine operation on the human mind is fully ascertained, and by every sincere Christian pleasingly experienced; and that, though "all the Lord's people" are not "prophets," the language of kind encouragement can never be expunged from the sacred page, "If ye being evil know how to give good gifts unto your children, how much more shall your heavenly Father give THE HOLT SPIRIT to them that ask him?"

In obedience to the orders of Deborah, Barak immediately put his little band of intrepid warriors in motion. The result was such, as under these circumstances might, however astonishing, have been reasonably expected; for "if God be for us, who can be against us?" The mighty hosts of Canaan, amounting, according to the estimate of Josephus, to three hundred thousand foot, and ten thousand horse, vanished before the valiant arm of Israel, nerved as it was by an energy from heaven. Barak poured the irresistible torrent of war upon his presumptuous foes, and swept them away.

Josephus states, that "when they were come to a close fight, there came down from heaven a great storm, with a vast quantity of rain and hail; and the wind blew the rain in the face of the Canaanites, and so darkened their eyes, that their arrows and slings were of no advantage to them; nor would the coldness of the air permit the soldiers, to make use of their swords; while this storm did not so much incommode the Israelites, because it came in their backs. They also took such courage upon the apprehension that God was assisting them, that they fell upon the very midst of their enemies, and slew a great number of them. So that some of them fell by the Israelites, some fell by their own horses, which were put into disorder, and not a few were killed by their own chariots."

Scarcely does the history of the world furnish an example of so complete a victory, accompanied by so utter an annihilation of the enemy. Curiosity might wish to trace the various movements of that memorable day, the plan of battle, the occasion of defeat, the exploits of individual heroes, and a thousand other circumstances, with which fancy often decorates the head of the hero, and amplifies the page of the historian; but with a majestic simplicity so eminently characteristic of the sacred narrative, it is stated that "the Lord discomfited Sisera, and all his chariots, and all his host, with the edge of the sword, before Barak; so that Sisera lighted down off his chariot, and fled away on his feet. But Barak pursued after the chariots, and after the host, unto Harosheth of the Gentiles: and all the host of Sisera fell upon the edge of the sword; and there was not a man left." Who will compare with this simple record the language of Cæsar, though so often celebrated, "*Veni, vidi, vici*--I came, I saw, I conquered;" words at least as remarkable for egotism as for laconic force: or who would represent the battle of *Zela*, and the defeat of the *Pharnaces* as worthy of being named in connection with the memorable victory of Tabor.

Sisera, defeated, dispirited, and alone, fled to the tent of Jael, the wife of Heber the Kenite, a family which was at this time at peace with the king of Canaan. It was an additional reason to hope for security from the enemy's pursuit, that the custom of the country interdicted intrusion of all strangers into the woman's apartment. Jael moreover went forth to invite this defeated general under her protection, and encouraged him to expect every attention that humanity could dictate in this moment of extremity. No wonder he resigned himself with a fearless confidence to her care, and prepared to seek in "balmy sleep" an oblivion of all his distractions. She furnishes him with a refreshing draught of milk, though he only requested water; covers him with a mantle, and undertakes to guard him from all unwelcome intrusion, by standing at the door of the tent, to answer the interrogatories of any inquisitive stranger. But no sooner did he drop into a sound sleep, than, seizing upon the first weapons that her situation afforded, a nail and a hammer, and approaching softly to the unconscious general, she drove the nail into his temple, and transfixed him to the ground. Hastening from her tent, in the transport of success, to meet Barak, who was in eager pursuit, she conducted, him to the corpse of his prostrate foe. "So God subdued on that day, Jabin, the king of Canaan, before the children of Israel."

Let us dismiss Jael, for the present, from our meditations, and offer a reflection or two on the fate of Sisera.

I. No event recorded upon the page of history is more calculated to impress upon our minds the assertion of Solomon, than that to which we have just given our attention: "The race is not to the swift, nor the battle to the strong ... for man also knoweth not his time, as the fishes that are taken in an evil net, and as the birds that are caught in the snare; so ere the sons of men snared in an evil time, when it falleth suddenly upon them." Nothing could have been more improbable, according to human calculations, than the result of this extraordinary battle. Who that had seen the far-stretching troops of the king of Canaan overspreading, like a vast inundation, the vicinity of Kishon and Harosheth, whose polished armour glittered along the valley to the rising sun, accustomed to victory, breathing revenge, and headed by the most distinguished general of the age--who that had viewed their prodigious forces, consisting of infantry and cavalry, in contrast with the diminutive strength and contemptible numbers of the Israelitish army, but must have considered the attack as the feeble effort of an unaccountable infatuation? But though HE who "sitteth upon the circle of the earth," could have interposed at once to crush the foe by the thunder of his power, ten thousand men of Israel were appointed to execute his purpose against the devoted Canaanites, to show that it is his will to work by human means;--he required the employment of *only* ten thousand, to prove that all human skill and success is mere instrumentality, and that the honour of victory is to be attributed to the God of battles.

2. The enemies of God and his people shall perish ingloriously. This is not the only instance. Pharaoh makes ready his own chariot, and takes with him all the chariots of Egypt, in eager pursuit of Israel, just escaped from his relentless oppression. In the pride of his strength he proclaims, "I will pursue, I will overtake, I will divide the spoil, my lust shall be satisfied upon them--I will draw my sword, my hand shall destroy them;" but there was an arm of superior might that seized the unresisting elements, and launched them upon the rash adventurer and his guilty myriads. "Thou didst blow with thy wind, the sea covered them; they sank as lead in the mighty waters. Who is like unto thee, O Lord, among the gods?"--Sennacherib, king of Assyria, sends Tartan, and Rabsaris, and Rabshakeh, with a great host against Jerusalem, in the reign of Hezekiah. Mark their insolent blasphemy: "Hearken not unto Hezekiah when he persuadeth you, saying, The Lord will deliver us. Hath any of the gods of the nations delivered at all his land out of the hand of the king of Assyria? Where are the gods of Hamath and of Arpad? where are the gods of Sepharvaim, Hena, and Ivah? have they delivered Samaria out of mine hand? Who are they among all the gods of the countries that have delivered their country out of mine hand, that the Lord should deliver Jerusalem out of mine hand?" A letter was afterward sent to the king to the same effect, commencing with this blasphemous sentence, "Let not thy God, in whom thou trustest, deceive thee." Hezekiah instantly repairs to the temple, opens his letter in the immediate presence of the Eternal, and supplicates his great name for that interference in the present extremity, which would deliver his people, and promote his own

glory. His prayer is heard. From the heaven of heavens an angelic envoy is despatched to the Assyrian encampment, and with the flaming sword of almighty indignation, smites *a hundred and eighty-five thousand* of the boasting foe; "and when they arose early in the morning, behold they were all dead corpses." Herod ventures upon the dangerous experiment of persecuting the church of God: he dares, with an untrembling hand, to put James to the sword, and ultimately imprison Peter for the same horrid purpose: but he who "sitteth in the heavens" held the presumptuous criminal in "utter derision," despatched an angel to break off the chains by which his servant was bound, and laid his finger upon the royal rebel to extinguish his glory and his pride for ever; "he was eaten of worms, and gave up the ghost." Ah! the immortality of the soul elevates it above mortal power, and the utmost that a persecutor can do is, by a painful stroke, to put a Christian into speedier possession of his promised blessedness. "A tyrant is mortal, his empire expires with his life; and were he to employ the whole course of his life in tormenting a martyr, and in trying to impair his felicity, he would resemble an idiot throwing stones at the lightning, while in an indivisible moment, and with as inconceivable rapidity, it caught his eye as it passed from the east to the west."

"Thou dull stupid man, who art not stricken with the idea of a God, whose will is self-efficient, and who alone can act immediately on an immaterial soul, come and behold some sensible proofs of that infinite power, of which metaphysical proofs can give thee no idea! And thou, proud insolent man! go aboard the last-built vessel, put out to sea, set the most vigilant watch, surround thyself with the most formidable instruments: what art thou, when God uttereth his voice?' What art thou, when the 'noise' resounds? What art thou, when torrents of rain seem to threaten a second deluge, and to make the globe which thou inhabitest one rolling sea? What art thou when lightnings emit their terrible flashes? What art thou when the 'winds' come roaring 'out of their treasures?' What art thou *then*? Verily, thou art no less than thou wast in thy palace. Thou art no less than when thou wast sitting at a delicious table. Thou art no less than thou wast when every thing contributed to thy pleasure. Thou art no less than when at the head of thine army, thou wast the terror of nations, shaking the earth with the stunning noise of thy warlike instruments: for, at thy festal board, within thy palace, among thy pleasures, at the head of thine armies, thou wast *nothing* before the King of nations. As an immaterial and immortal creature, thou art subject to his immediate power; but, to humble and to confound thee, he must manifest himself to thee in sensible objects. Behold him, then, in this formidable situation: try thy power against his: silence 'the noise of the multitude of waters:' fasten the vessel that 'reeleth like a drunken man;' smooth the foaming waves that 'mount thee up to heaven;' fill up the horrible gulfs whither thou goest 'down to the bottoms of the mountains;' dissipate the lightning that flasheth in thy face; hush the bellowing thunders; confine the winds in their caverns; assuage the anguish of thy soul, and prevent its melting and exhaling with fear. How diminutive is man! How many ways hath God to confound his pride! He uttereth his voice, and there is a noise of a multitude of waters in the heavens. He causeth the vapours to ascend from the ends of the earth. He maketh lightnings with rain, and bringeth forth the wind out of his treasures. Who would 'not fear thee, O King of nations?"

It is necessary, however, to remark, that we are not authorized always to expect the strict exercise of retributive justice in the present state. Some remarkable visitations have, in all periods, roused the attention of an astonished world, and powerfully appealed to the understanding of men, in vindication of the character, and in proof of the existence, of a superintending Providence. Tyrants have been hurled from their thrones, empires uprooted from their foundations, and the "poor set on high from oppression;" but these dispensations have not been regular, nor can they be calculated upon as certain, or in general, perhaps, as probable. They have been sufficiently numerous to indicate an observant though invisible eye fixed upon human affairs; but not so frequent as to supersede the Christian's anticipations of a day of final and impartial judgment. The present may indeed be considered rather as a time of permitted, confusion, the period of moral chaos, in which the elements of a new creation exists, but in a disorganized state; in which the principles of depraved human nature are permitted to develope themselves, and human passions are suffered to act in an ample field of exertion with comparatively little control, and for the purpose of ultimately promoting the glory of God. Hereafter "the morning stars" will "sing together," and all "the sons of God" again "shout for joy," when "all things that offend shall be gathered out of his kingdom," when sinners shall be everlastingly degraded, Christ for ever exalted, the most mysterious dispensations shine with transparent brightness in the light of eternity, and the unfading paradise of the saints bloom amidst the wrecks of time.

3. "Boast not thyself of to-morrow, for thou knowest not what a day may bring forth." Little did Sisera imagine the fatal reverses he was destined to suffer, when in all the pride of fancied superiority, sustained by the recollection of the successes of twenty years, he made his arrangements for the battle with Barak and Deborah. What a contrast between the moment of confident preparation, and that of disgraceful retreat! What a mighty and unexpected contrast between the high-spirited general at the head of his

army, and the trembling fugitive hiding himself in a tent, and slain by a woman.

Let us apply the reflection to ourselves. How often do we form our schemes, and calculate on temporal prosperities, without any due regard to the will of Providence, or any proper consideration of the uncertainty of life. "We live without God in the world," an omniscient Deity has no existence in our minds, and we inquire "Who will show us any good?" as if God were not the chief good, or could not supply our happiness.

Alas! how often have we boasted of to-morrow by neglecting, in a religious sense, the most important business of to-day. It is not easy to imagine a more dangerous state of mind, than that of a person, whose resolutions of repentance and amendment all respect futurity, because he makes these very resolutions an excuse for his negligences, and even considers them as an expiation of the guilt of his procrastinating temper. It is indeed an affecting thought, that so thick a mist surrounds us, we are not only unacquainted with the events of YEARS to come, we do not know what a DAY may bring forth. It may produce a change in our circumstances--our faculties--our friendships--our hopes.--An hour--a moment, may waft us from time into eternity! "Now," then, "is the accepted time, behold, NOW is the day of salvation."--"Seek the Lord while he may be found, call ye upon him while he is near."

4. Mount TABOR has been repeatedly mentioned as the place where Deborah directed that the forces of Zebulon and Naphtali should be concentrated, and its immediate vicinity as the scene of the celebrated contest between Barak and Sisera; but though it may appear a digression from the present subject, it would be scarcely pardonable to omit a reference to that still more wonderful circumstance, the transfiguration of Jesus Christ, which probability and tradition concur in assigning to the same remarkable spot. Three of his disciples, Peter, James, and John, accompanied him to this mountain, where two bright spirits from among the glorified saints, Moses and Elias, descended to join their society. Delightful pledge of that inseparable union which will one day take place upon the summits of immortality, when "the general assembly and church of the first-born" shall associate together in the realms of bliss!

> "O happy, happy company,
> Where men and heavenly spirits greet,
> And those whom death hath severed meet,
> And hold again communion sweet;
> O happy, happy company!"

What though death at present divides them, and while some of this glorious family have reached their destined habitation, others are left on earth to struggle with the calamities of life; the separation is but temporary, and will serve to heighten the raptures of union, when they shall come from the east and from the west, from the north and from the south, and sit down with Abraham, and Isaac, and Jacob, in the kingdom of God.

And what will constitute the heaven of believers? Doubtless the vision of the Lamb, converse with Jesus, and perpetual intercourse with saints of all nations and ages. Moses and Elias descended from the raptures of immortality to talk with Jesus on the mount, and the same divine communion will form a considerable portion of our felicity in the invisible world. To be for ever near him, and to "see him as he is"--to converse of the things of his kingdom--to learn from his own lips the purpose of all his most inscrutable dispensations to the church and to each believer, the reason of every sorrow, and the nature of its connection with our ultimate happiness--to hold fellowship with all his redeemed, holy patriarchs, distinguished apostles, and victorious martyrs--to be encircled with all his family, emparadised in his embraces, and united to all who love him in bonds of indissoluble affection; no sea to separate, no discord to agitate, no enemies to infest the unbroken circle of friendship--this will be "joy unspeakable and full of glory." Not the delight of Moses, when conversing with God in the burning bush, at the door of the tabernacle, or in mount Sinai--not the transports of David, when his enchanted spirit waked the lyre of praise and gratitude--not the bliss of the three favoured disciples, even on this mount of transfiguration, can be compared with this perfect happiness. All the little streams of felicity which flow to the church of God in the desert, will then be collected into one vast ocean, in which the tears and sorrows of time will be eternally lost. The pleasures of a moment which now solace us by the way, will be exchanged for the permanent joys of that celestial inheritance, in which "the Lamb, which is in the midst of the throne, shall lead us, and feed us by fountains of living waters; and God shall wipe away all tears from our eyes." By the anticipations of faith, we are "come unto mount Sion, and unto the city of the living God, the heavenly Jerusalem, and to an innumerable company of angels, to the general assembly and church of the firstborn which are written in heaven, and to God the Judge of all, and to the spirits of just men made perfect, and to Jesus the Mediator of the new covenant."

Section II

"On a favoured few," says an elegant writer, "has been conferred the combined glory of acting nobly and writing well; of serving their own day and generation with credit to themselves and advantage to their country, and of transmitting useful information to regions remote and generations unborn. On the list of those illustrious few, stands, with distinguished honour, the name of Deborah, the judge, the prophetess, the sweet singer of Israel; and it is with exultation we observe the most dignified, arduous, and important stations of human life filled with reputation by a woman; a woman who first with resolution and intrepidity saved her country in the hour of danger and distress, and ruled it with wisdom and equity, and then recorded her own achievements in strains which must be held in admiration so long as good taste and love of virtue exist in the world."

[Sidenote: Years before Christ, 1285.] The remarkable victory we have just related and remarked upon, is celebrated by Deborah in a poem, which claims our attention as one of the most ancient in the world, having been composed upwards of four hundred years before the birth of Homer, and which is characterized by unusual pathos and sublimity. Many passages in it are confessedly obscure, which will not be deemed surprising, when it is recollected how imperfectly we are acquainted, in this distant period, with the various circumstances, incidents, and localities of the memorable event it celebrates, and even with the original language in which it was written.

Dr. Lowth [26] very properly divides this poem into three parts; first, the exordium: next, a recital of the circumstances which preceded, and of those which accompanied the victory; lastly, a fuller description of the concluding event, the death of Sisera, and the disappointed hopes of his mother; which is embellished with the choisest flowers of poetry.

It is proposed in the present chapter to furnish an extended paraphrase of this fine specimen of ancient poetry, for the purpose chiefly of illustrating its meaning. Its various beauties as a composition can scarcely fail of striking the most superficial reader. It occupies the fifth chapter of the book of Judges.

[Note: In the original book, the text and paraphrase were displayed side-by-side. In this case, for each verse, the paraphrase follows in brackets.]

1. Then sang Deborah, and Barak the son of Abinoam, on that day, saying, [Deeply impressed with a grateful sense of that remarkable interposition of Providence for the deliverance of Israel from the long tyranny of their inveterate enemies, which Deborah and Barak saw accomplished by their own instrumentality, the one directing by her wisdom, what the other performed by his valor, they sang a sacred ode on the very same day; a day so wonderful for its dangers, anxieties, and triumphs. It was to this effect.]

2. Praise ye the Lord for the avenging of Israel, when the people willingly offered themselves. [Give thanks, ye tribes of Israel, to the God of battles, who has smitten the daring foe, and thus avenged our wrongs. "The hearts

of all men are in his hands," and instead of internal dissention enfeebling our energies, he has graciously disposed the people of Zebulon and Naphtali to offer their zealous services in the war; a war which patriotism and piety have, under the blessing of Heaven, conducted to a glorious termination.]

3. Hear, O ye kings; give ear, O ye princes; I, even I, will sing unto the Lord; I will sing praise to the Lord God of Israel [Let the voice of praise, uttered from the thousands of Israel, resound to distant nations, so that Gentile princes and potentates may hear of the miracles of mercy wrought for the covenanted people of God. Ye idolatrous rulers of the world, reject forever your gods of wood and stone, for I am called to celebrate the majesty of Jehovah, who has triumphed over them; and will sing to the honour of him, who, though no local divinity, has chosen the children of Israel as his peculiar people.]

4. Lord, when thou wentest out of Seir, when thou marchedst out of the field of Edom, the earth trembled, and the heavens dropped, the clouds also dropped water.

5. The mountains melted from before the Lord; even that Sinai from before the Lord God of Israel. [This illustrious day revives the recollection of those ancient interpositions of the strong arm of Omnipotence for our ancestors, which have often excited the our admiration, and of which this appears like the continuation of a miraculous series. O God! what a period was that, when Israel marched round the confines of Idumea, and the majesty of thy protecting presence was displayed before the enemy, in the pillar of cloud by day, and of fire by night. Edom refused a passage through their land, but so terrible were thy signs, that the trembling earth, the tempestuated heavens--all nature seemed to avenge the cause of thine insulted people, and the surrounding nations were smitten with terror, as when mount Sinai herself quaked, and for a time disappeared amidst the tremendous glory of the divine presence. These wonders do not surpass what we have witnessed to-day, and which prove that none shall oppress thy people with impunity. [27]]

6. In the days of Shamgar, the son of Anath, in the days of Jael, the highways were unoccupied, and the travellers walked through byways.

7. The inhabitants of the villages ceased, they ceased in Israel, until that I, Deborah, arose, that I arose a mother in Israel [Turn your weeping eyes to the recent miseries of our country Shamgar, indeed, who succeeded Ehud as judge, effected something for Israel, and Jael shall never be forgotten for her heroism and her useful exertions, although in a private station; but alas! the long tyranny of our oppressors continued to produce the most disastrous effects--trade perished, for no caravans of merchants dared to occupy the

public ways, infested as they were with an armed banditti, the life of the unoffending traveller became endangered, and the dejected inhabitants of the country were afraid to venture abroad, except as thieves, stealing through the most unfrequented paths, and even there the most dreadful outrages were committed; until I Deborah, arose, and notwithstanding the weakness of my sex, and the desperate situation of affairs, became the happy instrument of benefiting Israel, by the restoration of public justice, general security, and national glory.]

8. They chose new gods; then was war in the gates; was there a shield or spear seen among forty thousand in Israel? [But trace our former miseries to their source. Israel relapsed into idolatry, and God punished them with the scourge of war. The insulting foe pressed to the very gates of our fortified cities--the means of defence were utterly neglected in consequence of general despondency, and no adequate supply of arms could be furnished to repel the infuriated enemy.]

9. My heart is toward the governors of Israel, that offered themselves willingly among the people. Bless ye the Lord. [My warmest affections are due to the chiefs of Israel, who, in the hour of calamity and apprehension, did not shrink from danger, nor tremble at death; but, in the true spirit of patriotism, accompanied the people to battle, placed themselves at their head, flew at my first mandate to defend the common cause, and animated our warriors by their noble enthusiasm. Let *them* unite in this anthem of praise to Jehovah, who had the best opportunities of knowing, that nothing but his gracious interposition could have procured such unparalleled success.]

10. Speak ye that ride on white asses, ye that sit in judgment, and walk by the way. [Rejoice, ye nobles and judges of the land, who have the honorable distinction of riding upon white asses, [28] the most valuable animal of the kind, and therefore appropriated to persons of your rank; shout for joy, because now there is no impediment to the exercise of your high offices; and ye, merchants, assist in the song, for no obstruction remains to commercial intercourse; the ways are clear, communications open, and your marauding foes shall alarm you no more.]

11. They that are delivered from the noise of archers in the places of drawing water, there shall they rehearse the righteous acts of the Lord, even the righteous acts towards the inhabitants of his villages in Israel; then shall the people of the Lord go down to the gates. [Ye shepherds, who a short time since scarcely dared to drive your flocks to the watering places, and ye maidens, who were afraid to go and draw for your daily supply, or went in silence lest the smallest noise should rouse your ever-watchful enemies, [29]

now sing with a loud voice, and without the least apprehension, and unite with the husbandmen and vine-dressers, in extolling that miraculous mercy which has restored to your most unprotected habitations the blessings of peace and security. The gates of our cities shall no longer be shut for fear of the enemy, and the people may again repair to these seats of justice and judgment. [30]]

12. Awake, awake, Deborah! awake, awake, utter a song! arise, Barak, and lead thy captivity captive, thou son of Abinoam! [Let not my exhausted powers drop the exulting strain; but rather, O Deborah, kindle with fresh enthusiasm upon every new view of the glorious subject! Exert thy utmost powers of praise, upon this inexhaustible theme! And thou, companion and instrument of victory, Barak, arise! exhibit the captive foe who once led Israel captive! let the spoils of triumphant war be shown, and thou and thy father's name shall be had in everlasting remembrance!]

13. Then he made him that remaineth have dominion over the nobles among the people; the Lord made me have dominion over the mighty. [Alas! to what a wretched state was Israel reduced: but even this remnant of former greatness, this weak and dispirited handful, God employed to crush the power of Canaan and the presumption of her nobles and, be it spoken to his glory, the Lord made even me, a feeble woman, the conqueror of formidable armies, and the saviour of a sinking state.]

14. Out of Ephraim was there a root of them against Amalek, after thee, Benjamin, among thy people out of Machii, came down governors, and out of Zebulun, they that handle the pen of the writer. [Those noble warriors who hastened to the conflict with so much courage, and conquered with so much glory, have not only rendered themselves, but their tribes, for ever illustrious, Ephraim originated the expedition, who had, on a former occasion, discomfited Amalek, and now manifested an heroic zeal against them and the confederates of Jabin, Benjamin caught the holy infection of hatred against the enemies of the Lord, and first rushed to the fierce encounter, Machir, the half tribe of Manasseh, despatched her great men with their forces, and Zebulon sent her sons more famed indeed, as a commercial tribe, for handling the pen than the sword, but who readily came forward to aid the common cause.]

15. And the princes of Issachar were with Deborah, even Issachar and also Barak; he was sent on foot into the valley. For the divisions of Reuben there were great thoughts of heart. [The chiefs of Issachar repaired to Deborah and Barak in Mount Tabor, and with them the strength of their tribe. They descended into the valley as foot soldiers, with Barak, and trembled not at the chariots and cavalry of Sisera. But alas! for Reuben,

whose internal dissentions issued in a shameful neutrality, a circumstance deeply perplexing and vexatious to their brethren.]

16. Why abodest thou among the sheepfolds, to hear the bleatings of the flocks? For the divisions of Reuben there were great searchings of heart. [Why didst thou obey the dictates of a selfish spirit and a carnal policy, and while engrossed with thy flocks and herds, refusedst to listen to the cries of thy brethren in distress, and the loud calls of Deborah and Barak? Alas, for the dissentions of Reuben! What painful thoughts, what dreadful anxieties were occasioned by such unaccountable and unpatriotic conduct!]

17. Gilead abode beyond Jordan, and why did Dan remain in ships? Asher continued on the sea-shore, and abode in his breaches. [Influenced by a similar temper, Gilead, or Gad, remained inactive, in their possessions beyond Jordan, as though, happy themselves, they were insensible to the miseries of others, and why didst thou, O Dan, regarding only thy merchandise and thy gainful navigation, continue motionless in the day of our calamity! And see how Asher imitated the base example, abiding within the ruined walls of his cities, and in his bays and havens!]

18. Zebulun and Naphtah were a people that jeoparded their lives unto the death in the high places of the field. [But Zebulon and Naphtah have acquired immortal renown, by cheerfully hazarding their lives and their all, when they assembled in the heights of Tabor, and impetuously rushed upon the foe in the valley where Kishon flows. [31]]

19. The kings came and fought, then fought the kings of Canaan in Taanach, by the waters of Megiddo they took no gain of money. [Dire was the strife and vast the struggle when the confederate kings of Canaan fought in Taanach, and near Megiddo, to which places in the tribe of Issachar their mighty forces extended. They pressed eagerly and freely to the war, but how were their vain hopes disappointed when they returned without spoils.]

20. They fought from heaven, the stars in their courses fought against Sisera. [The awful contest was decided by the God of heaven. His angels, his elements--all nature aided our righteous cause; and the stars of the firmament lighted our midnight pursuit, and shone disastrously upon the fugitive enemy.]

21. The river of Kishon swept them away, that ancient river, the river Kishon. O my soul, thou hast trodden down strength! [The river Kishon rising, as if elated with joy at the opportunity, and overflowing its banks, swept thousands away; that river, celebrated in ancient times, and the witness of former conflicts. O Deborah, thou art indeed thrice happy in becoming the favoured instrument of exciting this glorious war, and thus eventually of crushing a most formidable confederacy!]

22. Then were the horse-hoofs broken by means of the prancings, the prancings of then mighty ones. [The war-horse, urged in his rapid flight over the flinty soil, cut his hoofs to pieces; or entangled amidst the overflowings of Kishon, pranced, and foamed, and perished. [32]]

23. Curse ye Meroz, said the angel of the Lord; curse ye bitterly the inhabitants thereof, because they came not to the help of the Lord, the help of the Lord against the mighty. [The angel, who preceded our hosts as the sword of an irresistible Providence, denounced a curse upon the city of Meroz, and commanded us to cherish a holy indignation against its lukewarm inhabitants, who, instead of resisting the giant armies of Canaan, remained as uninterested or timid spectators of the dreadful battle.]

24. Blessed above women shall Jael, the wife be of Heber the Kenite, be; blessed shall she be above women in the tent. [But feminine heroism shall exhibited in honourable contrast with such shameful neutrality. Let the benediction of heaven rest upon the head of Jael, the wife of Heber the Kenite, above all other women! Blessed shall she be above all other female, heads of families who remained at home, having with masculine-courage completed in her tent, what was so happily begun in the field.]

25. He asked water, and she gave him milk; she brought forth butter in a lordly dish. [Sisera, famished and fainting, requested water to allay his thirst; she opened a leathern bottle, and with feigned respect presented him with butter-milk; yes, she poured him out butter-milk in a vessel of copper, such as nobles use. [33]]

26. She put her hand to the nail, and her right hand to the workmen's hammer; and with the hammer she smote Sisera; she smote off his head, when she had pierced and stricken through his temples. [Lulled into a fatal security by her deceptive homage, he slept to wake no more! She seized a nail of her tent, and a hammer, approached in cautious silence the sleeping adversary of Israel, and, animated by an irresistible impulse of patriotic zeal, she drove it through his temples, and cut off his head.]

27. At her feet he bowed, he fell, he lay down; at her feet he bowed, he fell: where he bowed, there he fell down dead. [Thus fell the great instrument of Canaanitish oppression at the feet of a woman; thus ingloriously he perished [34]]

28. The mother of Sisera looked out at a window and cried through the lattice, Why is his chariot so long in coming? Why tarry the wheels of his chariots? [O day of triumph! Methinks the mother of Sisera, anticipating the fruits of victory, and the final subjection of all Israel to their oppressor's yoke, stood at her window, chiding the tardy moments, and impatiently exclaiming from behind the lattice-work, Why is the chariot of our victorious

general so long in returning? Whence this painful delay? Hasten, ye fleet animals that draw his chariots, and restore him to our embraces!]

29. Her wise ladies answered her, yea, she returned answer to herself,

30. Have they not sped? have they not divided the prey; to every man a damsel or two, to Sisera a prey of divers colours, a prey of divers colours of needle work, of divers colours of needle work on both sides, meet for the necks of them that take the spoil? [Her maids of honour, who were scarcely less eager than herself to see the laurelled conqueror, answered her; yea, chiding for a moment her own impatient expressions, as if they indicated a doubt of success, she said within herself, Have they not succeeded in discovering the enemy?--Doubtless they have, Have they not enriched them selves with immense booty, and apportioned an Israelitish damsel two to our brave warriors?--Yes, yes, this must occasion some delay, and let them enjoy the reward of their valour. As for Sisera, the most beautiful captives are his portion, and shall be the slaves of his will; the most elegant dresses, curiously interwoven and wrought with the needle, such as may well be deemed worthy of heroes, shall grace his triumph and heighten his renown.]

31. So let all thine enemies perish, O Lord let them that love him be as the sun when he goeth forth in his might. [But who can describe their utter disappointment! So shamefully, so totally, let all the enemies of thy people, and all the opponents of thy dominion in the earth perish, O Lord, from before thy face forever! But let all those who are animated with a sacred zeal for thy glory resemble the morning sun as he advances rapidly to his meridian splendour; let them increase in usefulness, influence, and esteem, the honour of human nature, and the lights of the world.]

Manoah's Wife Chapter IX

Obscurity of station or of birth has no tendency to prelude the favour of God. In this respect, he "seeth not as a man seeth," but, in the past dispensations of his mercy, appears to have preferred the lowly as objects of high and distinguishing manifestations. This is the case in the Christian era, and to the present hour the stream of celestial goodness pursues its silent and chosen course, chiefly down the vales of poverty and wretchedness.

We see from the histories of Scripture, that in seasons of national defection, there have existed pleasing instances of individual piety. Amidst universal darkness, some stars of considerable magnitude have shed a light, though comparatively feeble, athwart the moral hemisphere. God has never totally suspended his intercourse with man, even in the worst of times, nor suffered the series of his communications to be entirely broken. If, during certain disastrous periods, truth has been eclipsed, it has not been extinguished: the watchful eye of Providence has never been removed from the earth, nor has the divine hand ceased to interpose in terrestrial affairs.

[Sidenote: Years before Christ, about 1156.]

The history of Manoah and his wife is introduced by an allusion to the state of Israel. This people, in consequence of returning to the commission of those sins for which they were so notorious, were delivered up to their oppressors forty years. The Philistines were, in fact, very inconsiderable, in comparison to the Israelites, having only five cities of any importance; yet they were the appointed scourge in the divine hand to chastise his people. Thus he imparts power to the weak, or enfeebles the energy of the strong, to accomplish his omniscient purposes.

On a certain occasion, an angel of the Lord appeared to the wife of Manoah with most welcome tidings. She was a sufferer from the same cause which tried the faith and patience of so many of the illustrious females of patriarchal age: and, to alleviate those painful anxieties which good people at that period were accustomed to cherish for a family, but especially to evince the unceasing regard of Heaven to the interests of Israel, the commissioned spirit announced to her the conception of a son; and giving her at the same time some directions respecting her own mode of living, and the devotement of the future Samson as a Nazarite from the womb, assured her that be should become the deliverer of Israel from Philistine subjection.

It does not seem as if she were commanded to tell her husband; nevertheless, she immediately hastens to disclose to him every circumstance that had transpired. To whom could she so properly confide this important secret? who, excepting herself, could be so deeply interested; or who so worthy of sharing her utmost confidence? Between relatives so dear, and so closely allied, there should be few or no concealments. On every subject they are entitled to reciprocal confidence, which is the life of friendship and the soul of love: and whither it be for advice or for congratulation, the husband should share the feelings, the sympathies, the unreserved affections of the wife, and the wife those of her husband. These tender relatives may derive advantage especially from reciprocal communications on religious topics, and points of pious experience. By this means, they may sweeten and sanctify domestic enjoyments; by this renew and purify the flame of affection.

The simplicity and veracity of the wife of Manoah appear in her address to him. "Then the woman came and told her husband, saying, A man of God came unto me, and his countenance was like the countenance of an angel of God, very terrible; but I asked him not whence he was, neither told he me his name. But he said unto me, Behold, thou shalt conceive and bear a son; and now drink no wine, nor strong drink, neither eat any unclean thing; for the child shall be a Nazarite to God, from the womb to the day of his death."

The injunction respecting her own abstinence was no arbitrary requirement, but was founded in nature and reason. The temper of the mind, is materially affected by the state of the body, and both may concur in communicating permanent impressions from the mother to her offspring, which often affect the comfort of existence.

The condition to which her child was thus devoted requires a brief historical elucidation. The term Nazarite signifies *separated*; and is commonly applied to persons who make a vow to live in a more holy manner than others, either during a certain specified number of years, or ever after the pledge is given, without recantation or change. The Nazarite abstained from every kind of intoxicating liquor, "from wine and strong drink," from vinegar of wine, or vinegar of strong drink, and from grapes, whether moist or dried; he was to let his hair grow, and upon no pretext whatever to approach a dead body, though it were to render funeral honours to a father or mother. If, during the period of a vow, the Nazarite neglected any of these injunctions, the whole ceremony was to recommence. The least admissible time for this consecration was, according to some of the Jewish Rabbins, thirty days; and the perpetual Nazarite whose hair had been allowed to grow for many years, might cut it once. At the expiration of the appointed term, various sacrifices were to be offered, a particular enumeration of which is given in the sixth chapter of the book of Numbers. After this, the priest shaved the head of the Nazarite at the door of the tabernacle, and burnt his hair on the fire of the altar. If the person died previous to the expiration of his vow, his son was required to fulfil the time, and offer the same sacrifices. Perpetual Nazarites, like Samson, were consecrated by their parents; but there is a peculiarity attaching to him above all others of whom we read, being devoted even before his birth. Similar rites were observed amongst the heathen, especially the Egyptians, the Greeks, and the Romans, the origin of which is unquestionably to be referred to the Jewish law. [35]

As soon as Manoah was informed by his wife of the visit she had received, and the delightful promises she had heard, he entreated God to permit the return of the messenger, whom he supposed to have been a prophet. "When," says Bishop Hall, "I see the strength of Manoah's faith, I marvel not that he had a Samson to his son: he saw not the messenger, he beard not the errand, he examined not the circumstances; yet now he takes thought, not whether he should have a son, but how he shall order the son which he must have; and sues to God, not for the son which as yet he had not, but for the direction of governing him, when he should be. Zachary had the same message, and craving a sign, lost that voice wherewith he craved it. Manoah seeks no sign for the promise, but counsel for himself; and yet that angel spake to Zachary himself, this only to the wife of Manoah; that in the temple like a glorious spirit, this in the house or field, like some prophet or traveller; that to a priest, this to a woman. All good men have not equal measures of faith; the bodies of men have not more differences of stature, than their graces. Credulity to men is faulty and dangerous, but, in the matters of God, is the greatest virtue of a Christian. Happy are they that have not seen, yet believed. True faith takes all for granted, yea, for performed, which is once promised.

"He that before sent his angel unasked, will much more send him again upon entreaty; those heavenly messengers are ready, both to obey their Maker, and to relieve his children. Never any man prayed for direction in his duties to God and was repulsed; rather will God send an angel from heaven to instruct us, than our good desires shall be frustrated."

Upon his reappearance, the angel did not present himself to Manoah, though he came in answer to his supplications; but to his wife as she sat alone in the field. She immediately hastened to her husband, who gladly returned with her to the spot; and hearing from her own lips, that it was the same remarkable visitor she had so recently seen, he expressed his faith in the promise, and his solicitude for the child. His wife concurred in every desire; and his inquiry was, in fact, equally her own. "How shall we order the child, and how shall we do unto him?" The angel repeated his former injunctions, which this pious female was ready to observe.

Good people commence their plans, and offer their prayers, in behalf of children, even before their birth; feeling the weight of that responsibility which the parental relationship incurs, and knowing well the early trials and dangers that await their little ones. The tears and concerns that attend the period of parental anticipation, mingle with the transports which accompany their nativity, and stimulate their future exertions to train them up in the ways of religion. How gladly do they make considerable sacrifices of time and property to this object; and how richly are the maternal pangs repaid, when true wisdom guides the steps of their youthful charge into paths of pleasantness and peace! The mercies of Providence are ill requited, when the parents never inquire, like Manoah and his wife, "How shall we order the child?" If incapable of properly cultivating the infant mind themselves, either on account of their own ignorance, from their too abundant occupation, or from an unprincipled disregard to the best interests of the little immortals intrusted to their care; it is a happiness for the present generation, that so many benevolent institutions exist, which invite the poor and the neglected to their parental guidance. But let parents, and especially Christian parents, consider it one of their first duties, one of their noblest privileges, to implant the good seed of knowledge in their hearts, which in its future developements, may not only expand their faculties and dignify their characters, but render them the ornaments' of society, the comfort of their parents, the guides and examples of posterity, and the objects of divine approbation.

Hitherto these two favoured individuals had no idea of the being they were addressing, but still supposing him to be an ordinary prophet, Manoah, in the true spirit of eastern hospitality, requested permission to dress a kid for his refreshment. He was, besides, animated with a sense of gratitude for the joyful news he communicated. The angel declined his offer, assuring him, though he remained with him a little while, he should not take any food; but that if he designed to offer a burnt-offering, he ought to be careful not to imitate the prevailing enormity of sacrificing to strange gods, but to worship God.

Manoah now became anxious to know the stranger's name, that he might have an opportunity of hereafter expressing his gratitude and affection, by informing him of the birth of his predicted offspring, and making suitable acknowledgments for his kindness. This request was refused; and he was assured it was "a secret," and must remain concealed. This was a sufficient reply to Manoah and his wife, who did not presume, with an impertinent eagerness, to press the question. Many secret things belong to God; and it is the province of true piety to repress curiosity, where it is not authorized, or would be useless. All impatience, we should often take wing, and pursue our adventurous flight through all the regions of possible knowledge, and beyond the limits of Scriptural revelation; but, "Why askest thou?"--"What is that to thee?"--Truth is disclosed in all its essentials--regard thy duty, and listen to thy Saviour--"follow me."

Many expositors have concurred in rendering the words of the angel thus, "Why askest thou after my name, seeing it is WONDERFUL?" and for an explanation of the epithet, they refer to the sublime description of Isaiah, "His name shall be called WONDERFUL, Counsellor, the mighty God, the everlasting Father, the Prince of Peace." If this be correct, the ministering spirit, concealing his glory in the form of a man, was no other than the Angel of the covenant, the Wisdom, the Word, and the Son of God. If, after his resurrection from the dead, and immediately previous to his reascension to the glories of eternity, when invested with the character of the Conqueror of death and hell, he appeared to two of his disciples on the way to Emmaus whom he had so recently left, without their suspecting who it was, "for their eyes were holden, that they should not know him?" it cannot be deemed an improbable circumstance in itself, that on this occasion he should have been divested of all his splendid peculiarities, to fulfil so interesting a mission to these worthy Danites, to authorize so unusual a sacrifice, and to accomplish so glorious a mode of disappearance.

Manoah now proceeded to present an offering to the Lord, presenting, as was customary, a meat-offering with his burnt-offering. He was not indeed a priest, nor was this the place; but it was not requisite to go to the tabernacle in Shiloh, when his divine visiter had already dispensed them from the circumstantials, by sanctioning the sacrifice here. "Audit came to pass, when the flame went up towards heaven from off the altar, that the angel of the Lord ascended in the flame of the altar; and Manoah and his wife looked on it, and fell on their faces to the ground." This was, at once, a proof of the full acceptance of their sacrifice; and irresistibly convinced them, they had been conversing with a divine personage. "And Manoah said unto his wife, We shall surely die, because we have seen God. But his wife said unto him, IF THE LORD WERE PLEASED TO KILL US, HE WOULD NOT HAVE RECEIVED A BURNT-OFFERING AND A MEAT-OFFERING AT OUR HANDS; NEITHER WOULD HE HAVE SHOWED US ALL THESE THINGS, NOR WOULD, AS AT THIS TIME, HAVE TOLD US SUCH THINGS AS THESE."

Considering all the circumstances, this was very remarkable language, and merits attention; not only as illustrative of the character of this excellent woman, but as furnishing a principle of sound and legitimate reasoning in the concerns of religion.

At first, being overawed by the majestic manifestation, both these pious people fell prostrate in the dust. A reverential awe pervaded their bosoms, at a sight so wonderful and so unexpected. The sentiments they felt were, doubtless, allied to those which dictated the exclamation of Jacob, "How dreadful is this place! this is none other than the house of God, and this is the gate of heaven:" or the humble tone of Isaiah, "Wo is me, for I am undone; because I am a man of unclean lips, and I dwell among a people of unclean lips; for mine eyes have seen the King, the Lord of Hosts." But if the divine appearance in mercy proved so terrific and overwhelming to pious persons in those extraordinary times; how tremendous will the second appearance of Christ in judgment be to his enemies, with the glory of his Father, and all the holy angels! If the splendour of his grace confound a mortal eye; what must be the lightning of his indignation, how intolerable the flaming fire of his displeasure!

On this occasion, Manoah appears the weaker believer. He thought of nothing but death; he expresses his confidence of perishing, and assigns a reason, which, however weak, is sufficiently accounted for by the extreme terror of his mind, and the universal prejudice of that age: "We shall surely die, for we have seen God." Even good men are sometimes tempted to listen to the suggestions of nature, rather than to the assurances of revelation; and to dread as an evil, what in their better moments is anticipated as a good. If death were the extinction of being, it might excite alarm; but, if it be only the means of our purification, and the preparatory process to fit the spiritual character for the felicities of a higher existence, it should, and often does, awaken pleasure. If, even while the shroud is worn by the body, the spirit is clothed with the garments of salvation, and that shroud will soon be exchanged for the white robe of purity and heaven; what is there to prevent our adopting the words of an apostle, "I have a *desire* to depart, and to be with Christ, which is far better?" If the apprehensions of Manoah had been really well founded, and himself and his beloved partner had yielded Up their spirits on that memorable spot; who can say it would have proved an undesirable exchange? As the servants of the living God, they were prepared for all events, and for either world. Their union could never have been dissolved, and the sphere of their spiritual discoveries would have been amply enlarged. To see God is the antidote, and not the occasion, of death; the hope, and not the terror, of the believer.

It is not difficult, however, to ascertain the reason why this prejudice so early and so extensively influenced the pious in primitive times. It arose from a consciousness of guilt, and a dread of merited punishment. As a sinner, man must necessarily tremble at the thought of his approaching God, or at the communication of any message from his throne: when God opens his mouth, he naturally fears the sentence; when tidings arrive from the invisible world, he dreads their purport, and conscience suggests that even the most favourable manifestations may be blended with tokens of displeasure. Every approach of the Deity is liable to excite confusion to a guilty world; and a sense of demerit may lead us not only to expect a warrant for execution when a reprieve is coming; but at first, like Manoah, to mistake and misinterpret the sign.

The wife of this good man entertained no such fears. With a faith which penetrated the divine intentions, at least in part, and which elevated her not only above the prejudices of the age, but gave her a decided superiority over her trembling partner, she suggested a far different conclusion, and intimated the reason on which it was founded. Her conclusions, the very opposite to his--so different are the *degrees* of grace in different characters--were deduced from three considerations. Each of these, in her view, was a decisive evidence against his suggestion, and a consoling reflection in this extraordinary and ambiguous moment.

The first was, *the acceptance of their sacrifices.* "If," said she, "the Lord be pleased to kill us, he would not have received a burnt-offering and a meat-offering at our hands." The law which prescribed the presentation of sacrifices, expressly represented them as "a *sweet savour* unto the Lord;" which implied not only an approbation of the offering, which was indeed of divine appointment, and could not therefore be rejected, but complacency in the worshipper. The *person* could not be disowned, while the *presentation* was acknowledged. If this sentiment needed any corroboration, the history of Cain and Abel would have furnished it. The acceptance and rejection of each was evinced by the divine treatment of their respective offerings. "The Lord had respect unto Abel, and to his offering: but unto Cain, and to his offering, he had not respect." When God entered into a solemn covenant with Abram, "a smoking furnace and a burning lamp passed between the divided pieces of the sacrifice, and consumed them." At the dedication of the tabernacle, when "the glory of the Lord appeared unto all the people, there came a fire out from before the Lord, and consumed upon the altar the burnt-offering and the fat; which when all the people saw, they shouted and fell on their. faces." The dedication of the temple was signalized by a similar manifestation. "Now, when Solomon had made an end of praying, the fire came down from heaven, and consumed the burnt-offering, and the sacrifices; and the glory of the Lord filled the house!" The same principle is fully-recognized by David, in the following supplications: "The Lord hear thee in the day of trouble, the name of the God of Jacob defend thee: Send thee help from the sanctuary, and strengthen thee out of Zion: Remember all thy burnt-offerings, and accept thy burnt-sacrifice." The argument, therefore, of Manoah's wife was pious, legitimate, and conclusive: "if *we* were to be destroyed, our *services* could not be approved."

The people of God too frequently resemble Manoah; but their doubts and fears would soon subside, could they be persuaded to adopt the reasoning of his wife. Past experience is a solid basis for future expectations. A succession of spiritual mercies is a pledge of kind intention, and of continued favour. In periods of despondency, recur to days of religious prosperity and happiness, when the candle of the Lord shone upon you, and spiritual enjoyments were dispensed in the use of means. Have you not good evidence, that your sacrifices *have been* received--your prayers heard, your dedication to God accepted? Have the spirit and efficacy of his promise evaporated in the lapse of time, "I will never leave you, nor forsake you?" or have you no reason to say with holy anticipation, "Surely goodness and mercy *shall* follow me all the days of my life, and I will dwell in the house of the Lord for ever?"

Feeble, imperfect, and disproportionate to our obligations, as all our offerings must be, they are acceptable to God by Jesus Christ. He has presented a sacrifice, "once for all," upon the cross, to which this subject naturally directs our attention, which constitutes the foundation of human hope, and secures a welcome reception, and gives an available power to all the future offerings of faith. The figurative nature of the ancient dispensations renders it not improbable, that these humble Israelites perceived, in the memorable transactions they witnessed, some typical representation of the work of redemption, some glimpses of the great atonement, and of the principle upon which what they offered was accepted. This event was not intended merely to astonish or overawe, but to instruct; and the wife of Manoah presents a noble example of that profound attention, which it becomes us to pay to all the revelations of Heaven. If, in particular, the "angels desire to look into" the mysteries of redeeming love, and consider the sabbath of eternity well employed in this research; mortals surely, who are more nearly interested, cannot devote the less sacred hours of time to a more important inquiry. Nor should they be satisfied with superficial, or indeed with *any* attainments in spiritual wisdom, which is so unfathomable in its depths, and illimitable in its extent.

The second consideration, which led to the inference in their own favour drawn by Manoah's wife, was *the wonders which the angel had shown them.* These were of a nature, in her belief, to justify her conclusion, that God did by no means purpose their ruin, but the reverse. It appears from the general expression, that "the angel did wondrously," in connection with the mention of "*all* these things," that some other manifestations, probably of a hieroglyphic or typical nature, were given antecedently, or as an immediate preparation to his miraculous ascent in the flame of the altar. This at least is certain, making a general application of the statement, that we are not only authorized to conclude from the privileges we enjoy, but from the spiritual discoveries we have made, that God is our Father and our Friend. He would not have pointed out our danger, and exhibited our remedy, if he had designed our ruin. Were we appointed to perish in our guilt, "the Physician of souls" would never have been commissioned to visit us. To be shown, by Scriptural statement, by ministerial instruction, and by providential guidance, the way to heaven, is no indication of an appointment to destruction. Have you not discovered the evil of sin, the value of the soul, and the excellency of Christ? Have you not felt the sorrows of repentance, and the joys of faith? Have you not touched the outstretched sceptre, submitted to the chastising rod, and gloried in the cross? God does not impart a fixed aversion to all iniquity, an intense desire after holiness, habitual delight in his word, and desire after his presence and glory; he does not impress a sense of the infinite excellence of the Saviour, and a readiness to sacrifice every thing to his will, and for his sake, excepting to holy souls, which are "born, not after the flesh, but after the Spirit."

The wife of Manoah adverted to a third source of consolation, at the period of this miraculous disappearance. She refers to *what they were told*. The assurances they had received of the birth of a son, rendered it impossible they should die. She had received very minute directions, both respecting her offspring and herself, who was to be consecrated as a Nazarite, and to rise up as the deliverer of his country from the yoke of Philistia. Possibly, during the preparation of the sacrifice, the inquisitive spirit of this thoughtful woman induced her to seek a conversation, which the celestial messenger was not unwilling to encourage, and during which they might have received some further instructions. Our fears are apt to betray us into absurdities, and confuse the memory; so that good men, like Manoah, speak or act inconsistently with themselves, and their own more deliberate convictions. Happy they who are blessed with an intelligent awl pious companion, whose kind suggestions may detect their errors, refresh their recollections, quell their fears, and comfort their desponding hours! Thus "two are better than one, because they have a good reward for their labour. For, if they fall, the one will lift up his fellow: but wo to him that is alone when he falleth; for he hath not another to help him."

Obvious but important considerations are deducible from this narrative, which seem capable of an application to the general concerns of life, as well as to the inquiries of religion.

1. We should avoid precipitancy of judgment. The wife of Manoah, in this view, appears in advantageous contrast to her hasty husband. She

did not suffer herself to be hurried into a discouraging inference, without reviewing the circumstances of the case, and allowing time for reflection. In the common affairs of life, an inconsiderate eagerness, either to escape from danger or to possess good, is often itself productive of the disappointment it dreads; while a proper deliberation prepares the mind either for failure or success: and, in the pursuit of moral and religions inquiries, the same precipitancy is calculated to plunge into error, which, if it do not always endanger our salvation, may disturb our peace. Jesus Christ has expressly exhorted us to close and deliberate investigation, intimating that our labour will be repaid by discovery; for "searching the Scriptures," and acquiring a knowledge of him respecting whom they "testify," and "whom to know is life eternal," are inseparably connected. On another occasion, when describing the true hearer of his word, he suggests a comparison equally and beautifully illustrative of the necessity of a diligent use of the means of instruction, and that serious, profound, and careful inquiry, which is calculated to prevent an implicit submission to the opinion of others, or taking our religion upon trust. "Whosoever cometh to me, and heareth my sayings, and doeth them, I will show you to whom he is like. He is like a man which built a house, and digged deep, and laid the foundation on a rock; and when the flood arose, the stream beat vehemently upon that house, and could not shake it, for it was founded upon a rock."

2. It is wise, and may be useful, on all proper occasions, to avow our convictions. Selfishness and timidity may concur to suggest a different proceeding: but religion requires that we act upon principles superior to those of worldly policy. Manoah had every reason to be grateful to his wife, for the distinct and prompt avowal of her sentiments; which, though contradictory to his, were adapted to rouse him from his despondency and stupor. She was, no doubt, ready to sympathize with his distress; but duty to God, attachment to her husband, a consciousness of knowing the truth, and even a proper respect to herself, prompted a statement of her disagreement with his opinions. When religion claims our services, we must not withhold the offering of our lips, or the labour of our hands, through fear of danger or hope of gain. When truth demands that we should speak, or Providence that we should act, it would be criminal--it would be disgraceful, to continue silent or inactive.

To generalize and apply these remarks to the circumstances in which Christianity has placed us--it is required not only to believe in Christ, but explicitly to avow our sentiments of attachment to his Gospel by a public profession, whether we meet with the concurrence, or suffer the opposition, of our dearest friends. Timidity is natural to the female mind; but religion requires even the youngest and the weakest of the sex, not to suffer even natural delicacy to degenerate, by excessive indulgence, into criminal shame. It does more, it enables women to become heroes and martyrs! Inflamed with the love it inspires, they have learned to see no lions, to fear no dangers, to feel no pains in the path of duty; not only evincing patience, but expressing joy.

Jesus Christ was "not ashamed to call us *brethren*," to assume our nature, to fill our humble station, to suffer our sorrows, or to die for us an ignominious death; he is not ashamed to own his connection with us now he is in the highest heavens, or to be engaged in preparing a mansion, in his Father's house, for our final reception. Shall we be ashamed of him, or of his cause? Shall we tremble to avow our attachment, if we feel it? This would expose us to the censure of our own consciences, to the reproach of a dishonourable, hesitating, indecisive conduct; and, above all, to the Saviour's final malediction, as the Judge of mankind. It is the design of Christ to establish an interest in the world; and this is to be maintained, not by fear, but by firmness: not by temporal compliances, but by holy resistance; not by sloth, inactivity, and shrinking into a corner, but by "putting on the whole armour of God." Not to be *for* Christ is to be *against* him--neutrality is enmity--a refusal to enlist under his banners is disloyalty, rebellion, and treason!

3. The providence of God does never *really*, though it may *apparently* and to human apprehension, contradict his word or discredit his character. The present manifestation of the angel in flame and terror, did not subvert the confidence which the wife of Manoah felt in his past declarations, nor excite despondency respecting future events. The fears of her husband did not shake her faith in the promises of God, nor did the incomprehensible nature of the mystery blind her perceptions of the concealed mercy. We are very inadequate judges of the divine conduct. It is neither possible, nor proper, that we should know the mighty plan of his operations; and it can never be a sufficient reason, even under the most disastrous circumstances, for questioning the goodness or wisdom of his dispensations that *we* cannot comprehend them. The designs of God are very imperfectly unravelled in the present world. We can see but to a short distance, nor is it necessary that we should. *Some* light from the sacred page beams across the path of life; but if we cannot at present attain all we may wish to know, let us be contented to wait for the manifestations of eternity. In the mean time we may rest assured, that whatever is thought contradictory in the dispensations of Providence to the written word, is but *seemingly* so. It is so merely because we cannot now see the connecting links, the unbroken chain of events, which, when the clouds that obscure this earthly atmosphere shall be finally dispersed, will become distinctly and for ever visible.

Hannah Chapter X

Section I

"Where there is *piety*," says an excellent commentator, "'tis pity but there should be *unity*." There is, however, too frequent occasion to deplore the dissentions of families, whose religious profession induces us to expect the prevalence of peace and harmony. Nevertheless, these inconsistencies are so far from being justly chargeable upon religion, that they furnish the most decisive evidence of its value. It is in consequence of a departure from its genuine spirit, and a compliance with the suggestion of evil principles and passions, that individuals are rendered miserable and families distracted. The renewal of that "right spirit" which it inculcates, is the direct means of restoring personal comfort and domestic tranquillity.

The Psalmist represents "the law of the Lord" as "*perfect:*" it is the only solid-basis of human felicity; and every hope that is differently founded, must prove, inevitably prove, a shadowy super-structure. A deviation from the order and appointments of Heaven is a proportionate departure from happiness; for this order and these appointments do not result from caprice, but a perfect combination of goodness and wisdom. The divine system of legislation is formed with a merciful regard to our best interests, and an entire knowledge of our nature. Its arrangements are not arbitrary, but kind; and obedience is no less essential to our real welfare, both present and eternal, than it is expressive of a just regard to our obligations. In opposing the requirements of God, man is an enemy to himself; his resistance is not only culpable, but ruinous.

These observations are fully exemplified in the history of Hannah, and the family of which she was the female head. Her husband, whose name was Elkanah, resided at a place in the tribe of Ephraim, called Ramathaim-zophim. He is mentioned as having descended from Zuph an Ephrathite, or inhabitant of Bethlehem-Judah, which is Ephratah, probably with the view of showing his connection with David. As persons have sometimes conferred distinction upon places, so places have occasionally dignified persons. Who would not have thought it an honour to be born at Bethlehem, whence the light of the world first proceeded, and where such wonderful events were to be afterward transacted? And yet it is but an adventitious honour, which will soon fade, if it be not sustained by personal character and real excellence.

Elkanah had two wives; Hannah, the subject of this history, and Peninnah. Here we trace the origin of the infelicity of this religious household. It is strange that the experience of past ages, the incongruity of such a practice in itself, and the unauthorized nature of such a proceeding, should not have prevented him from forming two matrimonial connections at the same time. If polygamy were not expressly interdicted by a law, but rather tolerated in an age of imperfect revelation, like the plan of divorce to which our Saviour alludes, for "the hardness of their hearts;" it had plainly no foundation in reason, no sanction from Heaven; and not only no good consequences attached to it, but it was commonly attended with calamitous results. Every recorded instance of it proves its extreme inexpediency. It seldom failed to involve the comfort of all parties, and must be regarded as a proof of weakness, if not absolutely of a criminal indulgence of passion, even when adopted under the most plausible pretences. If the Creator had at first perceived that a plurality of wives was conducive to human felicity, he would have bestowed more than one upon man in his paradisiacal state. Infinite wisdom must have known what was really best; and the inspired narrative shows that infinite goodness pursued every conceivable method of completing the enjoyment of him who was placed, both in point of capacity and authority, at the summit of creation.

There is a marked difference between the two women whom Elkanah had espoused. In most cases of contention, considerable blame attaches to all the parties concerned. We hear of provocations and insults on the one hand, of recriminations and resentments on the other. Whoever originates the dispute, an irreconcilcable spirit in both usually perpetuates it. Hannah, reproached as she was by Peninnah for her barrenness, does not seem to have returned railing for railing. The haughty behaviour, indeed, of her rival, made her the more deeply sensible of her affliction, and fretted her almost into despondency. Day after day, she was ridiculed for what implied no blame, and admitted of no remedy. With how much greater reason might she have retorted upon Peninnah her malignant temper and provoking tongue! What was her natural infirmity, in comparison with the slanderer's moral defilement! How misplaced the censures of the one! How admirable the patience of the other!

This disagreement presents a fair occasion of remarking upon a practice too much tolerated in society, for which young persons especially cannot be too strongly reprehended. It is the cruel conduct of despising others for their natural imperfections, turning their blameless deformities into ridicule, and speaking ill of them for defects which ought rather to excite the deepest commiseration. Perhaps the persons who suffer this unmerited contempt, possess qualities of a mental and moral description, which ought to conciliate the esteem and excite the imitation of the fair and graceful slanderer. Perhaps they have a cultivated mind and a pious spirit, while she has nothing but a pretty countenance or an attractive form. But how ill is wisdom compensated by beauty, and how disgraceful is it to despise the work of God's hands! If the object of offensive remark should happen to be endowed with neither wisdom nor symmetry, is it becoming of you, my reader, to institute an arbitrary standard of gracefulness, and despise every one who has not attained it! Is it for you to aggravate as a crime, what reason teaches is, at worst, a misfortune? Is it for you to calumniate those who have given you no personal offence; who are, notwithstanding their disadvantages, good members of society; and if in some respects defective, may not be vicious? But if the latter were the case, if they exhibited a combination of exterior deformity and interior depravity, they would not then be the proper objects of *ridicule*. The former peculiarity would still merit pity, and indeed forbid observance; the latter would require more serious treatment.

In many instances, perhaps in the majority, young persons are guilty of this misconduct through inadvertency. They have been stimulated to it by others, or they have never been impressed with a sense of its impropriety. It has been the result of thoughtlessness, rather than of malignity. It was not their design to injure, but to seek amusement. Let parents and tutors, therefore, explain the evil of such practices; let such as read these pages meditate upon its enormity, and be solicitous of cultivating those benign and benevolent feelings which peculiarly adorn their early age, and are inculcated by the religion and the example of Christ.

To return to the family of Elkanah. This worthy man did not allow domestic dissentions to interrupt his religious duties. He went up to the worship of the Lord in Shiloh at the yearly festivals, according to the appointments of the law. "Unto the place which the Lord your God shall choose out of all your tribes to put his name there, even unto his habitation shall ye seek, and thither thou shall come; and thither ye shall bring your burnt-offerings, and your sacrifices, and your tithes and heave-offerings of your hand, and your vows, and your free-will-offerings, and the firstlings of your herds and of your flocks. And there ye shall eat before the Lord your God, and ye shall rejoice in all that ye put your hand unto, you and your households, wherein the Lord thy God hath blessed thee."

In the services of religion, it becomes us to ascend above all temporal considerations, and regard exclusively the will of God. Elkanah, however, even at the solemn and public festival, unhappily gave a worthy or double portion to Hannah, which was the ancient mode of expressing peculiar affection. This was likely to inflame, rather than to extinguish strife; and though done, no doubt, with the kind attention of alleviating the sorrows of his best beloved partner, was a sad display of weakness, and a miserable profanation of the worship of God. Peninnah had children, Hannah the affections of her husband; the former persecutes, and the other weeps. Who would not have indulged the pleasing hope, that the worship of God, that cement of society, that healing remedy for the disorders of the moral world, would have quieted contention; and that the flames of animosity would not have mingled with the hallowed fires of sacrifice! It was well meant in Elkanah to bring all his household together to the tabernacle in Shiloh--

"Religion should extinguish strife,
And make a calm of human life."

If we cannot be reconciled at the altar, it is an indication of rooted antipathy, and will neutralize the effect of our entreaties for divine forgiveness. "If I regard iniquity in my heart, the Lord," said David, "will not hear me." The salutary effect of Elkanah's measure was prevented by the continuance of discord. Year after year this mischievous spirit prevailed. Elkanah was unable to conciliate Peninnah, or to sooth Hannah. The good man was rendered wretched, both by the temper of the one and the tears of the other: the latter, however, was the most intolerable. "Hannah," said he, "why weepest thou? why eatest thou not? and why is thy heart grieved? Am not I better to thee than ten sons?"

There is something soothing and gentle in this remonstrance, which bespeaks the affection of Elkanah, and exhibits his pacific character in an advantageous light. He does not directly interpose to settle the point of domestic difference by the stern dictation of authority, but with a kind hand endeavours to wipe away the falling tears of his disconsolate wife. Nothing is more difficult than properly to administer reproof, except it be properly to receive it. Elkanah seems, on this occasion, to have managed it with extreme delicacy, and with happy success. He kindly insinuated, that she ought to feel consolation in her husband's regard; and that a becoming submission to Providence is at all times our duty. She might have suffered not only the affliction which she so deeply deplored, but the still greater distress of her partner's aversion. If he had been alienated, or even if his regard had been only diminished, there would have existed a more plausible pretence for incessant grief; but although Peninnah was blest with children, Hannah was best beloved. Would the latter have been willing to exchange advantages? would she have descended from a pre-eminence so justly valued, for the sake of a family? Doubtless it was her wish to unite these comforts; to retain the love of Elkanah, and to rival the children of Peninnah. But it is our duty, and would prove eminently conducive to our happiness, to improve the blessings we enjoy, rather than to cherish undue solicitude for what Providence does not see fit to confer.

There does, by no means, exist that inequality in the distribution of divine favours, which our impatience tempts us to imagine. One thing is set over against another; comforts are associated with crosses: and if we were in a situation, or possessed a capacity, to estimate with exactness the proportion of good and evil in the individual condition of mankind, it is more than probable we should find the balances by which these proportions are determined most accurately poised. We *may* safely, and *ought* unhesitatingly, to trust the hands in which they are placed, and the power that regulates their distribution.

If the language of Elkanah may be considered as honourable to his general spirit, the silent obedience of Hannah was no less illustrative of her extraordinary excellence. How many tempera would have been exasperated by such an appeal; and instead of drying up the tears of grief, and proceeding to partake food, would have instantly retorted both upon the intercessor and the rival! She might have demanded why her husband, instead of asking her to conceal her sorrows, did not rather reprove the provoking conduct of Peninnah, and silence her exasperating tongue? Availing herself of the decided preference shown her, she might have aimed at making her husband a party in the dispute; and, by his means, have triumphed over her adversary. But Hannah was influenced by far different sentiments. To her husband's remonstrances she appears to have returned no answer: nor was it a sullen silence; for she took food, interrupted no longer the festivities of the occasion, but, painful as the struggle must have been, heroically concealed her own feelings till the termination of the public solemnities.

"After they had eaten in Shiloh, and after they had drunk," Hannah continued in "bitterness of soul," and rose up to withdraw. But whither did she go? Whither, under circumstances like these, was it natural for her to fly? Perhaps into solitude to bemoan her sad situation, to pour out her unrestrained tears, to anathematize her insulting rival, to plot revenge, to curse the day of her birth. The stream of grief and complaint might be expected to flow, in the secret hour, with accelerated force and rapidity, proportioned to the restraint which publicity had imposed. She did not, however, yield to this influence, or retire for such a purpose. Perhaps she withdrew to seek the counsel of a friend, or solicit the prompt interference of others who pitied her sufferings, to check Peninnah, or to stimulate Elkanah to stronger measures. Such a proceeding was not unlikely; it was not, however, the one she adopted. Perhaps, then, it may be supposed, she went home to wait for some favourable opportunity of urging her husband to discard Peninnah, and of exasperating his prejudices against her. It was indeed *natural* for her to pursue either or of all these courses; but she chose a different one. The pious mourner has another and a better resource. If she look around her for comfort in vain, she can look above. She may be pressed on every side--difficulties and distresses accumulating in every direction--foes behind, and seas of trouble before--but the opening into heaven is free; the ear of mercy is not shut; the way of access to God never can be closed! "And she vowed a vow, and said, O Lord of hosts, if thou wilt indeed look on the affliction of thine handmaid, and remember me, and not forget thine handmaid, but wilt give unto thine handmaid a man-child, then I will give him unto the Lord all the days of his life, and there shall no razor come upon his head."

This solemn address to Heaven exemplifies some of the essential qualities of genuine prayer. It is marked by *reverence* and *godly* fear; for she appeals to "the Lord of hosts," whose prerogative it is to marshal the celestial armies, and to regulate with undeviating skill and irresistible influence the affairs of this lower world: it displays profound *humility*; for she repeats the simple and self-abasing term, "thine handmaid:" it expresses *submission* and *dependence* of spirit; for she refers with implicit obedience to the determinations of the divine will, as comprising whatever is best calculated to promote her real interests, though without presumption, she solicits Omnipotent interference to remove her affliction, if it should comport with the arrangements, and seem proper to the wisdom of God; it manifests an importunity which will always operate with more or less intenseness in every genuine prayer. Her solemn vow, her judicious repetitions, her whole phraseology, evince this prevailing disposition. She kindles with holy fervour, and seems to stretch forth her eager hand to take the blessing which she cannot persuade herself will be refused. She is fully aware that power and goodness combine in perfect proportions to influence the dispensations of the God whom she addresses, and pleads with success, because she pleads with fervour.

Nor is Hannah the first or the last witness to the apostolic assurance: "the effectual fervent prayer of the righteous availeth much." It is not indeed insinuated, that importunity in soliciting favours is invariably successful. Unquestionably, many considerations of propriety, necessity, and adaptation, must be understood to enter into the account. The spirit of dictation must not blend with that of earnestness, nor must we deem ourselves qualified to determine the time, the manner, or the proportion of divine communications; but, so far as relates to the spirit of prayer, importunity is materially connected with success, and coldness with failure: the former advances, and the latter negatives our supplications, even while we present them. There are cases of extraordinary ardour, which can be measured by no common standard; moments of outgoing after God, seasons of inexpressible sensibility, when the mind possesses an invincible persuasion of success, which is at once the dictate of the Holy Spirit, and the certain indication of acceptance. Faith discerns the blessing, with a distinctness hitherto unknown, and love burns with a vigour hitherto unfelt. A certain persuasion pervades the soul that its entreaties cannot fail, that the contemplated good is its destined portion; and amidst the deepest, the most unusual impression of unworthiness, its assurance is sustained by a vivid remembrance of the promises, and an overwhelming consciousness of personal interest in them: all obstacles seem to remove, or to vanish at the first touch; every thing yields before the pursuit of zeal, distance disappears, time dwindles into a moment, and the mind at once enters upon a paradise of possession. In the very midst of discouragements, the supplicant becomes a hero, and triumphs by *a prevailing power*, analogous to that of a great conqueror, whose very consciousness of superiority wins an otherwise doubtful battle, and gives him a victory even by anticipation. Amidst the provocations of her rival, and the soothings of her husband, Hannah could only weep and fast: but at the footstool of mercy, she wrestles like Jacob, and prevails like Israel. She rises above herself, no longer the despised and desponding mourner, but the accepted and the triumphant supplicant. Thus devotion not only sanctifies, but ennobles character. It awakens all the energies of our nature, directs them to their proper object, and supplies an ample sphere for their exercise. It produces extraordinary elevation, and creates a heaven in the exercise of faith, and in the sphere of duty.

It cannot excite surprise, that a mere spectator, even though he be a pious spectator, should, on such occasions as these, mistake the outward indications of inward feeling. Objections will sometimes arise in persons of cooler temperament or more constitutional apathy to the enthusiasm of younger and more ardent Christians, founded altogether in misapprehension, not like those of the world, in impious dislike. That the latter should miscal the holy ecstacies of religion enthusiastic and rhapsodical, we do not wonder; since they *cannot* understand them by that medium through which alone they become comprehensible, the medium of *experience*: nor need we feel much astonishment at the occasional mistakes of the former, when it is recollected, that the external indications of the passions are often equivocal.

This was the case with Hannah. Eli, the venerable priest, was sitting upon a seat by a post of the temple; and either from want of charity, or a defect of eyesight, he pronounced a precipitate judgment upon this good woman, whom he strangely imagined to have been in a state of intoxication.

Hannah, it appears, "spake in her heart; only her lips moved, but her voice was not heard." This excited the unjust suspicions of Eli, who immediately charged her with gross immorality. "How long" said he, "wilt thou be drunken? Put away thy wine from thee."

It may be admitted, as an extenuation of this rude attack, that the good priest was jealous for the honour of his God, whose temple he supposed was suffering profanation by indecent conduct: and that, instead of turning tale-bearer and whisperer, he openly expressed his sentiments to the party concerned, affording an opportunity for acknowledgment or explanation. Still his precipitancy cannot be justified. It was his duty to have obtained better evidence, before he ventured upon such a crimination; or, at least, to have been more ceremonious and considerate. Reproof may be well merited; but, in order that its end be answered, it should be properly administered. Gentleness and mercy should blend their benign influences with justice. We are ourselves liable to error, and have no right to assume the tone of severity, or the air of triumph, when required to notice blameable conduct. If we should be mistaken, either in the general fact, or in the circumstances, upon some of which we may have dwelt with unkind severity, the reproof will not only affect us by a strong and most unwelcome reaction, but in many instances furnish the transgressor with means of defending himself in what was actually wrong, and thus nullify *our* testimony, and harden *his* mind.

Admirable, indeed, was the reply of Hannah. "No, my lord," said she, "I am a woman of sorrowful spirit, I have drunk neither wine nor strong drink, but have poured out my soul before the Lord. Count not thine handmaid for a daughter of Belial; for out of the abundance of my complaint and grief have I spoken hitherto."

Nothing could be a more complete vindication of herself than this respectful, dispassionate, and dignified language. She merely disclaims the unjust imputation of her accuser, and explains the true cause of her emotions. If she had been resentful and clamorous, the suspicion of Eli would rather have been confirmed than removed; but her innocence shone forth as the noon-day, unclouded by irritability or violence.

There is usually a marked difference between innocence and guilt, in the mode of treating accusations: the latter boisterous and impatient; the former gentle, calm, and moderate, comparatively careless of misrepresentations, and often silent; the latter adopts any artifice to shun the light, the former affords every facility to investigation. If a character be free from the stain of guilt, it will not shrink from those proceedings which tend to hold it up to the light, and which of course only exhibit its perfect transparency.

Eli, perceiving his mistake, disdains to persist in it. Like a man of integrity and piety, he corrects himself at once, dismisses her with a blessing, and prays for her success. This was making the best possible reparation, and it was done with a promptness which evinced its sincerity. The good man was as ready to express his approbation, when convinced of Hannah's innocence, as he had been to censure her conduct, when he imagined it to be culpable.

In this transaction, we perceive him practising one of the most difficult of duties; and if the wife of Elkanah be worthy of imitation for a respectful and modest defence against a false accusation, the pious priest of the Lord is no less so for retracting a hasty judgment, and instantly exchanging frowns for smiles, reproof for applause, cursing for blessing. In most cases, the offending party is the last to be reconciled; and mistake is frequently adhered to with an obstinacy, and defended with a pertinacity, proportioned to the haste with which it has been adopted. Look inward. What is the present state of your minds respecting the errors you have committed, or the wrong steps you have taken, and of which you are deeply conscious? Have you adopted any measures to give satisfaction to an injured party, or, are you disposed to that concession which you know your past improprieties require? To trifle with the character of another is cruel--to persist in misrepresentation is wicked. Can you expect pardon of God, while living in the indulgence of an unforgiving spirit towards your fellow-creatures? Justice requires, and Christianity insists, upon reparation. O listen to their united voice! Hasten to wipe off the stain which your carelessness, or your malignity, has flung upon the white robe of innocence! Hasten to dry up the tears which you have caused the sufferer to shed: hasten to heal the wound you have foolishly, perhaps wickedly, inflicted.

This duty, remember, is not superseded even by the ill conduct of the person you have made your foe. If, instead of submitting to your unkindness, or bearing your mistake with the meekness of Hannah, you have been loudly denounced--if you have been represented as a calumniator, and railing has been rendered for railing--if the injured person have even taken advantage of your error to reproach you in turn, and circulated a thousand mis-statements to your disadvantage, you are still under the greatest obligations to correct and apologize for your original error. Never can you be justified in the eyes of impartial men; never can you stand upon the high ground of an unblemished reputation, and become invulnerable to attack; never can you obtain the divine approbation, till you have adopted this measure. Neither conscience, reason, nor religion, will admit that the aspersions of another justify your slanders. His persistance is no reason against your concession.

Restored to tranquillity and happiness, Hannah withdrew from the temple, and "her countenance was no more sad." Her innocence was apparent to the priest, her petition heard in heaven. She went up weeping, she returned rejoicing. Devotion had pacified her troubled breast, and since "committing her way to the Lord," the tide had ebbed, the sky had cleared. She knew that her request would be granted, or, if denied, that she should see occasion ultimately to feel perfect acquiescence and satisfaction in the determinations of Providence. She, therefore, wiped away her tears, and dismissed her anxiety. Such is the relief afforded by humble prayer. How often has sorrow been transformed into joy by religious exercises! From the dark vale of life, where the winds blow and the rains descend, how often has the pious mourner ascended to that sacred mount of communion with God, *the closet*, or to the "*holy hill of Zion*," and dwelt in the sunshine of heaven! Agitated no longer with conflicting elements, and mysterious events, the clouds have appeared far, far below; while the omnipotent hand has been seen engaged in regulating their movements, directing their course, and preparing to disperse them in every direction.

It is obvious that no combination of happy circumstances, no human power, no earthly friendship, could have afforded substantial consolation to Hannah, if she had not repaired to the mercy-seat. Already had her affectionate husband attempted, in vain, to sooth her grief. He had renewed his love, wiped off her tears, kindly remonstrated and reasoned with her.-- Hannah! "am not I better to thee than ten sons?" Ah! what avails it! Elkanah can sympathize, but he cannot relieve--he can reason, but he cannot remove the cause of her sorrows--he cannot turn the course of nature, or renew the springs of existence--he cannot change weakness for strength, or convert barrenness into fertility: but he who has all resources in his hands, all elements and worlds at his disposal, *can*; and, at the voice of prayer, *will* accomplish the holy desires of the mind. See, Christians, your best resource, your ultimate appeal, your distinguished privilege! "God sitteth upon the throne of his holiness."

Henceforward, the sacred narrative omits the name of Peninnah, and there is nothing in her history to induce a wish to penetrate the concealing veil. She was, in fact, originally introduced to notice for the purpose of illustrating the more valuable qualities of Hannah, whose excellence continues to shine with indiminished lustre to the end of her days. It is indeed profitable, as a warning, to contemplate specimens of moral deformity as well as examples of moral worth; but we naturally hasten from the offensive, to the pleasing and attractive forms of female character. Peninnah perishes unregretted from the page--Hannah continues to adorn it, and obtains an everlasting remembrance.

On the day fixed for the return of this pious family, it is stated that they rose early in the morning, and worshipped before the Lord. It is deplorable, that so many of our thoughtless race should live from day to day, and from year to year, in a state of perfect estrangement from the duties of devotion. Whirled about in the circle of dissipation, or busied with the cares of the world, they forget God their Maker; and, though the constant recipients of mercies which flow to them in uninterrupted succession, they never acknowledge, they can scarcely be said to know the Giver. The most important transactions, schemes, and journeys, are undertaken without once committing themselves to the guidance or protection of that Providence which is observant of their steps, and supplies them, notwithstanding their ingratitude. How pleasantly do *they* proceed, who, like the family of Elkanah, first solemnly present themselves before the Lord, and commence every business and every day with an act of worship! It is true they are not exempted from misfortune, or rendered invulnerable to the attacks of evil; but they are well prepared for, and will be graciously sustained in every vicissitude.

[Sidenote: Years before Christ, 1155.]

The predestined hour having arrived, a son was born to Hannah, whom she named *Samuel*; "because," said she, "I have asked him of the Lord." Sometimes, what has been sought with importunity, is received with coldness, or enjoyed with ingratitude. No sooner is the blessing bestowed, no sooner is the tear of agony dried up, than every pledge is forgotten, and the mind relapses into thankless indifference. The sun shines, and our impressions pass away with the storm. But Hannah adopted a measure well calculated to excite every member of the family, and his mother in particular, to a perpetual recurrence to the goodness of Providence. She was resolved upon an expedient, by which the flame of gratitude might be kept incessantly burning in her breast. Could she ever look upon *Samuel* without recollecting he was "asked of God?" Could she ever repeat the name of her beloved first-born, without thinking of the Hearer of prayer? Amidst the ecstasies of maternal love, when she witnessed the infant sportings, and traced the expanding faculties of her Samuel, how often would she remember the stirrings of her spirit, and the sad days of her reproach. Once she had scarcely indulged the hope of being a mother, much less the mother of so remarkable a child. Once she wept in bitterness of soul, now she shed tears of parental transport.

Assiduity in the discharge of maternal duties is the next distinguishing excellence of Hannah to which our attention is invited. The sensibilities of her character seemed to have remarkably qualified her for the new station she was called to occupy after the birth of her child.

Providence has so wisely and so kindly ordered the connection subsisting between the parent and the offspring, and has rendered human nature, even in its depraved state, so susceptible of fine impressions and feelings, that the moment this relationship commences, a sort of new character is superinduced.

When a dependant little being is presented, a careful and protecting disposition is generally displayed; the arm of support is readily held forth to the weakness of infancy, and the most inconsiderate and volatile of women are, by a natural instinct--a certain powerful, indefinable transformation--converted to sober habits and necessary attentiveness--Who can withhold his admiration of this singular economy, or refuse to admit the interference of an invisible and wonderworking God! If this be the effect in ordinary instances, it is easy to imagine that the wife of Elkanah proved an exemplary instance of diligence and goodness when she became a mother. For such an honourable situation she was peculiarly qualified by her gentleness and piety. The precious gift, for which she had been so solicitous, was nursed with fondness, and eventually presented with all a mother's, with all a Christian's joy, to the Lord in Shiloh.

At the next anniversary festival, Elkanah went up to fulfil a vow he had made, and to renew the dedication of himself and his family to the divine service. Hannah accompanied him in spirit, but was prevented from a personal attendance by her little lovely dependant: she intimated to her husband the propriety of her remaining at home, pledging herself to undertake the pleasing journey when the child was weaned. "Then," said she, "I will bring him, that he may appear before the Lord, and there abide for ever." It is no honour to religion for its professors to neglect the duties of civil life under the pretence of superior sanctity: in vain do those who disregard their families apologize for their misconduct by pleading their diligence in pious services. Religion not only requires a punctuality of observance in reference to its more public engagements, but demands an unremitted attention to those of a more private, social, and domestic nature: these ought not indeed to be viewed apart, in a separate and disunited form, but as constituting a beautiful whole. Religion, in fact, consists both in diligence and devotion, in the occupation of our stations in society, as well as in fulfilling the services of the sanctuary; in nursing and educating the child, as well as in presenting the sacrifice, or keeping the holy festival of saints.

Elkanah fully concurred with the arrangements of Hannah. Happy is it for that family where the domestic hearth is cheered by love and the altar by piety. Happy they, whose affection, planted in religion, resembles a flourishing tree that spreads its shade over the united household. Hannah consulted her husband, and stated the reasons of the plan she had devised- -Elkanah listened to the representations of his wife, and instantly assented.

"Do," said he, "what seemeth thee good; tarry until thou hast weaned him; only the Lord establish his word. So the woman abode, and gave her son suck until she weaned him."

How beautiful is the allusion of the royal psalmist to this important period in the history of infancy: "Lord, my heart is not haughty, nor mine eyes lofty, neither do I exercise myself in great matters, or in things too high for me. Surely I have behaved and quieted myself as a child that, is weaned of his mother: my soul is even as a weaned child."

It costs, indeed, a severe struggle to alienate the little offspring from the breast from which it has drawn the means of subsistence, and, for a short time, uneasiness and fretfulness may be the result; but when the days of weaning are accomplished, the long-valued provision is regarded with total indifference. Strong is the conflict and sharp the encounter between a sense of duty and an inclination to sin, when the world presents those fascinating pleasures which are so adapted to the appetites of nature; but having obtained the victory--having, through the grace of God, triumphed over the enticement, a real Christian will contemplate the glories of this world which once enchanted him, with an indifferent eye, and seek more substantial blessings. What naturally afforded satisfaction, will, in a renewed state of mind, excite aversion or be treated with neglect. The propensity being conquered, will never, or but partially return, and if not absolutely exterminated, it can never again acquire an ascendancy. The soul is become, in reference to the fleeting honours and possessions of time, like a "weaned child."

It is at once our duty and felicity to aim at this detachment of affection from the vanities of life, to cherish a holy disinclination toils allurements, and to seek our bliss in the unfading good which Scripture recommends and Heaven dispenses. An interest in the love of God, by faith in the Redeemer, is the supreme enjoyment to which we are encouraged to aspire, and which alone can fill the capacities and consummate the blessedness of intelligent and immortal creatures. Pitiable is the situation of those who are still attached, with childish fondness, to what cannot promote their spiritual growth, and befits not their advancing maturity. "Let Israel," then, "hope in the Lord from henceforth and for ever."

Section II

As soon as the time proposed by Hannah had elapsed, she thought of fulfilling her vow, and hastened to Shiloh. In the days of her distress she had pledged herself to devote her child to the service of God; in the days of her prosperity she does not forget the obligation. Never, so far as we can discover, was a more perfect example of female excellence and persevering religion: in adversity and in prosperity, in sorrow and in joy, the light of her piety shone with undiminishing splendour. She had virtues appropriate to every season, and conspicuous in every situation: in affliction she cannot be reproached with impatience, nor in success with ingratitude.

When Samuel was weaned, she took him with her, with three bullocks, an ephah of flour, and a bottle of wine, determining to leave him with the priest, for the purpose of being trained up to the service of the tabernacle. It was an equal honour to the pupil and the tutor, the one to have such a priest as Eli, the other to have such a child as Samuel. With all the dignity of innocence and all the pleasure of devotion, she presented the little stranger to Eli, reminding him of the occasion when she first pledged herself to consecrate the child she requested to the work of the sanctuary, and explaining a vow of which he was previously ignorant. It is true that God and her own soul were the only witnesses and hearers of this vow; but she did not deem it the less obligatory though it was made in secret, nor was her upright mind the less anxious for its punctual fulfilment: "And they slew a bullock, and brought the child to Eli. And she said, O my lord, as thy soul liveth, my lord, I am the woman that stood by thee here, praying unto the Lord. For this child I prayed; and the Lord hath given me my petition which I asked of him: therefore also I have lent him to the Lord: as long as he liveth he shall be lent to the Lord."

There is an exquisite delicacy in this language. The allusion to her former appearance in the house of God is as cursory as could be devised to enable the good priest to recognize her. Eli is reminded of her former prayers; but not a syllable is uttered tending to criminate or to reflect upon his past precipitancy and misrepresentation. She tells a simple story, in a candid and respectful manner. The points of deepest interest are introduced, and her darling child is devoted forever, and with unreluctant zeal, to the God of her salvation.

Let the impatient and revengeful study the example of Hannah, who did not allow herself to utter an angry word, or even to cherish a resentful feeling against Eli, when he preferred against her an inconsiderate and aggravating accusation; much less did she indulge a spirit of malignity. How many would have felt an invincible aversion, even though his frank acknowledgment had compelled them to a momentary reconciliation; and, viewing his character ever after through the medium of prejudice, would have magnified every feeling, and flung their public reproaches, or circulated their secret whispers and surmises against this venerable minister of the tabernacle. It becomes the people of God to be careful of the reputation of their brethren, and aim to wipe off the aspersions with which the world is apt to depreciate their characters, rather than to unite in the clamours of defamation. Men in official situations are placed upon a pinnacle which renders them conspicuous, and envy is always ready to shoot at them its envenomed darts. They have their faults indeed, but let charity cover them: they may have also their counterbalancing excellencies--let piety observe and imitate them. Should the criminal conduct of such persons belie their general profession, dishonour the religion they profess, and render it necessary to displace them, we ought to tremble for ourselves, and not triumph in their fall. Who would be qualified to cast the first stone, if his offences were all detected, exposed, and treated with merciless severity? The practice of dedicating children to God, is, we perceive, sanctioned by the usage of high antiquity; but, what is far better, it is conformable to reason and Scripture. Sometimes, indeed, it is accompanied with much absurdity and superstition; but, when properly attended to, it secures many advantages. Prayer, at all times important, is peculiarly effectual when offered in so solemn a manner: and if, in ordinary cases, it procure the blessings of Heaven, a well-founded hope may be excited, that the interesting little object of such a service will reap some substantial benefits. It tends besides to purify the domestic affections, and to regulate their exercise. The child which is bestowed in answer to prayer, and by prayer is, at the very dawn of existence, consecrated to God, and committed to the future care and guidance of his providence, is regarded with a new kind of feeling even by its parents; their fondness receives a peculiar tone and character from their piety; the motive to seek its spiritual interest is strengthened by their holy vows; and they cannot but feel an additional motive to impart early instruction, to cultivate its expanding faculties, and form the young immortal both for its present and ultimate destination.

Devote, then, ye mothers of Israel, devote your babes to piety and God! Hesitate not to incur the solemn responsibility which a vow implies in reference to your tender offspring: it is the most immediate method of making them your future comforts in this life, and your companions in a better. Your solicitude will at least afford you personal satisfaction; you will inherit the delightful consciousness of having done your duty: you may be happily instrumental in producing early impressions, and preparing them for their future crown. Then, should they depart from the world before you, to be "forever with the Lord," they will rise from their thrones of light to hail your approach, and mingle their thanksgivings and praises with yours in the songs of eternity.

Uniformity of character is a high attainment, of which Scripture history presents some pleasing specimens, though perhaps it affords more numerous instances of irregularity. The early life of some is nothing but the record of crime and folly, when the passions were indulged in unbridled licentiousness, and the moral creation groaned beneath the burden of their vices; but afterward retrieving their errors, they have become examples of sobriety, kindness, and religion. Others shone, forth at first with preeminent brightness, attracting the eyes of an extensive community to their juvenile excellence, and holding forth the best promises of futurity; but their goodness has proved like the morning cloud, and like the early dew, that passeth away; the eyes of parental tenderness, that once glistened with rapture and admiration, are suffused with tears; the church of God, that once hailed their zeal, is filled with regrets to witness its faded ardours and its altered nature. "How is the gold become dim, and the fine gold changed?" There is another, a sort of intermediate class, who have rather a doubtful complexion, some of whose actions indicate piety, others the reverse: at a distance they may be admired, but, upon a closer inspection, their principles are questionable, and, as our acquaintance with them increases, our respect irresistibly diminishes. Candour itself, which would put the most favourable construction upon them, is compelled to see new spots and blemishes in proportion as we perceive more distinctly their entire character.

The illustrious female, however, before us, exhibits a singular contrast to all these diversities. From the first to the last mention of her name in the page of Scripture, she challenges unmitigated admiration; she is uniform in every character: adversity and prosperity find her the same woman: she does not murmur in the one, she is not vain in the other. There is but a single variety in her character, arising from its progressive excellence. She is not *the same*, only because she is *better*; our veneration keeps pace with our knowledge. Her character does not, like that of many others, suffer by investigation; it does not resemble an object seen at some distance through a mist, which is magnified into unnatural dimensions, so that the illusion vanishes when you come near; but is like a tower seen afar off under a clear sky, swelling in majesty at every step of approximation.

We are now brought to the close of Hannah's history; it is even more splendid than its commencement. We have traced her through the various characters of a persecuted wife, a weeping suppliant, a misrepresented worshipper, a joyful mother, and a grateful saint, fulfilling her vows and devoting her first-born to the service of God. In some respects the latter must have proved a trying occasion, a duty of difficult execution; and we could have forgiven, we could have sympathized with the tears of a mother who was placed in the situation of violating her vows or giving up her darling;

we could have pitied her struggles, while we commended their successful issue, in leaving her Samuel behind her at Shiloh. But she assumes a higher tone and spirit: the mother is absorbed in the saint; and, at the moment when we expected the language of parting regret and anxiety, behold, she bursts into a song of praise, and soars to the heights of prophecy.

This holy effusion is somewhat analogous to that of the mother of our Lord, which we shall hereafter have occasion to illustrate. In the mean time the hymn of Hannah claims our examination. It is called a *prayer*, because it was addressed to God as an act of worship, and because the acknowledgment and celebration of divine mercies constitute an important branch of devotion.

"My heart rejoiceth in the Lord; mine horn is exalted in the Lord: my mouth is enlarged over mine enemies: because I rejoice in thy salvation."

A vain mother might have celebrated her *son,* and, if she had expressed a general sense of divine goodness in his bestowment, would have dwelt with satisfaction upon his premature indications of greatness. Inordinate attachment to the gift is apt to obliterate from the mind a grateful recollection of the giver; and to this forgetfulness we are liable to be seduced by our affections. But Hannah cannot taste of the stream without being led to the fountain; she cannot receive mercies without viewing the hand that bestows them; nor be so enraptured with the blessing as to sink the Creator in the creature. In fact, Samuel is unnamed. His beauty, his pliability--whatever he really possessed, or whatever the fond eye of a mother fancied he possessed--all was forgotten, lost, and annihilated in God. Every valued blessing--her child, her husband, her possessions;--the whole creation vanished into nothingness before the thought of the "eternal ALL!"

The "horn" is an emblem of power and pre-eminence, and Hannah speaks of its exaltation. She had been degraded and despised for the childless condition, and had suffered reproach from the daughters of Israel, in particular from Peninnah; but she had now, through the mercy of God, risen to distinction, and obtained the object of her warmest solicitude. The lips which before moved in secret whispers or inarticulate prayer, are now taught to praise! The horn was also an instrument of music, and was lifted up to be sounded in the sacred chorus. In the days of David we read of the sons of Heman, who were to "lift up the horn;" and this pious woman perhaps borrowed the allusion to represent the ardour of her worship and the triumph that inspired her tongue.

If, with her solemn praises, Hannah blended a momentary recollection of the unkindness with which she had been treated, it was solely to express her thankfulness for deliverance, and not to produce a charge against her enemies. "Her mouth was enlarged," indeed, but not to utter the language of retaliation, not in passionate exclamations or in threatening words, but to memorialize the goodness of the Lord. Nor was this her only source of joy. Temporal interposition served but to remind her of spiritual blessings; and, while her spirit exulted in the birth of Samuel, she looked forward to a more auspicious day, and rejoiced in the "salvation" which should hereafter be accomplished by the incarnation of the Redeemer.

Winged with holy rapture, she now ascends far above all earthly interests and concerns; and quiting the subject, to which she had made but a transient allusion, though of the deepest personal importance, she meditates alone on infinite perfection:

"There is none holy as the Lord: for there is none besides thee: neither is there any rock like our God. Talk no more so exceeding proudly; let not arrogancy come out of your mouth; for the Lord is a God of knowledge, and by him actions are weighed."

The attributes of the Divine Being excite in the bosoms of the wicked unmingled dread. Every manifestation of his character is an appeal against their impieties, and hence they "desire not the knowledge of his ways." In a state of innocence the presence of the blessed God enhanced the felicities of Paradise, and nothing but the estrangement which sin has occasioned could have so altered the views and perverted the inclinations of mankind as to render the best of beings an object of terror; but in proportion to the renewal of the mind will be the return of that feeling of complacency which was cherished by unfallen man, and is felt by sinless immortals.

In all the principal events of her own life, and in the general regulation of human affairs, Hannah perceived a display of those perfections which she now celebrates; the perfections of holiness, power, omniscience, and justice. Nothing is better calculated to suppress the arrogance of man than the contemplation of these divine excellencies, which are so many rays of one ineffable glory; distinct yet blended; separate, yet harmonious in their operations. The history of pagan nations supplies ample proof that the spirituality of the divine essence, which implies the existence and exercise of these attributes, is too high an idea for a creature sunk under the dominion of his senses: he cannot ascend to the conception of infinite purity and wisdom: God is not known, and cannot be discovered as the searcher of hearts, and the righteous dispenser of good and evil, life and death: he cannot realize his unlimited dominion, nor imagine the pervading presence of that all-seeing eye which looks through the universe, penetrates every concealment, and observes, with leisurely and perfect survey, every movement of the soul. It is the province of revelation to disclose these great facts, and the privilege of piety to triumph in them.

"The bows of the mighty men are broken, and they that stumbled are girded with strength. They that were full have hired out themselves for bread; and they that were hungry ceased: so that the barren hath borne seven: and she that hath many children hath waxed feeble."

The dispensations of Providence illustrate his perfections. Often, indeed, they do not accord with human plans or expectations, but they are nevertheless marked with wisdom and equity. In accomplishing the mighty purposes of omnipotence the strong are sometimes weakened, and the feeble supplied with power; the wealthy are impoverished, and the poor enriched; the childless blessed with families, and those whose tables are surrounded with a smiling offspring made to weep over their fading health and glory. For,

"The Lord killeth, and maketh alive; he bringeth down to the grave, and bringeth up. The Lord maketh poor, and maketh rich: he bringeth low, and lifteth up. He raiseth up the poor out of the dust, and lifteth up the beggar from the dunghill, to set them among princes, and to make them inherit the throne of glory: for the pillars of the earth are the Lord's, and he hath set the world upon them."

These changes are frequently ascribed, by unthinking mortals, to mere chance, or at least to the uncontrolled operation of second causes. Hannah ascribes them "to the Lord." Her faith discerned an invisible hand, and rejoiced in an omniscient superintendance. Whatever confusion appears to the eye of sense to prevail in the world, religion has access behind the scenes, observes the finger that touches the prime spring of this vast machine of providence, and sees nothing but harmonious movements, concurrent designs, merciful and intelligible plans, perfect and universal order. The perspective of human affairs is to such an one complete; he is placed by the fear of God in the very point of observance; he looks to the distant results, to the termination of the series, and every object, to his renewed sight, appears in just and proportionate dimensions. Unless seen from this point, every thing will be out of place and contradictory; and human arrogance will naturally arraign as irregular, imperfect, or unwise, what genuine piety will acknowledge to be best.

"He will keep the feet of his saints, and the wicked shall be silent in darkness; for by strength shall no man prevail. The adversaries of the Lord shall be broken to pieces; out of heaven shall he thunder upon them: the Lord shall judge the ends of the earth; and he shall give strength unto his king, and exalt the horn of his anointed."

There is a *progressive* energy in this sacred song. Hannah warms into enthusiasm as she proceeds, till, under the influence of a heavenly inspiration, she assumes the language of prophecy, and becomes "wrapt into future times." At the opening, she expressed her gratitude for personal blessings; hence she is led to celebrate the perfections of Jehovah: then she proclaims the interference of his providence in the vicissitudes of this lower world: and finally, proceeds to contrast the destinies of the righteous and wicked, as resulting from the manifestation of the Messiah to rule over all nations by a spiritual and everlasting dominion. In that name which is above every name, in the hallowed name of the ANOINTED ONE, the song of Hannah terminates. What greater honour could be conferred on a woman than to be gifted with that spirit of prophecy which first announced the approaching Redeemer, to whom all the prophets gave witness? She speaks of his authority as a "King," his administration as a "Judge," his work as a Priest and Prophet, prefigured by that oil which was poured upon the most eminent of mankind, who were types of the distinguished Personage who was to come, and who is therefore designated as the Lord's "Anointed." How great his influence! "he will keep the feet of his saints!" How terrible his power! "the adversaries of the Lord shall be broken in pieces: out of heaven shall he thunder upon them." Preposterous indeed is the hope of his enemies, that they shall evade the destruction of his iron rod; while pleasing and well-founded is the expectation of his saints, who bow with unreluctant submission, with grateful acceptance, to his golden sceptre.

Almost twelve hundred years were yet until when Hannah uttered this prediction of the Messiah; and yet her faith, overleaping the ages of intervening time, beheld his glory, and triumphed in his salvation. No darkness could blind her perceptions, nothing could repress her love: she lived as it were, in advance, and, like many of her illustrious predecessors and of her posterity, believed in Christ to the saving of her soul.

These ages are passed away, and many more are numbered since the actual manifestation of the Son of God in human nature. We are partakers of his day; we live in the light of his glory: from the ages of prediction, we are advanced to those of accomplishment; from the time of shadows to the era of reality. And have we *improved* upon the past, in the strength of our faith or in the warmth of our attachment to the Lord of glory? Would a fair comparison of our state of mind with that of early saints, in far distant ages, prove advantageous or unfavourable to our character? Is our piety proportionate to our privileges? Does the intensity of our love equal the clearness of our discoveries? These are salutary questions, and questions of practical importance. Let us aim to be able to put them often to our consciences without a blush.

Very little more information is communicated respecting Hannah: her history is merged in that of her distinguished son. We have, however, a beautiful picture of her maternal character, a record of the blessing which the aged priest pronounced upon the family, and an account of five other children which Providence gave them: "Samuel ministered before the Lord, being a child girded with a linen ephod. Moreover his mother made him a little coat, and brought it to him from year to year, when she came up with her husband to offer the yearly sacrifice. And Eli blessed Elkanah and his wife, and said, The Lord give thee seed of this woman, for the loan which is lent to the Lord. And they went unto their own home. And the Lord visited Hannah, so that she conceived and bare three sons and two daughters."

The good mother and the eminent saint are delightfully blended in the wife of Elkanah, and the influence of each is obvious in Samuel. Eli seems to have beheld him with unusual affection. He had been early trained to gentleness, docility, and goodness. Discipline at home commenced from his first infancy, and continuing to the moment of his removal to Shiloh, prepared him for the course of life to which he was so soon introduced. Too often the petulance and frowardness of children indicate the defective nature of their education: indulgence has permitted the wild plant to shoot forth its branches with irregular luxuriancy, and it has become both unsightly and enfeebled for want of being properly pruned. To suffer the propensities and passions of children to go unrestrained is the extreme of cruelty, being the most direct means of rendering them burdens to society and tormentors to themselves.

Hannah, with admirable firmness, relinquished her youthful charge to the care of Eli at the call of duty, and with no less admirable affection and prudence, continued to maintain that kind of intercourse which tends to promote mutual love. A *passionate* mother would have urged her husband to remove to Shiloh, for the sake of having her little darling perpetually under her eye; a *prudent* one chose to remain at Ramah, only bringing her present at the annual festivals. True love knows when to separate, and is ready to make necessary sacrifices to the good of a valued child. He was in excellent hands, training to a noble work, under a venerable priest, and in conformity to a solemn vow. Providence was not unobservant of his mother's heroism and piety, and she is amply repaid, not only by his superior excellence, but by her own increasing family. *One* child is lent to the Lord, *five* are given. She possessed with gratitude, she resigned with magnanimity, and she is recompensed by multiplication.

Let children never forget the debt they owe to maternal tenderness, a debt which the devoted affection and kindness of a whole life can scarcely discharge. Let the fond parent who nursed your infancy, corrected your frowardness, sowed the seeds of knowledge and piety in your heart, watched, wept, and prayed over you, be ever dear, ever respected, and loved. She who has sustained your weakness, may live to need support from your strength; she who hold you up in the helplessness of infancy, may require your supporting arm, and deserves your sympathizing aid in the years of her decrepitude.

Young persons need to be reminded, however, that even the impiety of parents is no sufficient reason for disrespecting them *as parents*; and if you possess the inestimable treasure of religion, it will be best evinced in soothing the cares, ministering to the necessities, and setting an example of every duty before the eyes of those who are still so unhappy as to be destitute of it. But you who are born of the children of God, and who have been nourished and educated under the wing of parental piety, can never be too thankful to the God of your salvation, and at some future period may have to adopt the poet's elevated strain:

"My boast is not that I deduce my birth
From loins enthroned, and rulers of the earth;
But higher far my proud pretensions rise--
The son of parents pass'd into the skies."

Cowper.

Abigail Chapter XI

Millions of the human race, naturally capable of great attainments and mighty exploits, had they been differently circumstanced, or had their mental and moral energies been properly cultivated, have died as they have lived, in a state of obscurity. Unknown to the rest of mankind even by name, they have scarcely wandered from the precincts of their native village, or the cottage that gave them birth; but, like the wild flowers of the untrodden wilderness, have sprung up, and bloomed, and perished upon the same spot. Successive generations have occupied the identical sphere of their ancestors, living in the same unenvied seclusion, and at last carried to the same undistinguished grave.

Whoever has had an opportunity of knowing the state of society and the character of man in retirement, must be aware that the amazing disparity subsisting between the extremes of rusticity and of polished life arises far less from original disproportions of capacity than from the accidental circumstances which attach to the two conditions. Education has a tendency to remove these differences, to elevate the inferior classes of society from their degradation, to raise them in the scale of being and to unite man to man: but still more important effects result from religion, which, by fixing the thoughts on holy and heavenly objects, and firing the breast with incessant ardour in the pursuit of them, advances the character to a dignity otherwise unattainable. How much humble piety has bloomed in the by-paths of life far from the crowded highway of the world, amidst the recesses of privacy! How often has the beauty of holiness adorned the most misshapen, or otherwise unattractive exterior! How many great and pious individuals have occupied the vale of poverty, the objects of divine approbation and of angelic joy; who, under different circumstances, might have been ornaments of the political world, or lights in the church of God; and will be pillars for ever in the celestial temple!

These dispensations of Providence are analogous to certain arrangements in nature. How many showers descend, and how many vegetable productions grow in barren wildernesses! It is not till after ages of research that a few species and varieties have been discovered; and it may be questioned whether an equal, if not a far greater number, still exist in the unfrequented solitudes of creation, which science may not visit for centuries yet to come: and of those which are at present known, a few only of their qualities, and the uses for which they were formed, have been ascertained. To pronounce a condemnatory sentence upon that wisdom which assigned them their places, merely on account of our incapacity to discover their precise destination, would be presumptuous and impious in the extreme; nor would it be less so to contemn the unsearchable mysteries of Providence, whose arrangements surpass the comprehension and confound the inquiries of man.

Some of those "lights shining in a dark place" have, however, been occasionally brought into view by unexpected circumstances; and more than one is exhibited through the medium of the inspired word. They would have for ever remained in concealment, and their names have perished, excepting from the book of God's remembrance, but for some apparent casualty. A history of *incidents* would furnish a most delightful record of Providence, showing its secret, but certain operations, and its connecting, though, to superficial observers, invisible links. One of these, in the life of David, presents the brief, but interesting account of ABIGAIL, who, like Job in Uz, Joseph in Egypt, and Daniel in Chaldea, exhibited a specimen of solitary excellence, which at length emerged from obscurity, and, by means of her connection with one of the most eminent of mankind, shone in an appropriate sphere.

[Sidenote: Years before Christ, about 1058.]

She is thus introduced to our notice, in the scriptural narrative, at a time when the son of Jesse was "hunted like a partridge upon the mountains" by his royal persecutor. "And David arose, and went down to the wilderness of Paran. And there was a man in Maon, whose possessions were in Carmel: and the man was very great, and he had three thousand sheep and a thousand goats: and he was shearing his sheep in Carmel. Now the name of the man was Nabal; and the name of his wife, Abigail: and she was a woman of good understanding, and of a beautiful countenance: but the man was churlish and evil in his doings; and he was of the house of Caleb."

The contrast which the characters of Nabal and Abigail exhibit, may well excite astonishment, that persons so dissimilar should have become united by the tender ties of matrimony, and may lead us to inquire a little into the sources of some incongruities of this kind, which not unfrequently make their appearance in society. How is it, that *adaptation to each other*, in point of mental and moral qualities especially, which seems so great a prerequisite to happiness, should seldom form the basis of an union voluntarily contracted, and incapable of dissolution--an union of the closest nature, and an union for life?

Frequently an ill-assorted connection arises from an *ambitious motive*; one party is wealthy, the other aspiring. Attracted by the gilded bait, it is seized too eagerly to admit of prudential considerations respecting the possibility of concealed mischief, from which, like the fish once caught by the hook, it is too late to be disentangled. It cannot be asserted that Abigail was induced to marry her churlish husband from such a motive, though it will not be deemed improbable by those whose experience of the world convinces them that even persons like her, of good understanding, beauty, and piety, are sometimes guilty of similar improprieties. Riches are, on many accounts, attractive to those whose immaturity of judgment is dazzled by the glare of life, and who are consequently too apt to associate in their conceptions things which, in reality, have no connection--*splendour* and *happiness*. The mind is naturally gratified by a sense of elevation above the usual level of mankind, as persons ascending in an air-balloon become elevated, even amidst their dangers, in consequence of attaining a height impossible to others, and attracting the idle gaze of spectators on the ground. It is supposed also, that wealth will furnish some covert from the storms of adversity, if not a perfect security against them; and, forgetting that it tends to multiply and extend our wants in a ten-fold proportion to the means of supplying them, the sheep and the goats of a Nabal are viewed with ardent but mistaken fondness. It is difficult to convince the young of their errors upon this subject; nevertheless, we forewarn them that the experiment is hazardous, the prospect delusory, the possessions of life uncertain, and utterly incapable of compensating for the absence of moral qualities and social suitabilities; above all, we proclaim the criminality of cherishing an avaricious disposition, and the practical falsehood of giving it the name of love. A young woman acting upon this principle literally fulfils the common representation of the case, by *throwing herself away*, and, in one rash moment, forfeits her reputation and her happiness.

This unsuitability of connexion in married life sometimes originates in a mutual, but foolish *wish to maintain the respectability of the family*. In such instances both are wealthy, and join their fortunes as a sort of compromise to the opinion of the world and their own pride, for the sake of maintaining their rank. It is true, an equality, or some fair proportion in point of fortune, as society is constituted, seems in itself *desirable*, and, if it can be accomplished, is as legitimate an object of pursuit as similarity of age or of mind; but the practice of making this an absolute prerequisite, of sacrificing to it the affections of the heart, and, qualifications of far greater importance, of rendering the want of it a sufficient ground of refusing a matrimonial alliance, though age, temper, religion, and every commendable quality, may be placed in the other scale, and of deeming the possession of it enough when other great requisites are absent, is both foolish and wicked. No reason can exist, in such a case, why an Abigail--a woman of "good understanding," should connect herself with a Nabal--a man "churlish and evil in his doings."

Occasionally the same evil arises from the *persuasion of others*, especially of those who are entitled to respect, and who sometimes, very improperly, interpose authority instead of suggesting advice. The parties immediately concerned would by no means, if left to themselves, select each other as companions for life, but marry merely to satisfy their friends. It can never be regarded as otherwise than extreme cruelty in those who compel their children to gratify *their* predilections, instead of allowing them their *own* choice. As this is a connexion, the happiness of which so essentially depends upon the affections, and as no argument can force the heart into an attachment from which it naturally, or perhaps capriciously revolts, and as moreover, the comfort of existence results from the state of the mind far more than from any external circumstances whatever; reason and religion prescribe, that, after due caution and admonition, persons should be permitted to determine ultimately for themselves, without being subjected to the miserable alternative of accepting parental choice or forfeiting parental fondness.

Incongruous connexions may also originate in one or both of the parties having suffered *previous disappointment*. Young persons under the pang occasioned by the failure of a romantic attachment, foolishly resolve no more to consult affection, or even to allow it any share in the determination of their choice. They imagine it needless any longer to expect happiness, because they cannot possess the individual they supposed alone capable of promoting it, and repair to marriage merely as a refuge from solitude or from reproach. In such cases, they deem it of comparatively trifling consequence with whom they connect themselves, refusing to admit it possible that they should ever more obtain peace of mind.

Nothing, however, can be more delusive than such a feeling. The immaturity of the judgment at the early age of first attachments, renders it probable that they may not, in reality, have made the best selection, and that their preferences were determined rather by casual circumstances and accidental impressions, than any knowledge of character or any perception of solid qualities. If the comfort of life depended upon the success of early predilections, it is probable few would be happy; but Providence has wisely ordered it otherwise, by constituting it independent of arbitrary associations. Let not the young, therefore, precipitate themselves into improper connexions--into connexions not founded on principle, and not cemented by love, through indulging the notion that the gratification of a first romantic attachment is essential to happiness, and that if disappointed, it is of no importance whether they become united to a gentle Isaac or a churlish Nabal; because, in reality, the prize is yet to be won, the jewel is yet attainable, and Providence may have kindly frustrated a present wish, to bestow ultimately a more substantial benefit. "The way of man is not in himself; it is not in man that walketh to direct his steps." Our utmost efforts cannot arrest or accelerate the wheel of destiny, which is turned by a secret and invisible power, that raises or depresses, subserves or frustrates our purposes, *irresistibly* indeed, but not *arbitrarily*; making "all things work together for good to them that love God."

The history before us represents David as still a wanderer from wilderness to wilderness, and reduced to great extremity. Hearing of the extraordinary festivities observed upon the occasion of Nabal's shearing his sheep, from which he inferred his opulence, ten messengers were sent to him to solicit, in the most respectful manner, a supply of provisions. It was intimated, that David had not availed himself of the power which the Arab emirs are accustomed to assume, of seizing whatever they need, but on the contrary, had afforded protection, instead of exercising violence. [36]

Nabal not only refused to comply with the request, but returned an insulting answer, which the young men carried to their master. David felt the utmost indignation, and instantly prepared to resent the affront. The persecutions of Saul being no more than he expected, were borne with a fortitude, and requited by a forbearance which cannot but excite our admiration; but the unlooked-for barbarity of Nabal took him by surprise, and threw him into a rage. We cannot justify his hostile preparations, nor look without regret upon his rash proceeding, in taking four hundred of his armed followers to destroy Nabal. How unlike David, the man after God's own heart, who had been so long trained in the school of affliction, and so often manifested a very different spirit! Alas, bow easily are the best of men "led into temptation;" and how necessary is it to exercise vigilance, not only over our "easy besetting sins," but over what we deem the least vulnerable points of our character! Neglecting the requisite precautions, we may be taken even on the strongest side, and at the most unexpected moment.

One of the servants informed Abigail of what had occurred, stating the message of David, and the behaviour of her husband; and, at the same time, representing the civility with which the former had conducted himself towards the shepherds.

A person of less understanding might have said, "Let these rival chiefs settle the matter between themselves; my husband had an undoubted right to do what he pleased with his own, and he has the means of defending himself from a vindictive stranger." But Abigail wisely listened to the information communicated by the servant, and instantly adopted a plan, which seemed indeed the only one calculated to avert the threatened blow. She took two hundred loaves, and two bottles of wine, and five sheep ready dressed, and five measures of parched corn, and a hundred clusters of raisins, and two hundred cakes of figs, which she hastened to present to David.

This was excellent management. Had she repaired to her husband, and endeavoured to pacify his turbulent spirit by remonstrance, reason, or entreaty, the probability is she would have met with a repulse, and disabled herself from any further interference. Had she merely *sent* the supply with which the asses were laden, the indignant son of Jesse might, very possibly, have returned it as insufficient, or pressed on with his armed men to compel Nabal to make reparation for the affront he had ventured to offer. This skilful negotiator, however, goes herself to settle the contention which had so suddenly arisen; and never, surely, was a better arranged or more successful expedition.

The moment Abigail perceived David, she alighted from her ass, and, falling prostrate at his feet, addressed him in language well calculated to accomplish her wishes. Every thing was in perfect contrast with the behaviour of Nabal--her suppliant posture--the respectful term she chooses, calling him *lord*--the appropriation of her husband's fault to herself--the apology she offers for him, by representing his conduct as resulting rather from a momentary impulse than any settled malignity, as the general failing of his nature, not the effect of any personal malevolence--the ignorance she professes of the request which David had sent, insinuating that otherwise he would have received a very different return--her apparent assurance of success, delicately intimating the happy circumstance of his being restrained from shedding blood in a momentary fit of passion--her offer of the magnificent present she had prepared--her congratulation upon his achievements--her confident anticipations of his future triumphs, and final establishment in the kingdom--her reference to Providence--her suggestion, that it would hereafter prove a source of satisfaction that he had been prevented from committing an act which, whatever were the provocation, must be painful to recollect, and which must rather afflict his conscience than grace his laurels--all these topics were well introduced, and urged with a tone of eloquence that proved irresistible. David takes the present, thanks Abigail for her interposition, and dismisses her, with the assurance that he had "hearkened to her voice, and accepted her person."

Upon her return she found Nabal in a state of intoxication, totally disregardful of danger, and ignorant of the ruin from which his prudent wife had procured his deliverance. Thus do multitudes sport upon the brink of everlasting destruction, heedless of the justice they have provoked, and solicitous only of consuming those hours, and days, and years, in indulgence, which ought to be devoted to repentance. Let the "lovers of pleasure" reflect on three short maxims, "He that will not fear, shall *feel*, the wrath of Heaven--He that lives in the kingdom of *Sense* shall die in the kingdom of *Sorrow*--He shall never truly enjoy his *present* hour who never thinks on his *last*." [37]

Abigail properly resolved to defer any conversation with Nabal till the morning, when she disclosed the whole affair. The surprise was so great that "his heart died within him, and he became as a stone." Ten days afterward he was smitten by the hand of God, and descended without honour into the grave. No one could esteem him while living, and no one regretted him when dead.

The news of this event having been conveyed to David, he expressed his grateful sense of the divine goodness in keeping him from the execution of his rash project, and in thus vindicating his cause by a signal interference. As he had been deeply impressed with the personal charms and good understanding of Abigail, and as no obstacle seemed to exist to prevent their union, he took the first opportunity of proposing to marry her; to which, with becoming expressions of humility and modesty, she consented.

"It was a fair suit," says Bishop Hall, "to change a David for a Nabal; to become David's queen, instead of Nabal's drudge! She, that learned humility under so hard a tutor, abaseth herself no less when David offers to advance her: 'Let thine handmaid be a servant to wash the feet of the servants of my lord.' None are so fit to be great as those that can stoop lowest. How could David be more happy in a wife? He finds at once piety, wisdom, humility, faithfulness, wealth, beauty. How could Abigail be more happy in a husband, than in the prophet, the champion, the anointed of God? Those marriages are well made, wherein virtues are matched and happiness is mutual."

The Queen of Sheba. Chapter XII

The pious solicitude of David, the king of Israel, in his last hours, for his son and successor, is thus recorded in the closing chapter of the first book of Chronicles: "Give unto Solomon my son a perfect heart, to keep thy commandments, thy testimonies, and thy statutes." With this prayer he connected suitable and impressive advice, "Thou Solomon my son, know thou the God of thy father, and serve him with a perfect heart and with a willing mind; for the Lord searcheth all hearts, and understandeth all the imaginations of the thoughts: if thou seek him, he will be found of thee; but if thou forsake him, he will cast thee off forever."

Parental piety does not always influence, as it ought, those who by their domestic privileges are most favourably situated for witnessing it: to all human appearance, the language of kind remonstrance or entreaty has been often useless, the petitions of fervent desire have failed, and the tears of pure affection have flowed in vain. The present instance, however, furnishes a pleasing exception to this remark; for upon Solomon's accession to the throne, he appointed a solemn festival at Gibeon before the tabernacle of Moses; and during the night, in which the God of Israel desired that he would ask what he should bestow upon him, he presented a petition, no less distinguished by its singularity in such circumstances, than by its excellence and success. "And Solomon said unto God, Thou hast showed great mercy unto David my father, and hast made me to reign in his stead. Now, O Lord God, let thy promise unto David my father, be established; for thou hast made me king over a people like the dust of the earth in multitude. Give me now WISDOM and KNOWLEDGE, that I may go out and come in before this people; for who can judge this thy people that is so great? And God said to Solomon, Because this was in thine heart, and thou hast not asked riches, wealth, or honour, nor the life of thine enemies, neither yet hast asked long life; but hast asked wisdom and knowledge, that thou mayest judge my people over whom I have made thee king; WISDOM AND KNOWLEDGE is GRANTED UNTO THEE; and I will give thee RICHES, and WEALTH, and HONOUR, such as none of the kings have had that have been before thee, neither shall there any after thee have the like."

The inspired description of Solomon's magnificence may justly excite astonishment--a magnificence which extended to "all his drinking vessels, which were of gold; and all the vessels of the house of the forest of Lebanon were of pure gold; none were of silver: It was nothing accounted of in the days of Solomon." It is natural to imagine, that the fame of so remarkable a prince, concurring with the comparative ease with which gold and silver were procurable, would contribute to establish that taste for splendour which has ever distinguished the potentates of the East. It is stated by Sir J. Chardin, that the plate of the king of Persia is of pure gold, originally made by Shah Abbas, the most glorious of the princes of the Sefi royal family; who, for this purpose, melted seven thousand two hundred marks, or nearly thirty six thousand English troy ounces of *the purest gold*. But Solomon, according to the testimony of Scripture, was the most opulent prince that ever sat upon a throne. His annual revenues were six hundred and sixty-six talents of gold, exclusive of the supply he received from the customs and from tributary nations. A talent weighed three thousand shekels, and a shekel two hundred and nineteen grains. The king employed a navy, which, with the assistance of Tyrian vessels and navigators, who were esteemed the most skilful in the world, fetched gold and silver, ivory, apes, and peacocks, from Ophir, by the way of the red sea. This voyage occupied three years.

In comparing the extremes of human society, the riches of a Solomon with the poverty of a Bartimeus, it becomes us to recognize the hand of a mysterious though wise Providence. He who fixed the stars of the firmament in their proper places, determines, independently of all human control, the orders of society and the sphere of the individual; and it is no less consolatory than obvious, that the equitable rule by which a final judgment of our character is to be determined, will measure the extent of our responsibility, by an impartial estimate of our situation, our opportunities, and our respective talents.

Attracted by the celebrity of Solomon, the QUEEN OF SHEBA came to Jerusalem, with a train and presents suited to his dignity and her own. Although the sovereigns of neighbouring nations paid similar visits of ceremony and of curiosity, yet this illustrious woman is particularly noticed in the sacred page, on account perhaps of her sex, her inquisitiveness, the remoteness of her situation, the magnificence of her equipage and offerings; but especially the piety of her views, and the impressive language of her devout admiration.

The date of this interview with the king of Israel may be referred, with sufficient accuracy, to the year of the world three thousand and twelve, or nine hundred and ninety-two before the Christian era. This was subsequent to the completion of the temple and of the royal houses. A variety of opinions have prevailed respecting the kingdom of Sheba; and some have supposed, though without sufficient reason, that this is the name of the queen herself, and not of her country or capital. The probability is, that *Sheba*, situated in the southern part of Arabia Felix, and on the eastern coast of the Red Sea, is intended. Moses speaks of Sheba, the son Joktan, a descendant of Eber, and more remotely of Shem; and ancient authors represent his descendants, the *Sabeans*, as peopling this district of Arabia, the metropolis of whose kingdom was denominated *Sheba* or *Saba*. It appears from authentic testimony, that they were accustomed to female government; and Bochart proves, by numerous citations, that the kingdom of Sheba was called by the Jews *the country of the South*, which explains the phraseology of our Lord in the twelfth chapter of Matthew. The geographical accuracy of this statement is further corroborated, by comparing the description which the inspired historian records of the gifts presented by this queen to Solomon, with the language of Pliny and Herodotus: the former of whom says, "that odoriferous woods were in use only in this country, and that the Sabean consumed them in dressing their food;" and the latter, "that the Arabians took a thousand talents of frankincense every year to Darius." We deem it proper to avoid involving ourselves in a labyrinth of geographical difficulties, and have therefore simply stated the result of our inquiries; which however may furnish us with, at least, one serious reflection. How transitory and how contemptible is human glory! It is not peculiar to the poor and the destitute to be forgotten, to have their dwellings and their names perish amidst the desolations of time; such is nearly the fate of one of the most remarkable sovereigns of antiquity, whose visit to the greatest potentate of the eastern world is so celebrated in Scripture. What mean our trifling cares--our incessant solicitude about temporal possessions and worldly distinctions? The house we now inhabit will soon be demolished and swept away by the flood of time--the name by which we are distinguished, and the annals of our short period of temporal existence, will soon be scarcely remembered by our successor--all our glory will be covered with the darkness of death! Shall we not, therefore, aim to secure an incorruptible inheritance in the skies, and an unfading pre-eminence in the records of eternity? "The *righteous* shall be had in everlasting remembrance."

The design of the queen of Sheba, in repairing to Jerusalem, was not merely to pay a visit of ceremony. She "heard of his fame concerning the name of the Lord," and "she came to prove him with hard questions." The report, not only of the riches, splendour, and wisdom of Solomon, but also of the miraculous interferences of the God of Israel on behalf of his people, and of his peculiar favour to this monarch, had reached the distant residence of this Arabian queen; and so deep was the interest it excited in her bosom, that she determined to undertake a journey, long and hazardous as it might be, for the sake of investigating these extraordinary facts. It is evident she attached a considerable degree of credibility to the representations she had received; and relying no longer upon subordinate means of information, she resolved upon a course of diligent inquiry. When and where shall we discover a similar zeal to acquire a knowledge of "the glorious Gospel of the blessed God?" How often have Christian ministers occasion to adopt the prophetic strain, "Who hath believed our report, and to whom is the arm of the Lord revealed?" How often do all the personal excellencies, the moral glories of him who is described as "a greater than Solomon," fail to attract mankind? Satisfied with mere report--few apply to the sacred Scriptures as the immediate and purest means of instruction in "the truth as it is in Jesus," after the long-recorded example of the ancient Bereans, who "received the word (of Paul and Silas) with all readiness of mind, and searched the Scriptures daily, whether those things were so."

Bishop Hall very pertinently remarks, "No doubt many, from all coasts, came to learn and wonder, none with so much note as this noble daughter of Cham; who herself deserves the next wonder to him whom she came to hear and admire: that a woman, a princess, a rich and great queen, should travel from the remotest south, from Sheba, a region famous for the greatest delicacies of nature, to learn wisdom, is a matchless example. We know merchants that venture to either Indies for wealth; others we know daily to cross the seas for wanton curiosity; some few philosophers we have known to have gone far for learning; and among princes, it is no unusual thing to send their ambassadors to far distant kingdoms, for transaction of business either of state or commerce: but that a royal lady should in person undertake and overcome so tedious a journey, only to observe and inquire into the mysteries of nature, art, religion, is a thing past both parallel and imitation. Why do we think any labour great, or any way long, to hear a greater than Solomon? How justly shall the queen of the South rise up in judgment, and condemn us, who may hear wisdom crying in our streets, and neglect her?"

Among princely cares, the ardent search of truth can seldom be enumerated, though it be a most honourable and beneficial employment. Those whom Providence has placed in an elevated situation are usually too much occupied with themselves, their pleasures, their pomp, and their ambitious projects, to listen to the dictates, or to search out the mysteries of wisdom. The concerns of an extensive empire furnish a plausible pretext for neglecting the great interest of piety, which a deceived heart is ready to plead in extenuation of a conduct condemned alike by reason, conscience, and revelation. But let the rulers of nations observe David, Solomon, and others of the kings of Israel; the splendour of whose earthly glory was eclipsed by the superior brightness of their heavenly wisdom; and whose names are written upon, the sacred page, not so much, because they were *men of rank*, as because they were *men of God*. The command of Jesus Christ is of prime importance and of universal obligation, "Seek FIRST the kingdom of God and his righteousness;" and unless it can be demonstrated that he has made one code of laws for the prince and another for the peasant, or that his precepts possess an accommodating flexibility suited to the prejudices and passions of mankind, no exception can be for a moment admitted. As there is no royal road to the heights of human science, but all who attain them must ascend by assiduous and persevering application, so there is none to the summit of celestial felicity; but persons of every class, rank, sex, and age, must follow Christ in the same unsmoothed path of repentance and self-denial. Hence, such is the bewitching influence of worldly splendour, so numerous and so powerful the attractions of opulence, that we have daily and hourly proofs of the apostle's statement: "Not many wise men after the flesh, not many mighty, not many noble, are called; but God hath chosen the weak things of the world, to confound the things which are mighty; and base things of the world, and things which are despised, hath God chosen, yea, and things which are not, to bring to nought things that are; that no flesh should glory in his presence." But happily the long scroll of history is here and there embellished with a name, which combines the glory that confers pre-eminence in the present world, with the grace that secures everlasting distinction in the next.

[Sidenote: Years before Christ, about 892.]

This celebrated princess is said to have visited Solomon, "to prove him with hard questions," by which have generally been understood enigmatical puzzles. Some of these are to be found in sacred writ, of which the riddle which Samson proposed to the young men of Timnath, is a very ancient and curious specimen. It appears from the writings of the ancients, that the Greeks and all the Eastern nations, were singularly attached to enigmas. Plutarch, in his Feast of the Seven Sages, introduces the following questions proposed by Amasis, the king of Egypt, to the king of Ethiopia: "What is the most ancient thing--what the most beautiful--what the largest--what the wisest--what the most common--what the most useful--what the most hurtful--what the strongest--and what the most easy?" To which the king of Ethiopia replied, "The most ancient thing is time--the most beautiful is light--the largest is the world--the wisest is truth--the most common is death--the most useful is God--the most hurtful is the devil--the strongest is fortune--and the most easy, to follow one's own inclination." In the book of Proverbs, we find several series of this description, which originally might have been answers to questions of a similar nature. Among others, we have this very curious and beautiful statement: "There be four things which are little upon the earth, but they are exceeding wise; the ants are a people not strong, yet they prepare their meat in the summer; the conies are but a feeble folk, yet make they their houses in the rocks; the locusts have no king, yet go they forth all of them by bands; the spider taketh hold with her hands, and is in kings' palaces." To the same class may be referred the following paragraph in the third chapter of Ecclesiastes: "To every thing there is a season, and a time to every purpose under the heaven: a 'time to be born, and a time to die; a time to plant, and a time to pluck up that which is planted; a time to kill, and a time to heal: a time to break down, and a time to build up; a time to weep, and a time to laugh; a time to mourn, and a time to dance; a time to cast away stones, and a time to gather stones together; a time to embrace, and a time to refrain from embracing; a time to get, and a time to lose; a time to keep, and a time to cast away; a time to rend, and a time to sew; a time to keep silence, and a time to speak; a time to love, and a time to hate; a time of war, and a time of peace."

Enigmatical questions and answers may easily degenerate into mere childish amusement: but it is due to the celebrity of the queen of Sheba, to suppose that her inquiries were principally directed to the great purpose of information. She was indeed curious to *prove* Solomon, to ascertain whether his reputation for wisdom were the result of mere courtly panegyric and flattering report, or whether it really originated in a supernatural endowment--but still more anxious to acquire knowledge "concerning the name of the Lord." While, therefore, she discovered a laudable desire of information upon subjects connected with the improvement of her mind, in general knowledge, and in political wisdom; she aspired after a more intimate acquaintance with that heavenly truth, which had hitherto been almost exclusively communicated to the descendants of Abraham. In this she may be exhibited as a pattern for the particular imitation of her own sex. No exterior accomplishments, no personal attractions can reconcile an intelligent observer to an ignorant mind; while such an one would be easily persuaded to dispense with external beauty, for the sake of mental and moral worth. He would prize the jewel, and overlook the inferiority of the casket. Curiosity is one of the most powerful principles of our nature, and may be indulged where it is not perverted. Let a woman assiduously cultivate, in early life especially, her mental faculties, and cherish an inquisitive spirit upon all the subjects of knowledge within the reach of her pursuit, still under the constant regulation of modesty and her sister graces; and let her never for a moment imagine, that knowledge is inimical either to her personal happiness and influence, or to her domestic duties. So far, indeed, as an intemperate persuit of learning disqualifies a woman for the sphere which Providence has allotted her, so far as she is rendered proud, pedantic, unsocial, assuming, and negligent of the proper business of every day in her family, it is to be discouraged; not from the consideration that *knowledge* is an evil, but the *misuse* of it. Its legitimate tendency is to improve the female character--to polish off the asperities and roughnesses occasioned by the indulgence of pride--to teach her the proper duties of her station, and the best means of discharging them--to elevate her into the interesting and intelligent companion of social and domestic life--to constitute her the best instructor of her children, at that early period when the first buddings of intellect are discernible, the first tendencies of the mind begin to be developed, and the character for time, perhaps for eternity, is to be formed. It is then under the hand of maternal tenderness the model of the future man or woman is to be made; for it is seldom, even in the most unhappy cases of apostacy, that traces of this early formation are by any circumstances totally obliterated.

But while we plead for the cultivation of the youthful mind, by a diligent use of all the advantages which are afforded to impart knowledge, be it remembered, that the "wisdom which is from above" must not only be sought--but sought *first*, as of paramount importance. With all our conscious superiority in other respects, if destitute of the knowledge of "the only true God, and Jesus Christ whom he hath sent," we shall prove but as "a sounding brass, and as a tinkling cymbal." Our boasted attainments, as enhancing our responsibility, will minister to our final condemnation; and while imagining we have been defective in nothing, we shall feel the everlasting remorse connected with the conviction of having forgotten or despised the "ONE thing NEEDFUL."--

"'Tis Religion that can give
Sweetest pleasures while we live;
'Tis Religion can supply
Choicest comforts when we die."

Solomon conducted himself to the queen of Sheba in a manner highly worthy of his wisdom, and instructive to those who are distinguished from others by any natural or acquired superiority. He was neither reserved nor impatient, but suffered her to "commune with him of all that was in her heart. And Solomon told her all her questions; there was not any thing hid from the king, which he told her not." It ill becomes those who can teach, to be supercilious and uncommunicative. As the rich are required to supply the necessities of the poor with a judicious liberality, being expressly appointed as the trustees of Providence, and dispensers of its bounty; and as those who withhold, when it is in the power of their hands to give, are unfaithful stewards; so, persons qualified to be the instructors of others, or who assume a station which presupposes such a qualification, ought to exert their talents and employ their time for the benefit of the uninformed. Is not this a lesson for the ministers of the sanctuary? For what purpose is "heavenly treasure" committed to "earthen vessels?" Is it not for distribution? Are they not made rich in spiritual gifts, graces, and knowledge, that, instead of monopolizing their spiritual possessions, they may aim to supply and enrich an impoverished world? The true ministerial spirit breathes in the language of Peter to the lame man, who was laid daily at the gate of the temple, "Silver and gold have I none, *but such as I have give I thee*; in the name of Jesus Christ of Nazareth, rise up and walk."

Every thing her eyes beheld at Jerusalem produced, in the queen of Sheba, surprise and admiration. Accustomed as all the eastern nations were to splendour, she had never before witnessed such an universal and surpassing magnificence. Solomon's wisdom--his house--his luxurious table--his servants--his ministers--the temple, and the devotional manner of his attendance upon its services, struck her with overwhelming astonishment. When she had seen all these, "there was no more spirit in her."

It is easy to imagine that the TEMPLE, a structure which has been admired in every age for its unparalleled glory, and for which such minute directions were given by Jehovah himself, must have attracted particular notice; especially when it is considered, that the science of architecture was, at that period, in a very infantine state, compared to its subsequent progress amongst the Greeks and Romans, and that temples were a species of building probably unknown to the queen of Sheba. It is notorious that the Persians, who worshipped the sun, erected no temple, from a persuasion it would be derogatory to his glory who had the whole world for his habitation; and hence the magi exhorted Xerxes to destroy all the temples in his expedition to Greece. The Bithynians worshipped on the mountains, the ancient Germans in the woods; and Diogenes, Zeno, and the Stoics, expressly condemned the erection of such edifices. The Arabians rendered homage to the sun, stars, and planets; and their religion resembled the ancient Chaldean superstition. The illustrious visitor of Solomon must, therefore, have been confounded at an architectural magnificence so superior to any thing she had ever before witnessed.

The inspired historian also mentions the house of the forest of Lebanon; his own palace, which occupied thirteen years in building; a house for Pharaoh's daughter whom he married; with other expensive erections. "All these were of costly stones, (according to the measures of hewed stones, sawed with saws,) within and without, even from the foundation unto the coping, and so on the outside towards the great court. And the foundation was of costly stones, even great stones; stones of ten cubits, and stones of eight cubits. And above were costly stones, (after the measures of hewed stones) and cedars."

Josephus gives the following amplified description of these buildings: "This house (the king's palace) was a large and curious building, and was supported by many pillars, which Solomon built to contain a multitude for hearing causes, and taking cognizance of suits. It was sufficiently capacious to contain a great body of men, who would come together to have their causes determined. It was a hundred cubits long, and fifty broad, and thirty high, supported by quadrangular pillars, which were all of cedar, but its roof was according to the Corinthian order, with folding doors, and their adjoining pillars of equal magnitude, each fluted with three cavities; which building was at once firm and very ornamental. There was also another house so ordered, that its entire breadth was placed in the middle; it was quadrangular, and its breadth was thirty cubits, having a temple over against it, raised upon massy pillars; in which temple there was a large and very glorious room, wherein the king sat in judgment. To this was joined another house, that was built for his queen. There were other smaller edifices for diet, and for sleep, after public matters were over; and these were all floored with boards of cedar. Some of these Solomon built with stones of ten cubits, and wainscotted the walls with other stones that were sawed, and were of great value, such as are dug out of the earth for the ornaments of temples, and to make fine prospects in royal palaces, and which make the mines whence they are dug famous. Now the contexture of the curious workmanship of these stones was in three rows, but the fourth row would make one admire its sculptures, whereby were represented trees, and all sorts of plants, with the shades that arose from their branches, and leaves that hung down from them. Those trees and plants covered the stone that was beneath them, and their leaves were wrought so prodigiously thin and subtle, that you would think they were in motion: but the other part up to the roof was plastered over, and, as it were, embroidered with colours and pictures. He moreover built other edifices for pleasure; as also very long cloisters, and those situate in an agreeable place of the palace; and among them a most glorious dining-room, for feastings and compotations, and full of gold, and such other furniture as so fine a room ought to have for the conveniency of the guests, and where all the vessels were made of gold. Now it is very hard to reckon up the magnitude and the variety of the royal apartments; how many rooms there were of the largest sort; how many of a bigness inferior to those; and how many that were subterraneous and invisible; the curiosity of those that enjoyed the fresh air; and the groves for the most delightful prospect, for the avoiding the heat, and covering of their bodies. And to say all in brief, Solomon made the whole building entirely of white stone, and cedar wood, and gold, and silver. He also adorned the roofs and walls with stones set in gold, and beautified them thereby in the same manner as he had beautified the temple of God with the like stones. He also made himself a throne of prodigious bigness, of ivory, constructed as a seat of justice, and having six steps to it; on every one of which stood, on each end of the step, two lions, two other lions standing above also; but at the sitting-place of the throne, hands came out and received the king; and when he sat backward, he rested on half a bullock, that looked towards his back, but still all was fastened together with gold." [38]

If human happiness were uniformly proportionate to the degree of elevation in the scale of society, and the extent of worldly riches, some plausible pretence might be framed for that eager ambition which characterizes so large a part of mankind; but, if Solomon may be congratulated as remarkably happy, this arose not from his being unusually rich, but pre-eminently wise. In vain does any one expect substantial enjoyment, who despises or neglects religion; while he who possesses it can never be miserable. "Having nothing, he yet possesses all things." If it be not our condition, but the state of our mind, that constitutes the blessedness of life, exterior circumstances can neither confer nor deprive us of real peace. The "contentment" which "godliness" imparts, is "great gain;" because it renders its possessor, in a high degree, independent of the vicissitudes that agitate this terrestrial scene, raises him above the tempests of this transitory state of existence to a higher sphere, and admits him into the very precincts of heaven. If Solomon had been endowed with *wealth*, but remained destitute of *wisdom*, we should have looked down upon his earthly splendour as a fading dream, or as the tinsel decoration of a littleness which, by this means, became the more contemptible; had he been possessed of *wisdom* without *wealth*, we should still have regarded him as the first of our species, and rich in all the requisites of real felicity.

Having recovered from the ecstacy which the first impression of Solomon's wisdom and magnificence produced, the queen of Sheba said to the king, "It was a true report, that I beard in mine own land of thy acts and of thy wisdom. Howbeit, I believed not the words, until I came, and mine eyes had seen it; and, behold, the half was not told me; thy wisdom and prosperity exceedeth the fame which I heard. Happy are thy men, happy are these thy servants which stand continually before thee, and that hear thy wisdom, Blessed be the Lord thy God which delighteth in thee, to set thee on the throne of Israel; because the Lord loved Israel for ever, therefore made he thee king to do judgment and justice."

Many reflections occur upon reading this noble panegyric. Nothing is so conducive to the true glory of a monarch, and the real interests of his people, as an entire self-devotement to the proper business of government. He who avoids the splendid course of ambition, to cultivate the arts of peace, and to promote, by judicious regulations, the internal welfare of his dominions, may not always glitter upon the page of history; but will live in the hearts of his people, and be embalmed in their grateful recollections. He will have the satisfaction, when commanded by Providence to lay aside his crown, to leave to his subjects what is infinitely better than extended empire, an *example* worthy of their imitation.

It becomes us to recognize a superintending providence in the appointment of rulers to their stations--to remember that "promotion cometh neither from the east, nor from the west, nor from the south; but God is judge, he putteth down one, and setteth up another"--and that the gift of a good king is a mark of favour, and ought to excite a people's gratitude. It was because "the Lord loved Israel forever," that Solomon was placed upon the throne. Confining our attention solely to second causes, and the limited horizon of the political theatre, we may frequently perceive nothing but confusion--the struggles of ambition--the uproar of passion--the ravings of impiety--the clash of arms--the subversion of thrones--the desolation of provinces--the flow of human blood--and an interminable series of changes, both unexpected and mysterious;--but when the light of Scripture breaks upon the dark and troubled scene, it discloses the footsteps of Deity walking in the midst of the storm, regulating all human affairs, and rendering every occurrence subservient to his own omniscient purposes. With these discordant elements he is moulding future events, and preparing to exhibit to the admiration of the intelligent universe, "a new heaven and a new earth, wherein dwelleth righteousness."

Comparing, further, the situation of the servants and courtiers of Solomon, with that of others in Pagan countries, we cannot help uniting in the congratulations of his noble visiter, and remarking the advantage of religious connexions in general. Wicked association is the bane of human society, and fatally conducive to the confirmation of evil habits and principles, or to the excitement of them. Such persons, therefore, as are connected with the people of God, who have pious parents or friends, or who are servants in religious families, cannot be too grateful to Providence, or too solicitous of improving their advantages. Let them be attentive to the instructions they receive, and anxious to understand and join in the devotions which are offered on the domestic altar.

But this congratulatory strain of the queen of Sheba may be applied to the Christian age, and to "a greater than Solomon." Jesus Christ is "king in Zion," and happy are his servants which stand continually before him, to hear his wisdom; happy they who have "the glorious Gospel" in their possession, and, by means of the evangelical historians of the New Testament, witness the actions and hear the words of this divine Instructor! The intelligence that distinguished the king of Israel was but a single beam of light from the "Sun of Righteousness," by whom all spiritual knowledge is communicated to the world--who is the fountain of all wisdom, and whose glory will for ever irradiate and beautify a redeemed universe. When believers ascend above this inferior state of existence into the presence of God and the Lamb, notwithstanding all the communications of inspired penmen in the sacred page--owing to the imperfection of human language, and the circumstances of man, which, in some cases, render further instructions *impossible*, in others *improper*--such will be their discoveries of the glory of Jesus Christ, that the language of the queen of Sheba will prove peculiarly descriptive of their feelings, "behold, the half was not told me." And even here experienced piety exclaims, "whom having not seen we love; in whom, though now we see him not, yet believing, we rejoice with JOY UNSPEAKABLE AND FULL OF GLORY."

The queen of Sheba did not return to her country till she had given Solomon a hundred and twenty talents of gold, besides a great quantity of spices and precious stones; a present, for which the king made suitable acknowledgments, by giving her "all her desire; whatsoever she asked, besides that which Solomon gave her of his royal bounty." Harmer remarks, "this appears strange to us; but is perfectly agreeable to modern Eastern usages, which are allowed to be derived from remote antiquity.

"A reciprocal giving and receiving royal gifts has nothing in it strange; but the supposition of the sacred historian, that this Arabian queen *asked* for some things she saw in the possession of king Solomon, is what surprises us. However, the practice is very common to this day in the East--it is not there looked upon as any degradation to dignity, or any mark of rapacious meanness.

"Irwin's publication [39] affords many instances of such a custom, among very considerable people, both in Arabia and Egypt, though not equal in power to the queen that visited king Solomon. They demanded from time to time, such things as they saw, and which happened to please them; arms, vestments, &c. What the things were that so struck the queen of Sheba, as that *she asked* for them, and which Solomon did not before apprehend would be particularly pleasing to her, the sacred historian has not told us, nor can we pretend to guess.

"Many other travellers have mentioned this custom, and shown that the great people of that country not only expect presents, but will directly, and without circumlocutions, ask for what they have a mind to have, and expect that their requisitions should be readily complied with; while, with us, it would be looked on as extremely mean, and very degrading to an exalted character." [40]

This reciprocation of presents may be considered as illustrative of that homage which it becomes every heart to render to the Son of God, and of those divine communications of grace with which he will ever enrich the believer. We cannot indeed enhance his glory by the most splendid liberalities, or the most costly offerings; but he solemnly requires, and graciously deigns to accept our penitence and our obedience. "The sacrifices of God are a broken spirit; a broken and a contrite heart, O God, thou wilt not despise." Whatever be the present state of the world, it is pleasing to reflect that an omnipotent Providence is hastening the triumphs of Christ; and to this wise and glorious King of Israel, all the tribes of the earth shall ultimately present their best offerings and their united affections. "The kings of Tarshish and of the Isles, shall bring presents; the kings of Sheba and Seba shall offer gifts. Yea, all kings shall fall down before him; all nations shall serve him."

But what shall be said to those who refuse submission to the authority of Jesus Christ, and reject the blessings of his salvation? How pungent was his address to the Jewish nation, and how applicable to such characters in the present age! "The queen of the south shall rise up in the judgment with this generation, and shall condemn it: for she came from the uttermost parts of the earth to hear the wisdom of Solomon; and, behold, a greater than Solomon is here." The queen of Sheba only had access to the wisdom of *Solomon*--but you have access to the wisdom *Christ*--she came from a *very distant region*--but "the word is *nigh thee*, even in thy mouth and in thy heart; that is, the word of faith which we preach"--she came *uninvited*, and upon the hazard of a favourable reception--but you are *requested* and *urged* to come to Jesus, and partake of the provisions which cover the well-spread table of his grace. His supplies are spiritual, and therefore invaluable. He does not promise gold, but dispenses "grace and glory."--He confers not the fading honours and transient distinctions of this life, but the joys of *salvation*, the blessedness of *heaven*, the riches of ETERNITY!

The Shunammite Chapter XIII

Section I

How strikingly different is the course of profane and sacred history! The former, searching out the most prominent characters that figure upon the stage of life, exhibits them in pompous language, and, by emblazoning their actions with the lustre of high-wrought description and extravagant panegyric, conceals from view those moral blemishes which a nearer inspection, through the medium of a more dispassionate narrative, would discover in all their enormity. Hence the Alexanders and Cæsars of the world, whose mighty ambition, in marching to take possession of unoffending empires, has trampled on the rights of man, the fruits of industry, and the comforts of domestic life, and whose laurels are died with the blood of humanity, have nevertheless had their names transmitted with loud applause from age to age. High station, noble birth, great talents, or marvellous exploits, though associated with daring crime, constitute a sufficient passport to the historic page, which too often extols where it ought to censure: and instructs us to venerate a name which should rather be execrated.

Sacred history pursues a different course. It records, indeed, the actions of the unworthy as well as of the pious; not that we should be roused to rapturous admiration of their achievements, but, by tracing the dreadful outline of their characters, and the fatal consequences of their guilt, be incited to avoid their vices. In general, those individuals whom civil history overlooks, are found in the inspired records, while "the mighty" and "the noble" remain unnoticed. Some few instances, indeed, of the lives of great men, in point of station and rank, furnish exceptions to this observation; but they are introduced, not because they were *great*, but because they were *pious*; or, if impious, because they stood connected with the church of God. Scripture does not so much furnish the history of the world as the history of the church and of human nature. It aims to instruct, not to amuse or astonish; and that, by the exhibition of characters remarkable in any respect for their efforts to oppose or to promote the purposes of eternal wisdom, or for the exhibition, in a private sphere, of those principles, the knowledge of whose diversified operations might prove useful to posterity.

Shunem, or Sunam, a city of the tribe Issachar, would have been scarcely noticed or known but for the residence of an opulent female, who is Herself rendered forever illustrious in consequence of her friendship for the prophet Elisha, and the eminence of her religion: but, though "a great woman," her name is omitted in the narrative--of so little importance are those distinctions upon which mankind value themselves so highly! She is simply designated *the Shunammite*, after the name of her city.

[Sidenote: Years before Christ, about 835]

The inspired narrator notices, in the first place, the warmth of her hospitality, and its unabating continuance to Elisha. On a certain occasion, when he went to Shunem, she urged him to visit her, which issued in such a mutual esteem, that "as oft as he passed by, he turned in thither to eat bread." Among the ancients, and in a simple state of society, where the accommodations of modern travelling were unknown, the entertainment of strangers was considered as one of the first of duties. In all the Arab villages this necessary practice prevails. The sheikh, or principal person, generally invites strangers to his house, furnishes them with eggs, butter, curds, honey, olives, and fruit, when there is not sufficient time to dress meat: and, if they choose to remain during the night, they are treated with the utmost kindness. The Arabs value themselves highly upon their hospitality. "How often," says one of their poets, "when echo gave me notice of a stranger's approach, have I stirred my fire that it might give a clear blaze. I flew to him as to a prey, through fear that my neighbours should get possession of him before me." [41]

The Scriptures furnish many examples of this duty. Abraham, in entertaining three strangers, is said to have "entertained angels unawares;" Lot received two angels into his house, who appeared as strangers in the streets of Sodom: Job affirms of himself, "The stranger did not lodge in the street; I opened my doors to the traveller;" a good widow, in the apostolic age, is described as washing the saints' feet, relieving the afflicted, and *lodging strangers*; and Gaius is represented as receiving Christian ministers into his house as his own children.

Although a considerable difference of circumstances exists in more civilized countries, and in this age, so as to render such an extensive hospitality impossible, as well as in many cases unsafe; yet no change of custom and no lapse of time can preclude the duty itself, or diminish the force of the apostolic admonition, "be not forgetful to entertain strangers, for thereby some have entertained angels unawares." If an indiscriminate admission of strangers into the domestic circle might, in our case, be productive of great inconveniences, benevolence requires that those acts of kindness should be shown to others which comport with our means and opportunities, and that we should aim at such moderation in our usual expenditure as shall enable us to discharge the obligations of Christian charity. How, otherwise, can we "do unto others as we would that others should do unto us?" The wheel of Providence is perpetually revolving, and who knows but that he who is now at the summit of worldly prosperity, or in the full enjoyment of an easy competence, may soon be brought down to the level of the needy; and, though he may be in a condition to *confer* kindness to-day, may have to *solicit* it to-morrow? Who can be insensible to the privilege of the Saviour's final benediction, "Come, ye blessed of my Father, inherit the kingdom prepared for you from the foundation of the world: for I was an hungered, and ye gave me meat; I was thirsty, and ye gave me drink; I was a stranger, and ye took me in; naked, and ye clothed me; I was sick, and ye visited me; I was in prison, and ye came unto me."

The Shunammite did not entertain a stranger merely, but a prophet; and, from the conversation of Elisha, doubtless derived that spiritual edification which induced her to solicit his future friendship. Others came, departed, and were forgotten; but religion in each heart converted these strangers into friends, and cemented a holy union, which neither time, nor change, nor death, could dissolve.

It is to be lamented, that the converse even of holy men in Christian families is not always tinged with that piety which renders it as "a sweet savour," and too frequently the ministers of the sanctuary fail to enforce the admonitions of the pulpit and fix the sacred impressions of the sabbath by "a conversation becoming the Gospel of Christ." What fine opportunities do they possess of "winning souls to Christ," or "building up the saints in their most holy faith," by the very nature of their office, and the extensive private intercourse to which it admits them! It would be well for *all* to cultivate that sort of spiritual adroitness for which *some* are truly remarkable, who can, with the utmost facility, glide from general topics of discourse to religious communications, which are so piously, and yet so delicately managed, that the most hostile are in some degree conciliated, and even pleased. The apostle of the Gentiles thus exhorts Timothy, "Be thou an example of the believers in word, in conversation, in charity, in spirit, in faith, in purity."

This excellent Shunammite proposed to her husband to accommodate Elisha with a *little chamber* appropriated to his own use, with which he seems readily to have complied. This is much to the honour of both; to the one for her proposal, to the other for his compliance. It is a happy circumstance where those who have joined hands are united in heart, and, avoiding the spirit of domination, are equally anxious to fulfil the respective duties of their domestic character. The ground of her solicitation, was that of his being "a holy man of God," which, it is to be feared, would prove a very decisive *objection* to such a measure in many families, who wish to conceal their gay and licentious habits from such observance. The suggestion of this pious lady to her husband respecting the accommodation of their agreeable visiter, may remind us of the duty of women, 'to avail themselves of the opportunities with which providence favours them in married life, to give such useful hints to their husbands as their benevolence will naturally dictate. The multiplicity of engagements in which the husband is involved, in the prosecution of his daily concerns, often precludes those thoughts which might issue in plans of public utility or more private kindness; while the wife has leisure for this very important purpose. And to the honour of the female sex let it be recorded, that the poor and the destitute are indebted to the ladies of Britain for originating, and in many cases carrying into execution, some of the noblest schemes of Christian charity.

Separate buildings, resembling the prophet's chamber, are frequently attached to houses in the East, sometimes rising a story higher than the house, at other times consisting of one or two rooms and a terrace: others are built over the porch or gateway, having most of the conveniences belonging to the house itself: they communicate by a door, into the gallery of the house, which the master of the family opens or shuts at his pleasure; besides another door, which opens from a private staircase immediately into the porch or street, without giving the least disturbance to the house. These back-houses are called *olee* or *oleah*, and in them strangers are usually lodged and entertained. The little chamber built by the Shunammite for Elisha was probably of this description. To this he had free access, without interfering with the family, or being interrupted by them in his devotions, and from it he might privately retire whenever he pleased. [42]

The peculiar simplicity of the furniture in the prophet's chamber cannot fail of striking attention: it consisted of a *bed*, a *table*, a *stool*, and a *candlestick*. This scanty fitting up of his room is by no means to be attributed to disrespect or negligence: it is rather to be considered as characteristic of the simplicity of the times. The intention certainly was to accommodate Elisha in a manner expressive of reverence and esteem. The original term, unhappily rendered *stool* in our English version, signifies one of the most honourable kind of seats usually placed in an apartment, and is sometimes translated *throne*. In ancient times, the nations of the East were not so universally addicted as they are at present to sitting on the ground upon mats or carpets, but accustomed themselves to raised seats or chairs, which were sometimes sufficiently elevated to require a footstool. The *candlestick* is likewise to be considered as a mark of respect, if not of magnificence, and its particular use was to keep a light burning the whole night. Dr. Chandler mentions a lamp being placed in his room for this purpose in the house of a Jew, who was vice-consul for the English nation, at the place where he landed when about to visit the ruins of Asia Minor.[43]

In general, however, the prophets chose to live in the plainest manner: they built their houses with their own hands, and wore a coarse dress of a dark brown colour. Instead of availing themselves of the opportunities with which they were often presented of acquiring riches, or of frequenting the luxurious tables of the great, they sometimes refused the most valuable presents. Of this we have a remarkable specimen when Elisha declined the gifts of Naaman, and inflicted a dreadful punishment upon Gehazi for his contrivance to secure them. If the mean attire and mode of living which distinguished the ancient prophets cannot be viewed in the light of an authoritative example to future ages, and if something may be reasonably conceded to the practices of different nations, this may be received as an axiom, that those whom Providence has appointed to the sacred office ought to avoid all unnecessary show in their appearance, and all ambitious aspiring after the vain splendours of life; for "the fashion of this world passeth away." On the other hand, it is the duty, and should be considered as the privilege of pious individuals, to whom Providence has dispensed riches or competence, to minister to the necessities of the poor servants of God, who, while devoting their lives to promote their spiritual comfort, and that of their families, have neither time nor means to rescue themselves from a state of dependence and poverty. "If they have been partakers of their spiritual things, their duty is also to minister unto them in carnal things."

Elisha was not insensible to all this kindness, but, on the contrary, feeling anxious to devise some means of requiting it, he intimated, during one of his visits, his wish to render his hostess any service in his power, and proposed what he thought might be the most acceptable; "Behold," said he, "thou hast been careful for us with all this care; what is to be done for thee? wouldst thou be spoken for to the king, or to the captain of the host?" It is gratifying to find that Elisha possessed so much influence at court, and that Jehoram, though an impious prince, honoured the man of God. But, perhaps, the king of Israel was more influenced in his attachment by the miracle which the prophet had lately performed in his favour, and the victory he had promised to him and his royal friends Jehoshaphat and the king of Edom, than by any proper regard to his person or his office.

The answer of this Shunammite to the prophet's proposal was brief, but expressive: it indicated a mind full of contentment, and actuated in all its liberal devices by the purest motives. "I dwell," said she, "among mine own people;" *q. d.* "I am satisfied with my lot--I am happy in the circle in which I move--I have no wish to emerge from obscurity, persuaded that though I or my family might gain in point of distinction or wealth by your kind interference, we should lose a considerable portion of that real comfort which, in our estimation, is better than the greatest of earthly possessions."

The sentiment of this pious lady is to be distinguished from the opinion which has prevailed in some parts of the world, that the perfection of religion consists in a total retirement from the intercourse of life to the cell of the monk or the cave of the hermit, and in passing the days and nights of existence in mere speculative contemplation. That separation from the world which the word of God enjoins, is a separation of *spirit*, a withdrawment of the affections from its criminal pursuits and guilty indulgences. It does not interdict all intercourse with mankind, or censure a diligent pursuit of business, but inculcates purity of character, and teaches us so to act in the particular sphere assigned us by the arrangements of Providence, that "our good works," may be "seen," and our "light" may "shine before men."

Religion is not an abstract principle, or a mere speculation; it is operative: God is its source and end, but society its proper sphere of action. In circumstances of perplexity and trial its real nature is best developed, as conquering the irregularity of desire, pacifying the turbulence of passion, purifying all the principles of the corrupt heart, and forming men into the future associates of angels and "saints in light." The Shunammite did not retire from her people, her family, or her friends; but "*dwelt* amongst them," exemplifying those virtues which adorn domestic and social life, and securing, as we may infer from her expressions, that general esteem which such exalted goodness is calculated to procure. She discharged scrupulously and zealously the appropriate duties of her situation, and shone in the orbit allotted to her by Him whose infinite wisdom disposes all the arrangements of the natural and moral worlds, with conspicuous brightness and useful influence.

Moreover, the language in question presents us with one of the finest specimens of contentment in the records of history. It may be affirmed without hesitation, that nothing can secure the exercise of this temper, in the present constitution of the human mind, but genuine religion. In cases where no such principle exists, dissatisfaction imbitters the cup of our earthly portion, and all those ambitious feelings which agitate and distress the life of man, acquire an uncontrolled ascendency. The discourse of Pyrrhus with Cineas is only a transcript of the impatient ambition of the generality of mankind. "If it please Heaven that we conquer the Romans," said the philosopher, "what use, sir, shall we make of our victory?"--"Cineas," replied the king, "your question answers itself. When the Romans are once subdued, there is no town, whether Greek or Barbarian, in all the country, that will dare to oppose us; but we shall immediately be masters of all Italy, whose greatness, power, and importance, no man knows better than you." Cineas, after a short pause, continued, "But after we have conquered Italy, what shall we do next, sir?" Pyrrhus, not yet perceiving his drift, replied, "There is Sicily very near, and stretches out her arms to receive us; a fruitful and populous island, and easy to be taken: for Agathocles was no sooner gone, than faction and anarchy prevailed among her cities, and every thing is kept in confusion by her turbulent demagogues."--"What you say, my prince," said Cineas, "is very probable; but is the taking of Sicily to conclude our expeditions?"--"Far from it," answered Pyrrhus, "for if Heaven grant us success in this, *that success shall only be the prelude to greater things*. Who can forbear Libya and Carthage, then within reach, which Agathocles, even when he fled in a clandestine manner from Syracuse, and crossed the sea with a few ships only, had almost made himself master of? And when we have made such conquests, who can pretend to say that any of our enemies, who are now so insolent, will think of resisting us?" "To be sure," said Cineas, "they will not; for it is clear that so much power will enable you to recover Macedonia, and to establish yourself uncontested sovereign of Greece. But when we have conquered all, what are we to do then?"--"Why then, my friend." said Pyrrhus, laughing, "we will take our ease, and drink, and be merry." Cineas, having brought him thus far, replied, "And what hinders us from drinking and taking our ease NOW, *when we have already those things in our hands at which we propose to arrive through seas of blood, through infinite toils and dangers, through innumerable calamities, which we must both cause and suffer?*" [44]

One motive to contentment, which probably influenced the Shunammite, and which is calculated to inspire a similar feeling in every situation, arose from the conviction, that *happiness is much more equally diffused than we commonly imagine*.

Whatever may be the diversities of human condition, and however preferable the situation of some above others may *seem*, to an inexperienced or careless observer, looking only at the *exterior* of society, Providence has so wisely adjusted its various inequalities, that it becomes extremely difficult to determine who possesses the most happy lot. Wherever particular advantages exist, they are balanced by proportionate evils, and the reverse: the golden cup often contains a bitter potion, while sweet is the draught and refreshing the supply, that is brought in a broken pitcher. The poor are apt to suppose, that opulence furnishes an inexhaustible fund of enjoyment; and that luxurious tables, sumptuous palaces, and a splendid retinue, confer a never-failing enjoyment; forgetting that riches create a thousand artificial wants, a thousand fantastic desires, which it is utterly impossible to supply. The wealthy look with pity upon the indigent, as condemned to an irksome and perpetual drudgery, and destitute of all means of enjoying life; a pity they might well spare, did they know that labour sweetens rest, and that unpampered appetite has none of those loathings which luxury superinduces. Riches and poverty are not then, according to the miscalculations of mankind, terms of synonymous import with happiness and misery. The most exalted have many afflictions, the most depressed many comforts. The shafts of envy fly over the lowly cottage, and smite the towers of greatness; and while the peasant sleeps soundly in his humble cottage,

"Uneasy lies the head that wears a crown."

It has been well remarked by Bishop Hopkins, that "there is scarcely any condition in the world so low, but may satisfy our *wants*; and there is no condition so high, as can satisfy our *desires*. If we live according to the law of nature and reason, we shall never be poor; but if we live according to fond opinion and fancy, we shall never be rich."

The diversities of our temporal condition, therefore, illustrate the remark which Solomon has connected with very important advice; "In the day of prosperity be joyful, but in the day of adversity consider; *God also hath set the one over against the other*, to the end that man should find nothing after him."

Independently of these considerations, it may be questioned whether that change after which so many eagerly aspire, would really conduce to their happiness. The probability is, that *any* material alteration of circumstances is unfavourable to enjoyment, and that our respective destinies are so wisely arranged, that each one is, upon the whole, most likely to secure the greatest proportion of temporal felicity in the sphere originally assigned him, than in any other. His habits, his views, his friendships, are all fixed by his position and place in society, and all his mental faculties have been trained, so to speak, to this very spot. Any removal or change would be hazardous and more likely to impair than consummate his happiness. After the growth of years, the tree cannot be transplanted into another soil and air without long exhibiting symptoms of languishing, and sometimes a total decay.

Another reflection calculated to promote a contented spirit is, that *if we were capable of tracing the tendencies, connexions, and ultimate results of all things as they are seen, by the eye of Omniscience, and established by omnipotent power, we should perceive as much reason to be thankful for what is denied us, as for what is bestowed.* The fancied good which we are so eager to obtain would, in many cases, be a real evil in possession. Our prejudices and passion prevent our forming a proper judgment, and were not our heavenly Father influenced by a truly parental solicitude for his people, the most fatal mischiefs would arise.

Providence has two ways of punishing a repining or an impatient temper; the one is by *counteracting* it, by placing the imaginary good beyond the reach of attainment, and forcing back the wandering heart to its home and its God, by disappointing its expectations of happiness in earthly possessions. Such refusals, or rather obstructions to temporal success, are indications of the purest regard, as parents, *severely* kind, take away from their froward children those destructive weapons which had attracted them by their glittering appearance. Another, and a more dreadful mode of inflicting necessary chastisement, is, by *complying* with their wishes, and making them feel the insufficiency of what they desired to render them happy. They "forsook the fountain of living waters," and the "cisterns" they resolved to possess, prove to be "broken" and empty. In this case, they suffer the double penalty of dissatisfaction *in* the imaginary good for which they had sacrificed so much, and of deep remorse for a misconduct which has incurred the divine displeasure. It is said of Israel, "he gave them their request, but sent leanness into their soul."

In considering the *denials* of Providence, it should not be forgotten, that what is in part an evil, may be a good upon the whole; the amputation of a disordered or fractured limb, as it necessarily produces great personal suffering, is in part an evil; but, inasmuch as it saves life, it is, on the whole, an important good. On the other hand, that which as in part good, may, on the whole, be an evil; the rich cargo with which a vessel is freighted may be considered in itself a good, but if it be retained to the destruction of the vessel tossed by a tempestuous ocean, and struck upon a sunken rock, it is, on the whole, a dreadful evil; and yet, in the vast concerns of the soul and eternity, what multitudes act upon this fatal principle--clinging to their treasures, though they sink them into perdition!

It is obvious, therefore, that in order to understand the dispensations of Heaven, it is necessary to know the circumstances of each particular case, which the very limited extent of our present knowledge and capacities renders utterly impossible; and it cannot be doubted, that if we were acquainted with the *whole* subject, the most afflictive events of life, no less than the most pleasing, would be seen to form essential parts of that great system of mercy, by which the universal Disposer is promoting the ultimate and perfect felicity of all his children. "But let patience have her perfect work," for eternity will discover these mysteries of time. "*Now* we see through a glass darkly, but *then* face to face; now I know in part, but then shall I know even as also I am known."

A third consideration, which, doubtless, influenced this contented Shunammite, was, *the vanity of the world.* The wise have always admitted, that the three principal objects of human desire, pleasures, riches, and honours, when weighed in the balances of truth, are "found wanting," and that, although the misplaced eagerness of mankind attributes to them a thousand charms, they are in reality, but "airy nothings."

"As bubbles blown into the air," says Bishop Hopkins, "will represent a great variety of orient and glittering colours, not (as some suppose) that there are any such really there, but only they appear so to us, through a false reflection of light cast upon them; so truly this world, this earth on which we live, is nothing else but a great bubble blown up by the breath of God in the midst of the air, where it now hangs. It sparkles with ten thousand glories; not that they are so in themselves, but only they seem so to us through the false light by which we look upon them. If we come to grasp it, like a thin film, it breaks, and leaves nothing but wind and disappointment in our hands; as histories report of the fruits that grow near the Dead Sea, where once Sodom and Gomorrah stood, they appear very fair and beautiful to the eye, but, if they be crushed, turn straight to smoke and ashes." If, from general reflections, we descend to the particular details of life, it will still be found, that "while we eagerly pursue any worldly enjoyments, we are but running after a shadow; and as shadows vanish, and are swallowed up in the greater shade of night, so when the night of death shall cast its thick shade about us, and wrap us up in deep and substantial darkness, all these vain shadows will then disappear and vanish quite out of sight."

The vanity of the world arises from the instability and mutation of human affairs, as well as from the comparative insignificance of all its best enjoyments. We say, "What a large estate does that distinguished personage *possess!*"--vain word and false--he is only a tenant for a day--to-morrow he will become the inhabitant of a sepulchre! What a mansion is yonder!--what a lovely family! what prospects in business! what admirable connexions! what charming society! O what an edifice of human happiness is here!-- The Providence of God blows upon the four corners of the house, and it falls! "Here we have no *continuing* city"--no fixed, unalterable enjoyments--no permanent rest. Mutation is inscribed in characters clear and legible to the eye of reason, upon all terrestrial things; and so uncertain are our property, our health, our enjoyments, our friendships, our ALL upon earth, that, as the thistle-down is scattered by the gentlest breeze, these light and fair possessions may be wafted away by the first wind that rises, or the first touch of unexpected adversity.

The impressive language of Scripture corroborates and illustrates these representations. Man that is born of a woman is of few days, and full of trouble. "He cometh forth like a flower, and is cut down: he fleeth also as a shadow, and continueth not." ... "Lord, make me to know mine end, and the measure of my days what it is, that I may know how frail I am. Behold, thou hast made my days as a hand-breadth, and mine age is as nothing before thee: verily, every man at his best state is altogether vanity. Surely every man walketh in a vain show: surely they are disquieted in vain; he heapeth up riches, and knoweth not who shall gather them." ..." We spend our years as a tale that is told." ... "My days are like a shadow that declineth; and I am withered like grass," ... "As foreman, his days are as grass, as a flower of the field, so he flourisheth; for the wind passeth over it, and it is gone; and the place thereof shall know it no more." ... "Man is like to vanity; his days are as a shadow that passeth away." ... "I have seen all the works that are done under the sun; and, behold, all is vanity and vexation of spirit." ... "What hath man of all his labour, and of the vexation of his heart, wherein he hath laboured under the sun? For all his days are sorrows, and his travail grief, yea, his heart taketh not rest in the night. This is also vanity." ... "Who knoweth what is good for man in this life, all the days of his vain life which he spendeth as a shadow! for who can tell a man what shall be after him under the sun?" ... "Vanity of vanities, saith the preacher, all is vanity." ... "Go to now, ye that say, To-day or to-morrow we will go into such a city, and continue there a year, and buy and sell and get gain; whereas ye know not what shall be on the morrow. For what is your life? It is even a vapour, that appeareth for a little time, and than vanisheth away."

A fourth reason for contentment, and which we cannot doubt influenced the pious woman of Shunem, is to be derived from a *view of that future happiness which infinite goodness has provided for the children of God*. In the early period to which we are now adverting, "life and immortality" were not so distinctly "brought to light" as they are in the Christian dispensation by "the Gospel;" but from the day of the first promise of a Saviour, the believing mind perceived the grand purposes for which he was to descend into the world, and enjoyed some pleasing anticipations of that paradise, which it was his prerogative to confer upon one of his fellow-sufferers on the cross. If, as we believe, the Shunammite were acquainted with the existence, and, in some degree, with the glory of a future state; if with Job she felt convinced, that "though worms destroy this body, yet in her flesh she should see God;" if she knew any thing of that inexpressible charm which attaches to the blessedness of "a better country," arising from its unfading permanence,--the language of contentment which she uttered, was but the natural expression of a feeling which such discoveries were calculated to excite. It was sufficient, in her apprehension, to all the purposes of real happiness, to "pass the time of her sojourning," among her "own people," without seeking those distinctions which constitute only the vain decorations of a scene that passeth away. Nor did her principles merely promote satisfaction with her lot: they fortified her against the assault of temptation, a temptation presented in the least exceptionable form, and recommended by the sanctity of a prophet, who deliberately proposed to her an interference with the king, or the captain of the host, for her temporal advancement. Her words express an unalterable resolution of mind: "I dwell amongst mine own people."

Every thing earthly possesses a character of insignificance from its transitoriness, while every heavenly object becomes inviting on account of its durability. A single hour may precipitate us from the highest worldly elevation--the proudest laurel that ever decked the brow of the proudest hero quickly fades; and he who sits out upon a journey of discovery to find the extent of human enjoyments, will soon "see an END of all perfection." But religion has laurels which never fade; crowns of glory which pass to no envious successor. Religion does not lay her foundations in the sand, but erecting her temple upon the shores of eternity, bids us enter in, to "go no more out."

An apostle states, that "godliness hath the promise of the life which now is, and of that which is to come;" intimating the certainty of the existence of a future state, the nature of its felicities, and the essential connection between the *pursuit* and the ultimate *possession* of it. The value of this promise respecting the life to come, is not a little enhanced by its being accomplished precisely at that critical moment when every earthly hope expires, and every human joy departs. Godliness has, indeed, the promise of the life which *"now* is;" but, if it had *not*, the life which "now is" will soon terminate: the successive generations of mankind are hastening to the grave; *our* breath will soon cease--our possessions must soon be left-- our days soon covered with the shadows of the last evening--all we fondly called *our own* scattered to the winds;--but at such a moment of desolation, the religion of Jesus points to regions of deathless felicity. His voice seems to sound across the gulf of death, in accents soft and sweet as the harps of angels, "I am the resurrection and the life." And the "life to come" is no other than the perfection of the Christian's life which "now is"--a life of love--a life of peace, purity, and praise--a life of incessant activity in the service of the blessed God. Hence his present spiritual life, is a kind of pledge and promise of his eternal life; the pantings and breathings of a holy mind after that world, are proofs that it is his *home;* and the believer in Christ becomes assured, that as he advances in spiritual attainments here, he is making so many approaches, hastening by so many steps, to the perfection and joy of eternity.

A few brief observations on the advantages resulting from a daily and deep impression of the transitory nature of terrestrial possessions, and keeping the scenes of another life in constant view, shall close the present section.

1. This will tend to moderate our earthly attachments. Affections were not implanted in our nature to be suppressed and extinguished. We may love, but we must not love inordinately. Love must be proportioned to the value of the object, and must be regulated by scriptural principles, otherwise we shall commit offence, and suffer injury. There is a remedy, and but one *effectual* remedy, for the errors of the heart. It is suggested by an apostle: "Set your affection on things above, not on things on the earth."

2. A due impression of the present, and a just conception of the future, will conduce to the purification of our moral principles. Intermixture with the world, its business and concerns, and those solicitudes which occupy the attention in reference to transactions merely temporal, tend to vitiate the mind. In the pursuits of traffic we seem to live, as if we were destined to live here always. The interests of a moment engross and captivate the passions, and kindle ardours which burn with incessant vigour. The mind is brought close to present objects, in consequence of which they assume an unnatural magnitude, filling the whole sphere of vision, and excluding external realities from view. The effect of this is depraving: it contracts the soul, misdirects its energies, and blunts the edge of its spiritual sensibility.

3. The sentiment we are wishing to inculcate will furnish us with consolation amidst adversities, and reconcile the spirit to bereaving dispensations. The present is a probationary state; and although the particular mode of suffering be unknown, afflictions are not unexpected by Christians. But whatever is transitory is tolerable--

"----the darkest day,
Live till to-morrow, will have pass'd away."

As their own condition is subject to vicissitude, they know also the uncertainty of every other, and realize the possibility of separation from their nearest and dearest connections. The severity of disappointment is here diminished; for what cannot be retained, or is precarious, or *ought* to be resigned, is dispensed with, if not without a sigh or tear, at least without a resentment against the smiting hand of Providence.

4. This comparative view of our two states of being, and this just estimate of their proportionate importance, will prepare us for our own dissolution. The feeling that we have no fixed, no permanent abode on earth, will familiarize the mind with the consideration, that "it is appointed

unto men once to die." If, when a fatal disease attacked the constitution, we thought for the first time of our removal from the present scene, the effect would be unspeakably painful, and hence arises the despondency which often pervades the mind of such as have moved only in circles of gayety and dissipation; but a Christian frequently meditates upon the final hour. While looking at this or that valued possession, he reflects, "I must soon leave it: the loan will, in a short period, be reclaimed."

Nor is this all. The prospect before him is exhilarating. "To die is gain." If the death of a man resembled that of a beast, if the termination of life were the extinction of being, the prospect would be inexpressibly alarming: but the religion of Jesus confers a victory over every fear by revealing immortality. A Christian knows there is something worth dying for; and this animates him to walk with a firm step down "the valley of the shadow of death." He is guided through a darkness impervious to reason. A beam from the "excellent glory" lights him HOME!

Section II

Defeated in his benevolent intentions by the unambitious spirit of the Shunammite, Elisha consulted his confidential servant Gehazi, through whom the former communication had been made, respecting what could be done for her benefit. Sincere as her refusal had been, he found it impossible to satisfy himself without some further attempt to express his gratitude; and upon the suggestion of Gehazi that she had no child, the prophet directed that she should be again called into his presence. "And he said, About this season, according to the time of life, thou shall embrace a son."

It is not improbable, that although Elisha addicted himself to great retirement, Gehazi might be in the habit of familiar intercourse with this pious family, by which means perhaps he found that they were anxious upon this point; at least, if that spirit of perfect contentment which breathed in the language on which we have already offered some observations, influenced them on this as well as on other occasions, they no doubt had intimated, in a moment of unreserved intercourse, that a child would prove a most acceptable gift of Providence.

The brevity of the sacred history precludes that detail of circumstances attending any particular transaction which it sometimes seems necessary to suppose.

In the present case, it is not to be presumed that Elisha would have ventured, *immediately*, upon the mere suggestion of Gehazi, to give so important a promise to the Shunammite as that which is here recorded, without first consulting the will of Heaven, or receiving some divine intimation of an event which no human being could foresee, much less make the subject of a solemn prediction.

Upon his announcing so unexpected a mercy, she manifested that sort of incredulity which extreme astonishment blended with joy is calculated at the first moment to produce; and the well-known effect of which accounts for what, under other circumstances, would appear like disrespectful language: "Nay, my lord, thou man of God, do not lie unto thine handmaid." She was too much acquainted with Elisha's character to intend to charge him with deliberate falsehood; but her feelings were suddenly overpowered, and consequently, she was at no leisure to weigh her words. The prophet's prediction was completely verified; and she had a son, "at that season that Elisha had said unto her, according to the time of life,"--"Lo! children are a heritage of the Lord; and the fruit of the womb is his reward."

In reviewing the scriptural account of remote ages, we cannot fail to be struck with several instances of the extreme anxiety of good women for the possession of children; an anxiety which requires some other reason than the general causes to be assigned for domestic and social congratulations common upon such occasions. Sarah, for example, the wife of Abraham, was induced by this desire to practise a piece of wretched and criminal policy, in giving Hagar, her Egyptian handmaid, to her husband. Rachel, the beloved wife of Jacob, was so impatient of her own barrenness, and so envious of her sister, that she exclaimed, "Give me children, or else I die." The fact was, that they were influenced by the promises of God to Abraham, whose posterity were to inherit the most invaluable blessings, and from whom the Messiah himself was to descend in the fulness of time. As in him "all the families of the earth were to be blessed," who can be surprised that the most distant probability or possibility of introducing him, who was to be "born of a woman," into the world, should excite an ardent wish in every pious woman to become a mother? And here it must be admitted, that whatever reproach the first transgressor might have cast upon the female sex by her misconduct, it is forever wiped away by the enviable distinction of becoming instrumental to a Saviour's birth.

The time hastened in which the Shunammite was to be subjected to a species of trial different from that with which she had been hitherto exercised. The congratulations of her connections on the birth of her child were scarcely expressed, and her earthly happiness consummated, when she was destined to suffer acutely by the death of her little favourite.

Those who have never felt a similar deprivation are necessarily disqualified from forming any adequate idea of the bitterness of parental grief, when the objects of their fondest solicitude are suddenly snatched from the grasp of their affections. It is difficult to say in what period of youthful history this stroke is severest, or when it is most tolerable; because every point of age has its peculiar attractions, and parental love will always imagine that to be the most afflicting in which the event occurs. Happy those who can adopt the language of one of the sweetest epitaphs that ever adorned a monument!--

"Liv'd--to wake each tender passion,
And delightful hopes inspire;
Died--to try our resignation,
And direct our wishes higher:--

"Rest, sweet babe, in gentle slumbers,
Till the resurrection morn;
Then arise to join the numbers,
That its triumphs shall adorn.

"Though, thy presence so endearing,
We thy absence now deplore;
At the Saviour's bright appearing,
We shall meet to part no more.

"Thus to thee, O Lord, submitting,
We the tender pledge resign;
And, thy mercies ne'er forgetting,
Own that all we have is thine." [45]

It is not unusual for the providence of God to deprive us of those objects we had too exclusively and too fondly called *our own*, and the long enjoyment of which we had confidently anticipated. This is no capricious proceeding: it is marked by wisdom and goodness, since our real happiness depends on the regulation of those passions which, but for such dispensations, would rove with unhallowed eccentricity from the chief good. It is necessary that we should be trained in the school of adversity; and that by a course of corrective discipline, nicely adapted to each particular case, our characters should be gradually matured for a nobler existence.

The manner in which the calamity to which we have referred overtook the Shunammite, is thus detailed by the faithful pen of inspiration. "And when the child was grown, it fell on a day that he went out to his father to the reapers. And he said unto his father, My head, my head! And he said to a lad, Carry him to his mother. And when he had taken him and brought him to his mother, he sat on her knees till noon, and then died."

From this brief statement it is evident that this child was smitten by the sun, in consequence of exposing himself in the harvest field to the intensity of the season. In northern climates it is difficult to realize the danger; but in the torrid zone great precaution is necessary to avoid such calamities. Observing the effects of the sun's rays, Apollo is represented, in heathen mythology, as holding a bow, and shooting his arrows upon the earth.

"Pay sacred reverence to Apollo's song,
Lest watchful the far-shooting god emit
His fatal arrows."

PRIOR'S Callimachus.

The heat in some parts of Judea has often proved fatal, even at a very early period of the year. In a battle fought by king Baldwin IV. near Tiberias in Galilee, as many are said to have died in both armies by the heat as by the sword; and an ecclesiastic of eminence, although carried in a litter, expired under mount Tabor, near the river Kishon, in consequence of the excessive heat. Shunem was in the neighbourhood of Tabor. [46]

As soon as the Shunammite found that her son was dead, she took him to the prophet's chamber, and laying him on his bed, shut the door and departed. The only reason of this proceeding probably was, its being the most retired part of the house, and therefore the best suited to such a melancholy occasion. But who can express the yearnings of her maternal tenderness, when she left behind her this precious, but now insensible clay! That tongue which had so often pleased her by its innocent prattle, so often uttered

----"the fond name
That wakes affection to a flame,"

was now silent in death; and those artless and attractive smiles, which to a mother's heart were more lovely than the looks of the morning, were subsided into the fixed and motionless aspect of one whose spirit has ceased to animate the body.

An impatient temper might have invented many reasons for discontent, on this affecting occasion. It might have reproached the father for permitting the child to accompany him, at this sultry season, into the harvest field--the child for an infantine eagerness to go--or herself for indiscreetly allowing of so dangerous a gratification. A comparison of the happier lot of other families might have been drawn, whose children went out on the same day, and returned unsmitten by the infectious atmosphere, or the burning sun; and by aggravating the painful peculiarity of her own affliction, she might thus have driven the barbed arrow still deeper in her bosom, and censured, at least by implication, the Supreme Disposer. But we have to admire a conduct which bespeaks the fullest conviction that it was a *providence* and not a *casualty* that occasioned the death of her beloved offspring, and evinces the most entire acquiescence in the mournful event.

While our attention is confined solely to second causes, the mind will be involved in a labyrinth of difficulties, in judging of the changes and trials incident to the present life; but when our faith ascends above this low and limited scene, to contemplate the arrangements of an universal Providence, the deepest mysteries become unravelled, and the greatest seeming inconsistencies in a considerable degree reconciled. Or, if we cannot develope the whole plan, and ascertain the reason of every movement of almighty Wisdom, we at least acquire a spirit of submission and obedience.

Some persons are so overwhelmed by their sorrows as to be totally disqualified for their duties: but, although the world may applaud this acute sensibility, religion condemns it. As the effect of mere passion, it has nothing in it which can secure the approbation of God; on the contrary, it is offensive to him, who, while he permits us to weep, does not allow us to despond, and who often sees it best to humble a refractory spirit by a repetition of chastisement.

This excellent Shunammite, after making the necessary arrangements for her poor departed son in the prophet's chamber, instead of sitting down to indulge her own melancholy feelings, or court the compassion of her domestics and friends, despatched a messenger to her husband, to request that a servant might be sent to her with one of the asses, for the purpose of going to pay a visit to the man of God. As she had not told him the motive of this sudden determination, he remonstrated, because it was "neither new moon nor sabbath," that is, neither the usual time of secular or sacred journeys. [47] He was, however, easily satisfied when she intimated that she had a good reason for wishing to pay this visit. "She said, It shall be well."

"See," says pious Matthew Henry, "how this husband and wife vied respects; she was so *dutiful to him* that she would not go till she had acquainted him with her journey, and he so *loving to her* that he would not oppose it, though she did not think it fit to acquaint him with her business."

Equipped according to the eastern mode of travelling, the Shunammite mounted an ass, and ordered the man appointed to attend her and goad on the animal, to make all possible haste to mount Carmel. As soon as Elisha saw her coming, he sent Gehazi to salute her with these inquiries: "Is it well with thee? Is it well with thy husband? Is it well with the child?" As she came at so unexpected a moment, and with such evident haste, the prophet was naturally apprehensive that some calamity had befallen her, and, as he felt a deep interest in all her concerns, first inquired respecting what he well knew lay near her heart, the welfare of her family. Her reply was short, but remarkable: "IT IS WELL."

Some have considered this merely as an evasive answer, made for the purpose of avoiding conversation with Gehazi, with whom she did not wish to enter into the particulars of her present situation. This, however, is an improbable interpretation, because it would by no means comport with the general integrity of her character, nor with the respect which was due, and which we know she cherished, for the prophet. This was doubtless the message with which Gehazi returned to his master, who, from his ignorance of her precise circumstances, could not, till her own subsequent explanation, comprehend the elevated sentiments implied in such a general reply. A pious mind in similar circumstances would not hesitate to affirm, "It is well"--well with the living--well with the dead--well with those who, notwithstanding all their bereavements, are under the care of Heaven and enjoy the smiles of God--well with those whose disembodied spirits, escaped from the imprisonment of time, have ascended to the unfettered freedom, the unbounded felicity, of eternity.

In this view the Shunammite recognized the sovereignty of God; his indisputable right to dispose of her and her affairs as he pleased. "Shall the clay say to him that formed it, What doest thou?" The unbending temper of infidelity will, perhaps, receive this as "a hard saying;" but it is affirmed in the inspired page, and must ever be admitted by him who is in his "right mind." Uncontrollable power, acting irrespectively of wisdom or goodness, would be indeed a terrific idea, and must issue in a state of universal anarchy; but the *perfection* of that Infinite Being who "sitteth upon the circle of the earth," secures the *righteous* exercise of the most irresistible authority; and of this we may ever be assured, that although his arm is omnipotent, it is never unmerciful.

The Shunammite intended also to express her confidence in the goodness of God, however disguised by the afflictive nature of his dispensations. In a proper state of mind it will not be requisite, in order to produce resignation, that we should comprehend the whole design of every sorrow. We should bow to the mysteriousness of the event; and the patience of our endurance will not depend on the full developement and explanation of the mystery. Whether events accord with our wishes or oppose them, "It is THE LORD" will strike us into silence and submission.

Upon this subject the declarations of the Scriptures are most encouraging. They affirm, that "he doth not willingly afflict or grieve the children of men"--that their own benefit requires the chastisement, of whatever description it may be--that not a needless sigh heaves the human bosom, or an unnecessary tear is made to flow--and that "all things work together for good to them that love God, to them that are the called according to his purpose." It cannot be doubted, that the all-wise Disposer could, if he had pleased, have prevented a single cloud from rising to darken the Christian's day, and by the interdictions of his Providence, as formerly by the blood sprinkled upon the door-posts of Israel in Egypt, have secured his people from the visitation of all the messengers of wo; but he knows that affliction is conducive to our real welfare, that it is a means of improving our character, and of preparing us for that state of perfect enjoyment where it shall be no longer necessary; and that it furnishes occasion for the exercise of those graces which adorn the Christian's character, and glorify his God.

"We should endeavour," to use the words of a profound writer, "not to be distressed about any thing, but to take every event for the best. I apprehend this to be a duty, and the neglect of it to be a sin: for in truth, the reason why sin is sin, is merely because it is contrary to the will of God. If, therefore, the essence of sin consists in having a will contradictory to the known will of God, it seems clear to me, that when he discovers his will to us by events, we sin if we do not conform ourselves to it." Again, "Our own will, though it should obtain all it can wish, would never be contented; but we are contented from the very instant that we renounce it. We never can be contented with it," [48] nor otherwise than contented without it.

It is highly proper to investigate the causes of our sorrows, to inquire how far they are occasioned by any thing sinful in ourselves. It becomes us to be humble and penitent before God, when we discover that our own misconduct has rendered it necessary for him who is "slow to anger" to inflict chastisement. It is to be feared that while we abhor the blasphemy of uttering the language of complaint, and of saying, like Jonah, "I do well to be angry," we often do not suspect the criminality of cherishing hard thoughts of Providence, doubting the propriety or repining at the continuance of afflictive dispensations. There exists, perhaps, a secret suspicion of his goodness, a latent spirit of revolt, which we dare not express, or which we flatter ourselves, because we give it another name, that we do not cherish.

The people of God sometimes receive affliction with a gaze of wonder, as if it were the most unlikely of all occurrences. We feel no surprise when it attacks *others*, but live in the true spirit of the poet's representation,

"All men think all men mortal but *themselves*."

In general terms we even acknowledge that we are not exempted; and yet, when actually visited by personal or relative troubles, we seem like a traveller suddenly overtaken by a thunderstorm; all is confusion and alarm: our faith, and hope, and joy, take wing, and leave us solitary and sad. In our alarm we forget God, think it "strange," brood with a melancholy, but guilty pleasure, over our sufferings, and act as if we thought that "God had forgotten to be gracious." But "let them that suffer according to the will of God, commit the keeping of their souls to him in well doing, as unto a faithful Creator."

"Four things," observes Melancthon, "ought to be well impressed upon our minds respecting afflictions.

"1. They are appointed. We do not suffer affliction by chance, but by the determinate counsel and permission of God.

"2. By means of affliction God punishes his people; not that he may destroy them, but to recall them to repentance and the exercise of faith; for afflictions are not indications of displeasure, but of kindness--'He willeth not the death of a sinner.'

"3. God requires us to submit to his afflictive dispensations, and to expend our indignation and impatience upon our own sins; and, since he determines to afflict his church in the present state, submission tends to glorify his name.

"4. Resignation, however, is not all; he requires faith and prayer, that we may both seek and expect divine assistance. Thus he admonishes us, 'Call upon me in the day of trouble, I will answer thee, and thou shalt glorify me.'

"These four considerations are applicable to all our afflictions, and are calculated, if properly regarded, to produce that truly Christian patience, which essentially differs from mere philosophical endurance." [49]

As soon as the Shunammite came to Elisha, she fell at his feet and embraced them. Gehazi attempted to thrust her away, but the prophet told him to desist, intimating that he perceived she was in some deep affliction with which he was unacquainted. Then bursting out in the abrupt language of impassioned grief, she exclaimed, "Did I desire a son of my lord? Did I not say, Do not deceive me?"

If these words wear a complaining aspect, we must make allowance for the strength of maternal feelings; perhaps, too, notwithstanding her characteristic equanimity of temper, and the elevated piety of her mind, she was betrayed, in this instance, into some degree of impatience. It is remarkable, that some of the most eminent of saints have failed, in particular periods of their lives, in the exercise of those very dispositions for which they are particularly celebrated. That faithful page, which delineates the characters of men with perfect impartiality, represents Moses, distinguished for his *meekness*, as in a state of *violent irritation* when he saw the idolatry of Israel; in consequence of which he broke the two tables of stone to pieces on which the finger of God had inscribed his own laws--Job, to whom sacred and profane history have assigned extraordinary *patience*, in language the most emphatical, "*cursed his day*"--Peter, whose *courage* and *ardent zeal* in the service of his Divine Master were apparent on every other occasion, not only *trembled* before the simple intimation of a servant-maid that he was one of his friends, but *denied* him with *oaths* and *curses*. Such is the inconsistency of human character! Such are the shades that darken the brightest names. Such the salutary warnings that preceding ages transmit to those who have to follow the long train of heaven-bound travellers to a better existence!

Let us turn our eyes for a moment from these specimens of mortal excellence to Him who was "holy, harmless, undefiled, separate from sinners;" and who has left us "an example, that we should follow his steps: who did no sin, neither was guile found in his mouth ... who his own self bare our sins in his own body on the tree, that we, being dead to sins, should live unto righteousness."

Compassionating the distressed Shunammite, Elisha immediately adopted measures to afford her effectual consolation. He commanded Gehazi to hasten to the chamber appropriated to his use, and lay his staff upon the face of the child. He was to avoid the usual compliments upon meeting friends or strangers, in order that not a moment might be lost. [50] The bereaved mother, in the mean time refused to quit the prophet, to whom she was so much attached, and in whom she cherished such unbounded confidence; and he, affected by her sufferings, arose and accompanied her home.

Gehazi fulfilled his commission; but finding no symptoms of life, he returned to inform his master, whom he met on the way. "And when Elisha was come into the house, behold, the child was dead, and laid upon his bed. He went in, therefore, and shut the door upon them twain, and prayed unto the Lord. And he went up, and lay upon the child, and put his mouth upon his mouth, and his eyes upon his eyes, and his hands upon his hands, and he stretched himself upon the child; and the flesh of the child waxed warm. Then he returned and walked in the house to and fro; and went up and stretched himself upon him; and the child sneezed seven times, and the child opened his eyes. And he called Gehazi, and said, Call this Shunammite. So he called her. And when she was come in unto him, he said, Take up thy son. Then she went in, and fell at his feet, and bowed herself to the ground, and took up her son, and went out."

It is observable, that the attempt to reanimate the child by despatching the servant to place the prophet's staff upon its face utterly failed, possibly because "this act was done out of *human conceit*, not out of *instinct from God*." [51]

Elisha, however, came, *prayed unto the Lord*, and succeeded in effecting a miraculous restoration of the departed child. The grateful mother may be classed among those who, through faith, "received their dead raised to life again." How animating the prospect of that moment when almighty power will be displayed in raising every human body from the grave, and reuniting it with its kindred spirit in a state of deathless existence! May we attain the "blessedness and holiness" of such as have "part in the *first* resurrection!"

Only one other circumstance is mentioned in the history of the Shunammite. When Israel was threatened with a famine of seven years, Elisha forewarned her of the danger, and advised her retirement into some place of security and plenty. She accordingly removed with her family into the land of the Philistines. At the expiration of this period she returned; but finding that her property had become the prey of rapacity, or was alienated by some royal edict, she applied to the king for its restoration. This was perfectly consistent with her former character; for although she felt no eagerness for worldly advancement, and, indeed, refused it, piety did not require a total negligence of her civil rights, or of measures calculated to preserve her and her beloved family from a state of indigency.

Providentially, at the precise moment of her application the king was conversing with Gehazi, who was informing him of Elisha's miracles, and in particular of the miracle he had performed upon the deceased son of the Shunammite. She was of course introduced under the most favourable circumstances; and having ascertained the identity of the present applicant, "the king appointed unto her a certain officer, saying, Restore all that was hers, and all the fruits of the field, since the day that she left the land even till now."

Thus is afforded a striking exemplification of the remark of Solomon, "The king's heart is in hand of the Lord, as the rivers of water: he turneth it withersoever he will."

Esther Chapter XIV

One of the most delightful employments of the heavenly state will probably be, to investigate the past dispensations of Providence, and to make perpetual discoveries of its mysteries. In that world of light, events which are now covered with clouds and darkness impervious to the eye of sense, will become obvious to the view of "just men made perfect" in all their proportions, connexions, and combinations. The shadows of the morning having disappeared, the brightness of eternal noon will irradiate our existence.

We are by no means to imagine, however, that it is inconsistent with the present arrangements of divine goodness to afford us information, even in this world, respecting his plans and purposes; we do "know," though it be but "in part." The book of providence is indeed the least intelligible to us of all that the wisdom of God has written: but we can read *some* of its pages, and understand *some* of its hieroglyphical characters. The histories of Scripture constitute a volume of elementary instructions, of which the narrative of ESTHER has always been regarded as singularly interesting.

[Sidenote: Years before Christ, about 460.]

In order to introduce this story, it will be requisite to take a cursory view of some previous occurrences. The scene is laid in Persia, in the days of Ahasuerus, another name, as learned men have generally agreed, for Artaxerxes Longimanus. After struggling with those perplexing competitions for empire which often obstruct the path to a crown, and agitate the first years of power in arbitrary governments, he at length secured the dominion of Persia with its hundred and twenty-seven provinces. To proclaim his undisputed possession, and to display his glory, he appointed a feast, which may perhaps be deemed unrivalled in the majesty of its circumstances and the length of its continuance. At the expiration of a hundred and fourscore days the king gave another entertainment of seven days, for "all the people that were present in Shushan the palace, both unto great and small." It was held in the court of the garden, for the purpose of accommodation, and with great magnificence. Vashti also, his royal consort, in conformity to the usages of the times, which, it must be admitted, were admirably calculated to preserve the purity of morals, prepared a separate entertainment for the women in another part of the palace. "Vashti feasted the women in her own apartment: not openly in the court of the garden, but in the *royal house*. Thus, while the king showed the *honour of his majesty*, she and her ladies showed *the honoux of their modesty*, which is truly the majesty of the fair sex." ... HENRY.

Alas! how little did Ahasuerus comprehend wherein true riches and dignity consisted; and how little are these heathen "lovers of pleasure" to be envied by us, who are invited as welcome guests to a nobler table and a better banquet! "Wisdom hath builded her house, she hath hewn out her seven pillars, she hath slain her oxen, she hath mingled her wine." Into the highways and hedges, into every quarter of the world, and amongst every class of mankind, the messengers of heaven are commissioned to go and call the poor as well as the rich, the peasant as well as the prince, to the "feast of fat things," which celestial mercy has provided in the Gospel, where admission is not exclusive, where indulgence cannot be construed into excess, where not a brutal appetite, but a mental and spiritual taste, is amply supplied. The princes of Persia congratulated themselves upon the favour of Ahasuerus; but how much greater reason have Christians to rejoice in the friendship of Christ! Now they are admitted to participate the blessings of his grace and the sacramental festival; hereafter they have substantial reasons to anticipate a diviner intercourse and a more exalted familiarity, when they shall drink new wine with him in his Father's kingdom.

On the seventh day of the feast already mentioned, the king commanded the seven chamberlains of his household to wait upon Vashti, and bring her before him arrayed in the crown-royal. His heart is said to have been "merry with wine," or he would not have thought of indulging his own vanity, and insulting his queen's dignity, by such an exhibition. She ventured to refuse a compliance with this royal order, in which she was probably countenanced by the concurring opinion and feelings of the ladies who were present at the entertainment. As a woman she felt for the honour of her sex, and as a queen for her individual reputation and dignity. It was unquestionably a foolish command, contrary to the Persian customs, and dishonourable to the character of Ahasuerus as a sovereign and a husband. It is not by indulging pomp that the glory of a prince is best displayed, but by useful enactments, virtuous associations, and an upright uniformity of conduct.

Unreasonable, however, as the demand of Ahasuerus was, Vashti ought not to have been so peremptory. In such an age, and under such a government, a moment's consideration must have excited in her an apprehension of danger. Besides, it was not the time for remonstrance. She was no private character; it was, therefore, an injudicious resistance of his authority. Obedience would have involved no guilt; but disobedience, even though the command were ridiculous, necessarily exposed her husband's authority to contempt. It must be admitted in Christian communities, that the Gospel requires submission on the part of a wife; nor is this requisition limited solely to those commands which the woman herself may deem just and proper, otherwise her own humour, caprice, or misconception, would perpetually infringe upon a positive law, and in fact, render it nugatory. On the other hand, if the husband would secure a cheerful obedience, and cherish, instead of spoil, an amiable temper, or regulate a peevish one, let his wishes be reasonable in themselves, and uttered without a look or a term expressive of an insolent consciousness of superiority.

Ahasuerus instantly resented the refusal of Vashti. His passion became outrageous, sensible that his dignity was insulted and his authority questioned. He not only felt the uncomplying message of the queen as a sufficient mortification to his personal vanity, but as a public attack upon his influence and power as a king. It was not in a retired apartment, or on a private occasion, but, in a sense, before the eyes of a *hundred and twenty-seven provinces!*

Immediate recourse was had to his counsellors, who concurred in the opinion of Memucan, that it was a public question of great importance to the future welfare of the state, and affecting the domestic felicity, not of the king only, but of every family in the Persian empire. The advice he gave them, which Ahasuerus promptly followed, was to divorce Vashti, and interdict her forever from reappearing in the royal presence. "If it please the king, let there go a royal commandment from him, and let it be written among the laws of the Persians and the Medes, that it be not altered. That Vashti come no more before king Ahasuerus: and let the king give her royal estate unto another that is better than she. And when the king's decree which he shall make shall be published throughout all his empire (for it is great,) all the wives shall give to their husbands honour, both to great and small." It is not surprising that such a gratifying, but *unchristian* proposal, should be adopted by an arbitrary heathen monarch. Neither Memucan nor his royal master had drunk at the purifying fountain of evangelical truth.

God was now making "the wrath of man to praise him." Human passions, prejudices, and errors were promoting divine designs. The feast, and the riot, and the vanity, and the rage of Ahasuerus, all concurred, though unconsciously on his part, to fulfil the mighty arrangements of Providence, and to introduce, a train of events which now march through the page of sacred history in rapid and wonderful succession.

After the divorce of Vashti, the ministers of Ahasuerus advised him to adopt speedy measures to fill up the vacancy in his affections and his throne. Their plan exhibits the barbarity of the age and the sensuality of the king. He was to have his choice of all the "fair young virgins," collected from the provinces of the empire: and it devolved upon Hadassah, or Esther, an orphan educated under the inspection of Mordecai, her cousin and guardian, one of the captive Jews at this period attached by some employment to the royal establishment. That God, who had bestowed upon this young Jewess unusual beauty, gave her favour in the eyes of the king, and secretly accomplished his own gracious purposes respecting his people by her advancement.

Little did any of the persons immediately concerned in this affair imagine the predestined results. Ahasuerus was gratifying his passions; Esther and Mordecai conforming to an irresistible influence; Hegai, the keeper of the women, following the impulse of a secret admiration, and, perhaps, aiming to ingratiate himself in the favour of one whom he might suppose likely to become the future queen; while the Supreme Disposer was making use of all this variety of feeling and design as the means of securing the ends in his omniscient view.

Esther retained her humility of spirit after her elevation of circumstances; for she "did the commandment of Mordecai like as when she was brought up with him." She was one of the very few that resist the allurements of splendour--that cherish kindness for their poorer relatives--and remember with gratitude the guardians of their youth.

Mordecai, having detected a conspiracy against the king, mentioned it to Esther, who named it to her royal consort; by which means the traitors were soon brought to execution. This circumstance rendered the faithful Jew known to his sovereign. It was attended, indeed, by no immediate recompense; but he felt a satisfaction in having done his duty, incomparably more grateful to an unambitious mind.

The danger to which the great king of Persia was exposed by the machinations of his domestics, shows the counterbalancing disadvantages which attach even to the most prosperous condition of human life; the conduct of Mordecai, on this occasion, teaches the allegiance we all owe both to our lawful king, and to the Sovereign of the universe; and the circumstances of the whole transaction, though for the present otherwise unnoticed, being "written in the book of the Chronicles before the king," reminds us of the "Lamb's book of life," that faithful register of the pious services of his people, which, if not in this life, shall be fully requitted in another.

Great princes often act capriciously, and advance to the highest stations those whose personal insignificance or baseness must otherwise have rendered them contemptible. Thus Ahasuerus promoted Haman, the Agagite, to the place of his prime minister; who received that homage from the multitude, which persons of rank and eminent station usually secure in all countries, but which is peculiarly exacted under arbitrary governments. The flattering incense of the king's servants was accepted by Haman as a fragrant offering, while his vanity feasted itself most luxuriously upon popular admiration.

But, in proportion to a man's eagerness after honour, will be his sensibility to the slightest affront, and his readiness to interpret, in the worst sense, even unintentional neglect. It will not appear surprising to those who are acquainted with the heart of man, that this new favourite should have felt even more pain from the disrespect of one individual, than pleasure from the reverence of ten thousand others: and this, not because of any extraordinary importance which the dissentient had acquired, but simply on account of the extreme susceptibility to applause which the dignity and the pride of Haman had superinduced. Mordecai, in fact, refused to pay that homage to the prime minister which the king commanded; and he persisted in his refusal, notwithstanding the remonstrances of the king's servants, who "spake daily unto him." The known loyalty of Mordecai renders it certain that this determination did not proceed from any disesteem of the king; his character is an equal pledge that it did not originate in envy, or any ridiculous pique: it must have been a conscientious scruple, and the probability is, that the king required for his favourite a *religious* homage, similar to what the Persian monarchs were accustomed to claim for themselves. The minister was, besides, an Agagite, and therefore, probably, of the race of Amalek, a people against which Jehovah had proclaimed a perpetual and exterminating war. If these were his motives, he is rather to be extolled for his heroism, than censured for his temerity. A man of God should persevere in his duty at all hazards, unseduced by the flatteries, and unawed by the threats of mankind. He must contend against spiritual wickedness, oppose internal lust, and resist external temptation. He must brave alike caresses and sneers; the importunity of the timid, and the insistance of the powerful; so, however reproached by men, he will be honoured by God.

The officers of the king, at length, resolved to inform his favourite of this determined omission to pay him reverence. Haman became incensed, and his rage burned with destructive violence. Having been told that Mordecai was a Jew, he instantly vowed to revenge his mortification, not only by punishing the individual, but by destroying the nation: and as the Persian monarchy, at this period, included Judea, had not Providence signally interposed, few if any could have escaped. How cruel is wrath, how outrageous anger! Thousands are devoted to death for an individual's conduct, who were utterly incapable of participating in it, and who had never even heard the name of their offending countryman! Supposed guilt and unquestioned innocence were doomed alike to perish in one indiscriminate massacre! O let us daily pray for that "wisdom which is from above, which is first pure, then *peaceable, gentle, and easy to be entreated, full of mercy*, and good fruits!"

With a view of discovering the will of the gods, according to the common practice of Pagan antiquity, Haman ordered the lot to be cast, which was supposed to discriminate between lucky and unlucky days, little aware that "the whole *disposing* thereof is of the Lord."

His address to the king was artful and insinuating. Instead of stating the real cause of his desire for the extermination of the Jews, he touches only upon what the principles of policy might seem to dictate; and induces Ahasuerus to accede to his sanguinary proposal, by lending him his ring to use at his own discretion. Thus the weakness of favouritism combines with the wickedness of pride, to destroy a people whose name was scarcely known to their prince, and whose crime was not even attempted to be proved by their malignant accuser.

The decree was at length issued, and letters were despatched into every province of the empire, "to destroy, to kill, and to cause to perish, all Jews both young and old, little children and women, in one day, even upon the thirteenth day of the twelfth month, which is the month Adar, and to take the spoil of them for a prey." After this inhuman proceeding, "the king and Haman sat down to drink; but the city Shushan was perplexed."

It is an outrage upon public decency, which even modern times and civilized nations have unhappily witnessed, to see princes dissipating their days in festivity, and enfeebling their reason by excess, riot, and intoxication, when the calamitous circumstances of their country have demanded a serious investigation, a sympathizing regard, and a prompt relief; but still more lamentable is it to observe such conspirators against the lives of mankind as Haman and Ahasuerus, sitting down to indulge in merriment, while Persia was bathed in tears, and innumerable of her inhabitants written for execution. Was not one governor then to be found, to return an answer similar to that which the king of France, in a later age received, who had commanded the massacre of the Huguenots? "In my district," said one of his virtuous lieutenants, "your majesty has many brave soldiers, but no butchers!"--This was a people, however, ignorant as the haughty favourite of Ahasuerus was of the fact, that no human power could annihilate--a people under the immediate protection of the eternal God--a people respecting whom important prophecies were yet unaccomplished--a people of whom it is affirmed, Jehovah "kept him as the apple of his eye."

Mordecai was no uninterested spectator of these transactions; but went about the city, and approached even to the king's gate, attired in sack-cloth, and uttering cries of grief and lamentation. Esther, who was no less accessary to sorrow in the palace than in the cottage, being informed of this circumstance, sent him a change of raiment, that she might enjoy a conversation to which he could not be introduced in the habiliments of mourning. Alas! though the *signs* of affliction may be interdicted, the unwelcome visitant herself will intrude even into the most splendid residences and most elevated conditions! Mordecai refused the dress, not out of disrespect to the queen, but to express his poignant anguish, and to incite her to deeper sympathy. Esther immediately despatched her attendant, one of the king's chamberlains, to inquire into the cause of his distress; and this faithful messenger soon hastens back to detail all the proceedings which had been adopted in reference to the Jews, with a request from Mordecai, that "she should go in unto the king, to make supplication unto him, and to make request before him for her people."

This was a dangerous requisition. She, therefore, sent back her attendant to Mordecai, to remind him that it was a matter of universal notoriety, whoever, man or woman, should venture into the royal presence without being called, must suffer death, unless the "golden sceptre" were held out as an intimation of mercy; and that she questioned the probability of this in case of her intrusion, since her not having been sent for during thirty days past seemed to indicate some alienation.

It must be confessed, there is less of the heroine and the martyr in this reply than we could wish to have witnessed; but, on the one hand, we may observe that a similar blemish disfigured the early conduct of Moses: and on the other, as some extenuation, that she does not *refuse* to comply with Mordecai's suggestion; but merely referred to the danger awaiting such a proceeding, in order perhaps to induce him, if possible, to contrive some safer and no less effectual expedient. The love of life is a principle of human nature implanted by our Creator for the purpose of self-preservation, a principle which, in ordinary cases, cannot be violated without guilt; and, on no occasion, can be dispensed with but from some imperious necessity. He who gave life, however, has a right to reclaim it; and that sacrifice which it would be a vice to make to our own passion, becomes a virtuous and pious offering when yielded to divine requirements.

Mordecai sent another message to Esther, at once spirited, pointed, and effectual. It was a moment that demanded instantaneous action; and if the timorous queen cherished apprehensions on her own account, he showed her that she was even more likely to suffer by an ignominious retreat than a bold advance. He reminded her of her Jewish extraction, and the consequent danger to herself in the arrangement to exterminate all that hated race. For though the prime minister probably would not have lifted his hand against the queen; and though her connexion with his master, who married her from affection as great as we can imagine a sensual and despotic prince capable of cherishing, seemed to promise security; yet there could be no absolute dependence, and the favourite of to-day might be discarded to-morrow. He added to this other and weighty considerations--"If thou altogether boldest thy peace at this time, then shall there enlargement and deliverance arise to the Jews from another place; but thou and thy father's house shall be destroyed; and who knoweth whether thou art come to the kingdom for such a time as this?"--*q.d.* 'Thy timidity may prevent thy becoming the means of rescuing the people of God; nevertheless, they shall assuredly escape--his resources are inexhaustible--his chosen nation shall not be annihilated--and he will not only perform the work without thy instrumentality, but inflict an awful but merited chastisement for thy misconduct. After all, I have better anticipations--perhaps thy wonderful advancement to the crown was intended by him who sometimes conceals his plans of mercy in clouds of mystery, for the very purpose of accomplishing the deliverance of Israel at this critical emergency.'

Mordecai, in this appeal, shines as a "wise reprover;" and it was "upon an obedient ear." He is, moreover, illustrious as a man of *faith*. The confident tone he assumed did not arise merely from that solicitude he felt upon the subject, and which will sometimes inspire a boldness not commonly manifested; but from a knowledge of the prophecies, and a trust in the faithfulness of God respecting their fulfilment. The lyres of Isaiah, Ezekiel, and Daniel, celebrated in accordant strains the restoration of the Jews from captivity, and the advent of Messiah; and he was persuaded that infinite Wisdom could not be deceived, nor infinite power frustrated. O that in every minute affair of our lives, as well as with regard to every great event of time, we could cherish a similar faith in the providence of the "God of salvation!"

Observe, in passing, that it is reasonable and just to expect services from us proportioned to the situations which we occupy. Favours involve obligations; and whatever influence, talent, or means of any kind we possess, ought to be conscientiously appropriated to the great Bestower. Every being in the universe has duties arising out of his condition by doing which he glorifies, and by omitting which he displeases, his Creator. Esther was, therefore, responsible for her actions as a queen, as a Jewess, and as one furnished with extraordinary opportunities at a crisis most singular and important, and the remonstrance of Mordecai proved irresistible. With what exultation must he have received this message from her--"Go, gather together all the Jews that are present in Shushan, and fast ye for me, and neither eat nor drink three days, night or day. I also, and my maidens, will fast likewise: and so will I go in unto the king, which is not according to the law; and if I perish, I perish!"

These devotional preparations for the experiment about to be hazarded, were not only highly proper in themselves, but expressive of the piety of Esther. Abstinence from food, an ancient practice of the church sanctioned by divine authority, is an evidence of humiliation before God; and at the same time, adapted to produce it, by inflicting a salutary mortification upon the corporeal appetites. If carried to excess, it will indeed hinder rather than promote piety; but when adopted on proper occasions, and observed with judicious regulations, it is attended with consequences manifestly beneficial. The queen did not impose a service on others which she was indisposed to practise herself; but sympathizing with the condition of her countrymen, she participated in their self-denying duties. Let us never forget the promise of eternal mercy, which has consoled the church of God in her deepest afflictions, and upon which every pilgrim in Zion may depend with unhesitating confidence, "Call upon me in the day of trouble; I will deliver thee, and thou shalt glorify me." [52]

When it is recollected, that the proceeding of Esther, in going in to the king uncalled, was a deliberate violation of a law of the state, and that Vashti had been discarded for an offence of far inferior consideration; we cannot but notice the overruling providence of God, in giving the queen acceptance in the eyes of Ahasuerus. On the third day she laid aside her mourning dress, and putting on her royal apparel, presented herself in the inner court of the palace, opposite the king's private apartment, where he sat upon his throne. What a moment of suspense and of secret agony! If previous devotion had not, in some measure, tranquillized the agitations of her bosom, and inspired a holy courage, it is scarcely conceivable how a woman could sustain the trial of such an hour. If the sharp conflict had smitten her to the ground, and she had expired upon the spot, we should not, religious considerations apart, have been greatly astonished; but hope in God, and a composure gained, no doubt, at the mercy-seat, and diffused over her spirit by recent intercourse with heaven, prepared her to hear the mandate of death, or receive the outstretched token of clemency. Her splendid attire--her attractive mien--her beautiful countenance, in which grief, anxiety, and devotion blending their influence, produced a new and interesting character, fixed the king's attention, and reinspired his love; but neither the one nor the other of these, nor all of them in the most happy combination, could have produced the effect, had not the tears, the prayers, the fastings of Israel and of Esther, brought down the blessings from above. How *important* are means! how *essential* is religion!

Behold the golden sceptre! The queen trembles with rapture at the anticipated sign--it is held out--she approaches--touches--triumphs--and lives! "Let us come boldly unto the THRONE OF GRACE, that we may obtain mercy, and find grace to help in time of need!"

Instead of rejection and death, Esther soon found herself treated with perfect familiarity, and more than usual kindness. Imagining that some important business had occasioned this visit, the king desired to know it, and promised to gratify the queen "to the half of the kingdom." She thought it prudent, however, at present, to waive the particular request she had to present, simply inviting Ahasuerus and his favourite to a banquet, by which mark of attention she hoped more effectually to confirm his reviving fondness, and thus secure the accomplishment of her ultimate purpose. Her invitation was accepted. He repaired with Haman to the festival, where, being highly delighted with the entertainment, he renewed his protestations in reference to whatever petition she might have to present. The wary queen ventured only to request a renewal of the royal visit on the morrow, at which time she assured him of a full explanation of her wishes.

There is an appearance of undue timidity in this procrastination; and yet, if we were better informed of her secret motives, we might perhaps award her the praise of wisdom. The partiality of the king for Haman might render her doubtful of success in the contest with that favourite; and she might think it necessary to excite both the curiosity and the affection of the king still more, in order that he might not, through being startled at the magnitude of her demand, instantaneously refuse it. Extremes are dangerous. It would be well for us always to avoid both dilatoriness and precipitancy in our conduct; in order to which we should implore, with habitual fervency, the "wisdom from above."

Whatever were the views of Esther, the designs of God were secretly maturing. Haman retired to his own house, full of mortification at the continued neglect of Mordecai, which disturbed him even when every external good seemed to concur in promoting his enjoyment. He called his friends together, expatiated upon all his possessions and glory, noticing with peculiar emphasis the favour of Esther in admitting him as the sole companion of his sovereign and queen at the day's festivity, to a repetition of which he had the honour of being invited on the morrow; "yet," he added, displaying at once the festering wound of his heart, "yet all this availeth nothing, so long as I see Mordecai the Jew sitting at the king's gate."

Never, surely, was a more complete exposure of the insufficiency of worldly glory to constitute happiness, and never a more impressive exhibition of the littleness of vanity. What an insignificant disappointment is sufficient to mar the comfort of him who depends upon creatures! The merest feather may be turned into a weapon of hostility, and destroy his peace; and whatever he may possess or acquire, he must necessarily he as remote from true felicity as at the first step of his pursuit, since something will always he wanting to *complete* his bliss, and the phantom of *ideal* good will continue to dance before his eyes.

Zeresh, the wife of Haman, advised him to have a gallows made of fifty cubits in height, upon which he should instigate the king to hang Mordecai. To this advice, in which all his friends concurred, he listened, and gave immediate orders for the construction of this instrument of death.

What is to be done--what can be *attempted* by Esther or by Mordecai, in this critical emergency? Neither of them were, indeed, aware of the murderous determination. The queen had delayed her petition till the succeeding day, at the intended banquet; but malevolence was hastening to frustrate her designs, without her knowledge, and previously to her intercession. Could she ever pardon herself for this delay, when Mordecai is suspended? Could she recall the past hours of festivity, in which so favourable an opportunity seemed to present itself for urging her supplication to the king?--

"Stand still and see the salvation of God!" He who "sitteth upon the circle of the earth," is about to fulfil his own purposes, which no human projects can frustrate, and no apprehension of contingencies need hasten. "On that night could not the king sleep." But little did he know the true cause of this unusual wakefulness, or suspect that God was about to render it subservient to accomplish his divine intentions. "And he commanded to bring the book of records of the chronicles; and they were read before the king." But why did not a prince like this, addicted to pleasure, seek a diversion of his restlessness, by calling in the aid of music, rather than that of history? It seems more natural, that, he should wish for temporary amusement, rather than sold instruction. What more soothing than the "concord of sweet sounds?" True; but that Providence which kept him awake, influenced him to the choice of this extraordinary expedient. "And it was found written, that Mordecai had told of Bigthana and Teresh, two of the king's chamberlains, the keepers of the door, who sought to lay hand on the king Ahasuerus." But how came this particular circumstance in his personal history, to be selected on this occasion? The Persian records contained events of astonishing magnitude, and romantic interest. They told of mighty exploits, and splendid conquests!--Again we discern that divine superintendence, by which Ahasuerus was *led* to a circumstance of his own time, in which that very individual was named, whose life was now in imminent danger, and upon whom depends so many of the incidents of this story. The king inquired, whether the fidelity of Mordecai had been properly rewarded! To which his servants replied, "There is nothing done for him." The cares of empire are so multifarious and complicated, that we ought to make considerable allowances for those omissions in princes, which would be utterly inexcusable in others; yet it does appear surprising, that so signal a service as that which Mordecai had rendered in the discovery of a dangerous conspiracy against the throne, should have been totally unrequited. Happily for Christians, they serve a Master who cannot forget even "a cup of cold water, given in the name of a disciple" to one of his "little ones!"

Early the ensuing morning, Haman hastened to the palace, for the purpose of obtaining the royal consent to his malignant preparations. Now he was about to rid himself at a stroke of the disdainful Jew that refused him homage; and anticipated the hour when he should witness his enemy on the gallows, so soon and so eagerly prepared! It was, indeed, a strange coincidence. Ahasuerus is as anxious to see his minister, as Haman to be introduced to the apartment of his king. Each has a great object in view, for which the other's concurrence is desired--each too is solicitous respecting the disposal of the same individual, and each ignorant of the other's wishes and projects.

After the usual salutations, the king entreated, the opinion of his favourite minister with regard to the best mode of expressing his attachment to one whom he "delighted to honour." Haman concluded that his royal master, of course, alluded to *him*, since he well knew no other shared so largely in the royal confidence; and thinking to gratify the vanity of his little soul, he proposed that the favourite alluded to should be, for once, clothed in the royal apparel and crown, carried through the city upon the horse which was appropriated to the king, attended by one of the first princes of the empire, and have proclamation made before him, "Thus shall it be done to the man whom the king delighteth to honour." Approving of this mode of testifying the regard he wished to express, extraordinary as it was, Ahasuerus instantly commanded its punctual execution. "Make haste, and take the apparel and the horse, as thou hast said, and do even so to"--whom? to my favourite Haman?--No--insufferable mortification;--"to *Mordecai the Jew!*"

Behold Haman again in his house, "mourning and having his head covered, and expatiating upon the misery of his situation." His wise men and his wife agree, that if Mordecai be of the seed of the Jews, all his contrivances to ruin him would prove ineffectual; so fully aware were even the heathen of the peculiar interposition of Providence, in former times, on behalf of that scattered people.

In the midst of their consultations, the king's chamberlain came to attend Haman to the banquet prepared by Esther. He goes--but rather like a man led to execution, than one invited to a festival. But he must conceal his chagrin, and assume the smile of gayety.

Having partook of the feast, Ahasuerus requires of Esther the fulfilment of her promise, in the explanation of her wishes. He assures her with reiterated protestations, that her petition shall certainly be granted, "even to the half of the kingdom." How was he astonished, when she entreated for her own life, and that of her people! It had never entered into the mind of the king, that such a request was necessary. Is it possible that he hears aright? Ignorant that he had really prostituted, his authority to sanction the destruction of the queen as a Jewess, he looks at her and Haman with wild confusion, while she proceeds in a strain of firm, dignified, and eloquent statement: "For we are sold, I and my people, to be destroyed, to be slain, and to perish; but if we had been sold for bondmen and bondwomen, I had held my tongue, although the enemy could not countervail the king's damage."

Who can paint the terrors that gathered, at this moment in the countenance of Haman, or the indignant frown of Ahasuerus, when he thundered forth--"Who is he? and where is he that durst presume in his heart to do so? The hour of detection was come. Detestable conspirator, thou shall not escape! Truth shall, at length, come from her concealment, and wither at a touch thy unmerited and unenviable distinctions!" Esther said, *"The adversary and enemy is this wicked Haman."*--"The word was loath to come forth, but it strikes home at last. Never till now did Haman hear his true title. Before, some had styled him noble, others great; some magnificent, and some perhaps virtuous; only Esther gave him his own, 'wicked Haman.' Ill-deserving greatness doth in vain promise to itself a perpetuity of applause." Bp. Hall.

Overwhelmed with astonishment and indignation, the king hastily withdrew from the banquet into the palace-garden: while the offender, who was too well acquainted with the countenance of his master not to perceive that "there was evil determined against him," writhing in all the agonies of despair, produced by a consciousness of guilt, and a dread of merited punishment, implored the queen to intercede for his safety. He who was profuse of the lives of others, with a consistency which is characteristic of villany and despotism cannot endure the thought of forfeiting his own, but betrays a cowardice proportioned to his recent insolence. The king returning at the moment in a state of the utmost exasperation, imputed the worst motives to his suppliant attitude, and allowed his servants to rush forward and cover Haman's face, as a person under sentence of death. The miserable criminal had, probably, many flatterers in the days of his greatness, but his adversity shows that he had no friends. Every one is eager to accelerate his destruction. Harbonah, especially, a chamberlain, proposed his being executed on the gallows of fifty cubits in height, which he had prepared for Mordecai; to which the king immediately assented. In this manner did Providence take the cunning persecutor in his own snare, and vindicate the cause of his oppressed people. Let the enemies of religion tremble, while the children of God are joyful in their King. The arrows which malignity shoots at the church of Christ shall either be broken against her walls, and fall pointless to the earth; or rebounding on the foe that ventures upon the attack, shall pierce his own heart.

The advancement of Mordecai was the natural result of Haman's ruin. Esther having fully informed Ahasuerus of her relationship to the much-injured Jew and his nation, she was empowered to bestow upon him the house of the fallen minister. The Jews, however, were not yet exempted from the decree which the wickedness of Haman had inveigled the king to issue against them! so that Esther, not merely solicitous for her personal security or that of her friend and relative, ventured again before the king, "and fell down at his feet, and besought him with tears to put away the mischief of Haman the Agagite, and his device that he had devised against the Jews." The king renewed the testimony of his kindness, by stretching forth the golden sceptre; and the queen addressed him in these words, "If it please the king, and if I have found favour in his sight, and the thing seem right before the king, and I be pleasing in his eyes, let it be written to reverse the letters devised by Haman the son of Hammedatha the Agagite, which he wrote to destroy the Jews which are in all the kings' provinces: for how can I endure to see the evil that shall come unto my people? or how can I endure to see the destruction of my kindred?"

The king was ready to concede every thing it was in his power to grant: but as the laws of Persia were irreversible, and he could not rescind an edict already issued in his several provinces, he adopted the plan of putting his ring into the hands of Mordecai and Esther, to seal whatever decree they might think it right to frame in the present emergency. Accordingly, they gave unlimited permission to the Jews to defend themselves, which it was likely would so plainly evince the royal wishes to nullify his former edict, that few if any would indulge their malice against this people, or endanger their own lives by availing themselves of the first order. Many, however, did so; and even in the royal city five hundred men attacked them, probably some of the partisans of the late minister; but their temerity hurried them on to their own destruction. The ten sons of Haman, were also slain, and at the request of the queen, hung on the gallows.

An annual festival, called *Purim*, [53] was established in commemoration of the deliverances we have recorded, which the Jews continue to observe at this day. It seems to have been appointed by Mordecai and Esther, as a civil, rather than a religious feast; unless it be supposed, that they received some special revelation to authorize such a measure. It is observed in the month *Adar*, which corresponds with our *February* and *March*.

The interesting history we have been reviewing, is calculated not only to impress those general sentiments of Providence, to which we cannot too often recur, but to awaken in the minds of Christians a pleasing conviction of that minute inspection of their affairs, and that unremitted care for their welfare individually, which God exercises towards them. Is it possible to imagine a doctrine more elevating than this, or more calculated to produce sensations of reverence, gratitude, and joy? It is not presumptuous, even in a mortal "worm," to believe that his interests engage the attention of the INFINITE BEING; and that to promote them, the immense machinery of moral and natural means is put in motion--the animate and inanimate creation--mortal agents and spiritual beings--events great and small, past and present. *Worm* as thou art, still the central point in the vast circle of Providence! *Worm* as thou art, God has "graven thee upon the palms of his bands, and thou shalt never perish." *Worm* as thou art, but for thee "the brightness of the Father's glory" had not left his radiant sphere to become incarnate, to endure reproach and execration, and finally to be "brought as a lamb to the slaughter!" To hear *thy* supplications the King of heaven has erected a *throne of grace*--to vindicate *thy* character, to condemn *thy* foes, to perfect *thy* felicity, he is preparing, and will soon come to sit upon *a throne of judgment!*

Review past dispensations, and gather encouragement for present confidence! "If God be for us, who can be against us?" Did he not choose *Abraham*, and call him his "friend?" Did he not release *Joseph* from the pit, and raise him to princely glory? Did he not rescue *Moses* from the destructive waters, and constitute him the leader of his people Israel? Did he not deliver *David* from the lion and the bear, from the giant of Philistia, and the royal madman of Israel! Did he not feed *Elijah*--advance *Esther*--promote *Mordecai*--support *Job*--save *Jonah*--rescue *Peter*, and honour *Paul*?

Has he not, in all ages, supplied the necessities of his saints--alleviated their sorrows--sweetened their bitter cup--turned death itself into life? Can he not extricate them from all difficulties--preserve them amidst ail temptations--render them invulnerable to all attacks--make them more than conquerors over external misery, internal pollution, and satanic malice?--Can he not eventually elevate them above the reach of all evil, the fear of death, and the possibility of falling? Can he not array them in the robe of light--adorn them with a crown of glory--make them "drink of the rivers of his pleasures"--associate them with holy angels, in a state of immaculate purity--stamp immortality on their blessedness, and "wipe away all tears from their eyes?"--HE CAN--HE WILL--"Our Father which art in heaven ...thine is the POWER and the GLORY, forever. Amen!"

Footnotes

1. : Bates.

2. : Young's Centaur not fabulous, p. 61.

3. : Sir William Temple's Gardens of Epicurus. Horne's Discourses, vol. I.

4. : This subject is more fully illustrated in the Essay prefixed to the second volume of this work.

5. : Dr. Johnson.

6. : Paley's Moral Philosophy, vol. i. p. 316, 8vo.

7. : SAURIN, Discours historiques, critiques, theologiques, et moraux, sur les Evenemens le plus memorables du Vieux et du Nouveau Testament. Tom. I. p. 41-43. 8vo.

8. : The following quotation is illustrative of this circumstance: "At ten minutes after ten in the morning, we had in view (says Dr. Chandler) several fine bays, and a plain full of booths, with the Turcomans sitting by the doors, under sheds resembling porticos; or by shady trees, surrounded with flocks of goats." Harmer's Observations, vol. i. p. 132.

9. : Fleury's Manners of the ancient Israelites.

10. : Newton's Diss. on the Prophecies, vol. i. p. 34--36.

11. : The ancient authors, Tacitus, Pliny, Diodorus Siculus, and others, furnish abundant testimony in undesigned confirmation of the scriptural account. The following quotation is from Strabo: "There are many indications that fire has been over this country; for, about Massada, they show rough and scorched rocks and caverns, in many places eaten in; and the earth reduced to ashes, and drops of pitch distilling from the rocks and hot streams, offensive afar off, and habitations overthrown; which render credible some reports among the inhabitants, that there were formerly thirteen cities on that spot, the principal of which was Sodom, so extensive, as to be sixty furlongs in circumference, but that by earthquakes, and by

an eruption of fire, and by hot and bituminous waters, it became a lake as it now is, the rocks were consumed, some of the cities were swallowed up, and others abandoned by those of the inhabitants who were able to escape." *Lib xii*

Tacitus states, that the traces of fire were visible in his time "At no great distance are those fields which, as it is said, were formerly fruitful, and covered with great cities, till they were consumed by lightning, the vestiges of which remain in the parched appearance of the country, which has lost its fertility." *Hist lib v*

A modern traveller, who was recently an eyewitness of the scene, is particularly entitled to be heard on this interesting subject, even at the risk of extending this note to a disproportionate length: "The Dead Sea below, upon our left, appealed so near to us, that we thought we could have rode thither in a very short space of time. Still nearer stood a mountain upon its western shore, resembling in its form the cone of Vesuvius, and having also a crater upon its top which was plainly discernible.

"The distance, however, is much greater than it appears to be; the magnitude of the objects beheld in this fine prospect, causing them to appear less remote than they really are. The atmosphere was remarkably clear and serene; but we saw none of those clouds of smoke which, by some writers, are said to exhale from the surface of the Lake Asphaltites, nor from any neighbouring mountain. Every thing about it was, in the highest degree, grand and awful. Its desolate, although majestic features, are well suited to the tales related concerning it by the inhabitants of the country, who all speak of it with terror, seeming to shrink from the narrative of its deceitful allurements and deadly influence. 'Beautiful fruit,' say they, 'grows upon its shores, which is no sooner touched, than it becomes dust and bitter ashes.' In addition to its physical horrors, the region around is said to be more perilous, owing to the ferocious tribes wandering upon the shores of the lake, than any other part of the Holy Land." *Clarke's Travels*, part ii. sect. i. p. 614.

12. : The design of this work being rather practical than critical, the author conceives it generally proper to avoid subjects of doubtful disputation; and rather, in particular cases, to give the *result* of his inquiries, than to detail the process by which it had been obtained. On this account, he has forborne to introduce the different notions that have prevailed among the learned respecting the real nature of the punishment inflicted upon the

wife of Lot, but has simply stated what is the most common, and, upon the whole, the most satisfactory opinion. It seems conformable to the words of the historian to suppose a *real conversion into a pillar of salt*, and not that Lot's wife was merely *smitten dead upon the spot*. If further information be wished, the reader is particularly referred to a French work of well-merited celebrity, and which contains on this and many subjects of Biblical criticism, much valuable and curious information--Saurin, Discours historiques, critiques, theologiques, et moraux, sur les Evenemens les plus memorables du Vieux et du Nouveau Testament. Tom, i.

13. : This appears to have been the ancient mode of concluding an agreement, or solemn covenant. Josephus says, that if two persons bound themselves mutually by an oath, they put their hand upon each other's thigh. Grotius states, that anciently they wore the sword upon the thigh, so that to swear by putting the hand upon the thigh, was intimating, "I am willing to be pierced through by this sword if I break my promise."

14. : "Sir J. Chardin observed this difference in the East between wells of living water, and reservoirs of rain water; that these last have frequently, especially in the Indies, a flight of steps down into the water, that as the water diminishes, people may still take it up with their hands, whereas he hardly ever observed a well furnished with those steps through all the East. He concludes from this circumstance, that the place from whence Rebekah took up water was a reservoir of rain water. This is the account that he gives us in his sixth MS. volume, and it explains very clearly what is meant by Rebekah's *going down* to the well, Gen. xxiv. 16." HARMER'S Observations, vol. ii. p. 184, 185, *note*.

15. : HENRY in loc.

16. : "We do not find that their (the Israelites') marriages were attended with any religious ceremony, except the prayers of the father of the family and the standers by, to entreat the blessing of God: we have examples of it in the marriage of Rebekah with Isaac, of Ruth with Boaz, and of Sara with Tobias. We do not see that there were any sacrifices offered upon the occasion, or that they went to the temple, or sent for the priests; all was transacted betwixt the relations and friends, so that it was no move than a civil contract." Fleury's Manners of the ancient Israelite, Part ii. chap. 10.

17. : Most commentators attribute a higher principle to the partiality of Rebekah; they imagine that it was founded upon the prophecies, choosing

him whom the Lord had chosen: but I can perceive no good reason for this opinion.

18. : "For I brought thee up out of the land of Egypt, and redeemed thee out of the house of servants; and I sent before thee Moses, Aaron, and *Miriam.*" Mic. vi. 4.

19. : Hieron, in Trad. Heb. ad 1 Kings 3. Calmet's Preface to Ruth, and Ch. iv. 22.

20. : Gray's Key to the Old Testament.

21. : Comp. HARMER'S Observations, vol. i. p. 78, 79.

22. : There is something inimitably beautiful in this ancient practice, and in language of their mutual address, which is preserved in the inspired narrative, "And behold, Boaz came from Bethlehem, and said unto the reapers, The Lord be with you. And they answered him, The Lord bless thee." Ch. ii. 4.

23. : Clarke's Travels, Part II, Sect, ii. p, 302.

24. : Comp. Harmer's Observations.

25. : It has been thought probable, that from the expression "Is not the Lord gone out before thee?" some angelic messenger or visible appearance, similar to that of the Shekinah, prompted the words and animated the zeal of Deborah. The Targum favours this sentiment: "Is not the angel of the Lord gone out before thee to prosper thee?"

26. : Lectures on the Sacred Poetry of the Hebrews.

27. : The historical reference appears to be to the narrative in the twentieth chapter of Numbers, in which the refusal of Edom to allow the children of Israel to go through their borders is recorded. Some extraordinary circumstances seem referred to, not mentioned in the sacred page, but possibly transmitted by tradition to the times of Deborah. Sen is a mountain of Idumea. The language is highly figurative, and denotes earthquakes and storms. "The mountains melted," that is, part of their surface was carried down, by the force of excessive torrents of rain.

28. : The ass derives its name from a Hebrew word signifying *redness*, the usual colour of this animal, but some are white. The word translated white is *zechorot*, and may, perhaps refer to the *zebra*, which the Ethiopians

call *zechora,* and which is generally considered as one of the most beautiful of living creatures. It is sometimes called the wild ass.

29. : "Dr. Shaw mentions a beautiful rill in Barbary, which is received into a large basin, called *shrub we krub,* (drink and away,) there being great danger of meeting there with rogues and assassins. If such places are proper for the lurking of murderers in times of peace, they must be proper for the lying in ambush in times of war; a circumstance that Deborah takes notice of in her song, Judges v. 11." Harmer.

30. : *Gates* were anciently the places where they held their courts of judicature. In the towers there were very spacious and handsome state-rooms.

31. : The Vulgate reads, *in the country of Merom,* alluding to the place where Joshua fought a former king of Canaan. The waters of Merom are supposed to be the same as Kishon. Comp. Josh. xi. 5 Ps. lxxxiii 9.

32. : There is a remarkable alliteration here in the original Hebrew, [Hebrew: *middaharoth daharoth.*] Some have supposed it a poetical imitation of the sound of the trampling of horses, and compare this passage with the celebrated line of Virgil--"Quadrupedante putrem sonitu quatit ungula campum." VIRG. Æn. viii. v. 595.

33. : Comp. HARMER'S Observations, volume i. pp. 216 and 445.

34. : It has often been inquired, on what principle this action of Jael, which is so apparently repugnant to the laws of honourable warfare, and even of common humanity, could be so eulogized by Deborah. The Kenites and the Canaanites were in alliance, and besides, the rights of hospitality have always been most scrupulously regarded, especially in the early ages of the world. To these considerations the ingenious Saurin replies, that in order to judge of this affair, it would be necessary to know the nature of the treaty between Heber and the Canaanites; because, according to Puffendorf, if two agreements cannot be performed, of which the one was made *with* and the other *without* an oath, the latter ought to yield to the former; and we cannot tell but this latter might be the nature of the agreement between the Kenites and the Canaanites. He conceives also, that a justification of Jael's conduct might be found in the character of Sisera, pleading that we are not required to keep good faith, or to show lenity to those execrable persons who only avail themselves of our regard to these virtues, to violate them in their conduct to others, to falsify their promises, and carry blood and carnage

wherever they go. Under this impression, he prays that Providence may never raise up among us Jabins or Siseras; but if the justice of God should see fit to employ such scourges for our correction, that his mercy would send Jaels to effect our deliverance. Comp. SAURIN Discours Historiques, tom iii. *La defaite de Jabin et de Sizera*, p. 318-322. I confess this reasoning is not quite satisfactory; nor indeed will any reasoning upon this remarkable transaction be so, till we allow that there were circumstances which the Spirit of God has not seen fit to disclose, and that Jael most probably acted under the influence of some divine intimation. Long was it the revealed will of God that the Canaanites should be exterminated, and Israel had been criminally negligent of his commands. It must, doubtless, be admitted, that the general authority which they had received, independent even of any acts of oppression, was paramount to every other consideration, and sufficient to justify the most implacable hostility.

35. : Illustrations may be found in Saurin, "Discours Historiques, Critiques, Theologiques, et Moreaux, sur les Evenemens les plus memorables du Vieux et du Nouveau Testament." Tom. iv. p. 14-20, 8vo.

36. : The Septuagint rendering of David's message to Nabal explains the rapaciousness of the Arabs, and the forbearance of David. "Behold, I have heard that thy shepherds are now shearing for thee; they were with us in the wilderness, and we have not *hindered* them, ουχ απεχωλυσαμεν, nor have we *commanded* them ουχ ενετειλαμεθα, all the days of their being in Carmel." "This," says Harmer, "is translating like people perfectly well acquainted with the management of the Arab emirs, whose manners David, though he lived in the wilderness as they did, had not adopted. One of them at the head of six hundred men, would have *commanded,* from time to time, some provisions, or other present from Nabal's servants, for permitting them to feed in quiet; and would have driven them away from the watering-place upon any dislike. He had not done either." *Observations,* vol. i. p. 173.

37. : Young's Centaur, p. 119.

38. : JOSEPHUS, Book viii. ch. 5,

39. : Voyage up the Red Sea, and Route through the Desarts of Thebais.

40. : Harmer's Observations, vol. iv. p. 192, 193.

41. : From the *Arabian Anthologia,* quoted by SCHULTENS.

42. : Shaw's Travels, p. 214-317, quoted in Harmer's Observations, vol. i. p. 251.

43. : Comp. Harmer's Observations, vol. ii. p. 503.

44. : Plutarch's Life of Pyrrhus.

45. : Epitaph in Bunhill Fields burying-ground on a child that died at the age of nine months. The writer of these pages knows not the author, or whether these lines have ever appeared in any other place than on the stone whence he has transcribed them.

46. : HARMER'S Observations, vol. i. p 4.

47. : The first day of the month was kept with burnt-offerings and peace-offerings. Vide Numb. x. 10. and xxviii. 11. In imitation of the Jews, the calends, or first days of the month, and the fourth and seventh of the week, were sacred to Deity.

48. : PASCAL'S Thoughts, pp. 229, 244.

49. : See The Life of Philip Melancthon, by the author of this work, p. 225, second edition.

50. : "The salutations of the East often take up a long time. The manner of salutation as now practised by the people of Egypt, is not less ancient. The ordinary way of saluting people, when at a distance, is bringing the hand down to the knees, and then carrying it to the stomach; marking their devotedness to a person, by holding down the hand; as they do their affection, by their after raising it up to the heart. When they come close together afterward, they take each other by the hand, in token of friendship. What is very pleasant, is to see the country-people reciprocally clapping each other's hands very smartly, twenty or thirty times together, in meeting, without saying any thing more than *Salamant aiche halcom?* that is to say, *How do you do? I wish you good health.* If this form of complimenting must be acknowledged to be simple, it must be admitted to be very affectionate. Perhaps it marks out a better disposition of heart than all the studied phrases which are in use among us, and which politeness almost always makes use of at the expense of sincerity. After this first compliment, many other friendly questions are asked about the health of the family, mentioning each of the children distinctly, whose names they know," &c. MAILLET, Descript. de l'Egypte.

"If the forms of salutation among the ancient Jewish peasants took up as much time as those of the modern Egyptians that belong to that rank of life, it is no wonder the prophet commanded his servant to abstain from saluting those he might meet with, when sent to recover the child of the

Shunammitess to life. They that have attributed this order to haste, have done right; but they ought to have shown the tediousness of Eastern compliments." HARMER'S Observations, vol. ii. pp. 331, 332.

51. : BISHOP HALL.

52. : Ps. I. 15. The thirteenth and fourteenth chapters of the apocryphal book of Esther contain appropriate prayers for this occasion, attributed to Mordecai and Esther, well worthy of perusal.

53. : In the Persian language *Pur* signifies a *lot*; and the reference is to Haman's casting lots to ascertain the lucky month for the execution of his iniquitous project against the Jews.